ANABAPTIST BAPTISM
A REPRESENTATIVE STUDY

Studies in
Anabaptist and Mennonite History

Edited by

John S. Oyer, Ernst Correll, Melvin Gingerich, Guy F. Hershberger,
J. C. Wenger, and John H. Yoder

1. TWO CENTURIES OF AMERICAN MENNONITE LITERATURE, 1727-1928.
    By Harold S. Bender. 1929.
2. THE HUTTERIAN BRETHREN, 1528-1931.
    By John Horsch. 1931.
3. CENTENNIAL HISTORY OF THE MENNONITES IN ILLINOIS.
    By Harry F. Weber. 1931.
4. FOR CONSCIENCE SAKE.
    By Sanford Calvin Yoder. 1940.
5. OHIO MENNONITE SUNDAY SCHOOLS.
    By John Umble. 1941.
6. CONRAD GREBEL, FOUNDER OF THE SWISS BRETHREN.
    By Harold S. Bender. 1950.
7. MENNONITE PIETY THROUGH THE CENTURIES.
    By Robert Friedmann. 1949.
8. BERNESE ANABAPTISTS AND THEIR AMERICAN DESCENDANTS.
    By Delbert L. Gratz. 1953.
9. ANABAPTISM IN FLANDERS, 1530-1650.
    By A. L. E. Verheyden. 1961.
10. THE MENNONITES IN INDIANA AND MICHIGAN.
    By John Christian Wenger. 1961.
11. ANABAPTIST BAPTISM: A REPRESENTATIVE STUDY.
    By Rollin Stely Armour. 1966.

ANABAPTIST BAPTISM:
A Representative Study

By
Rollin Stely Armour
Associate Professor of Religion
Stetson University

PUBLISHERS
Eugene, Oregon

Wipf and Stock Publishers
199 W 8th Ave, Suite 3
Eugene, OR 97401

Anabaptist Baptism: A Representative Study
By Armour, Rollin S.
Copyright©1998 Herald Press
ISBN: 1-57910-158-5
Publication date 9/22/1998
Previously published by Herald Press, 1998

To My

Mother and Father

In Affection and Gratitude

Editor's Foreword

It is at first sight astonishing that in the two generations of growing interest in Anabaptism, no one has made a thorough examination of the views and practices which gave the movement its opprobrious name. Virtually every scholar who works in the Anabaptist sources has found himself required to evaluate the Anabaptist view of baptism; but the search for the essence of the Anabaptist spirit has led past the question of baptism to such issues as ethics, ecclesiology, and later to *Weltanschauung*. As Rollin Armour himself is quick to point out, this bypassing of the baptism issue in the search for essences is proper. However, an examination of Anabaptist baptism is long overdue. Scholars will welcome the fact that Dr. Armour, at present Associate Professor of Religion at Stetson University, has seized the initiative in doing it.

Not all scholars have been willing to admit Armour's Anabaptists to the main stream of the movement. Armour fits each man's thought into the larger Anabaptist picture so persuasively that the necessity for their inclusion is beyond question. Scholars will want to notice his judicious assessment of the Anabaptists' relations to the basic Protestant groups and to the Catholics.

Our own age does not, on the whole, take Christian baptism very seriously. Armour's work can be of great profit to the Christian layman by disclosing the multiplicity of meanings baptism had for an age which valued the ceremony so highly that it literally fought over it.

The Mennonite Historical Society is pleased to become a partner in this publishing venture. It welcomes the opportunity to cooperate with the American Society of Church History, whose Brewer Prize has enabled the enterprise to move forward without the customary financial problems. It wishes to express its gratitude for the excellent working relation with Dr. Armour. He has been patient with what may have seemed to him the editors' idiosyncrasies.

John S. Oyer

Author's Preface

The work contained herein was first presented as the author's doctoral dissertation at Harvard University under the title, "The Theology and Institution of Baptism in Sixteenth-Century Anabaptism." It appears here in a revised and, hopefully, an improved form. There has been extensive editing and rewriting, but the content and argument remain essentially the same; and, as the reader will discover for himself, the book still bears some of the marks of a doctoral dissertation.

The author is especially pleased that this is being printed under the joint auspices of the American Society of Church History and the Mennonite Historical Society. That the work should have received the 1963 Frank S. and Elizabeth D. Brewer Prize from the American Society of Church History is of course a distinct privilege, and the author wishes to express his gratitude to the Society's officers for the award. He is also grateful that this is appearing as one of the Mennonite-sponsored *Studies in Anabaptist and Mennonite History*. For the book to be included in this series is natural in a way, because it treats an important aspect of Anabaptist history. But since some of the conclusions differ from the generally held opinions of Mennonite scholars, one might have expected that the editors would have refused it. The fact that they accepted it speaks well for their breadth of spirit, and the author wishes to express his own appreciation for this.

A brief explanation is necessary on one matter of form. In the original version the titles of primary sources were transferred into the modern spelling and Christian names were translated into English. In compliance with the policy of the Mennonite Historical Society, this has been changed and the original spellings have been used. Exceptions to this rule are works which have been critically reedited by modern scholars. Titles of these have been given as found in the modern editions. Untranslated words and quotations are reproduced as found in the original text, the only exception being the substitution of the modern *Umlaut* for the archaic German diphthong.

One source consulted in the early stages of research is not named in the notes, although it is listed in the "Bibliography." This is the English translation of Hubmaier's works done in 1939 by Dr. George D. Davidson, then Chairman of the Modern Language Department of William Jewel College. Since his translation includes all of Hubmaier's writings, it is a handy source of reference. This was especially significant before the excellent edition of the Hubmaier *corpus* by Drs. Westin and Bergsten appeared in the *Quellen zur Geschichte der Täufer* series. However, accomplished linguist though Dr. Davidson was, he lacked the theological background necessary for such a translation, and thus his work is usable for only the most general purposes. But for these it is helpful, and it could well be recommended to English language students for introduction or survey.

The original form of this study was written under the guidance of Dr. George Huntston Williams, now Hollis Professor of Divinity, Harvard Divinity School. Without question, his constant encouragement and exacting scholarship are due no small credit for whatever contribution is made by the appearance of this book, and the author gratefully and happily acknowledges this. Credit is also due the following: Drs. Robert Friedmann, Gordon Rupp, and Torsten Bergsten, who read portions of the original manuscript and offered many suggestions; Dr. Raymond Calkins, who carefully examined the earlier dissertation and made many helpful suggestions regarding style; Dr. Fritz Blanke, who gave generously of his time and counsel when the research was in its early stages; Drs. Hans J. Hillerbrand, Gunnar Westin, Leo Crismon, and Alvin Beachy, and Mr. Ernest Lashlee, who helped by conversation and letter; and Drs. Walter Klaassen, William Klassen, William Keeney, and Robert Walton, who very kindly made their own dissertations available to the author. However, even though aided by the knowledge and wisdom of this company of scholars, the author has still made many errors, and, since they are his alone, he acknowledges full responsibility for them.

In addition, special appreciation is due to Dr. John S. Oyer of Goshen College for his patient and helpful liaison between committee, press, and author; he has more than once made rough places plain and crooked places straight and has consistently shared his good counsel as the work of revision and printing has progressed. The author also wishes to thank: Stetson University, for granting the time and means which have made research and writing possible; Mrs. James Mitchell, the author's secretary, who has cheerfully and expertly assisted in the lengthy process of revision; Dr. Maria Grossmann of Andover-Harvard Theological Library and Miss Anne Hurst of Stetson University for their unfailing help in obtaining books and sources; Mr. Nelson Springer of the Mennonite Historical Library for his assistance in obtaining rare documents and materials; the University Library of Budapest for a microfilm copy of Hans Hut's tract on baptism; and my wife, who helped in unnumbered personal ways and did the original typing, doing it flawlessly. R.S.A.

DeLand, Florida
August, 1965

Contents

INTRODUCTION	17
CHAPTER I. BALTHASAR HUBMAIER	19
The Movement Away from Infant Baptism	19
Influences upon Hubmaier	24
The Case for Believer's Baptism	27
Zwingli, Hubmaier, and the Idea of the Covenant	36
Baptism and the Church	44
The New Testament	47
Tradition and the Church Fathers	49
The Administration of Baptism: *Eine Form zu Taufen*	54
The *Rechenschaft*	56
Summary	56
CHAPTER II. HANS HUT: BACKGROUND IN THOMAS MUENTZER AND HANS DENCK	58
Baptism According to Thomas Müntzer	59
Baptism According to Hans Denck	62
The Authorship of *Von dem Geheimnus der tauf*	64
The Evidence for Müntzer	65
The Evidence for Hut	68
Further Details	73
CHAPTER III. HANS HUT'S BAPTISMAL THEOLOGY	76
The Baptismal Sign and Covenant	76
Inner Baptism: *Das Wesen der Taufe*	79
The Gospel of All Creatures	81
The Inner and Outer Covenants	83
Baptism and Eschatology	86
The Three Baptisms: Spirit, Water, and Blood	92
The Baptisms of John and Christ	93
The Administration of Baptism	94
CHAPTER IV. MELCHIOR HOFMANN	97
Regeneration and the Baptismal Covenant	97
Baptism, Eschatology, and Redemptive History	102
The Administration of Baptism	107
Hofmann on Infant Baptism: A Recantation	109
Scriptural Texts	110

CHAPTER V. PILGRAM MARPECK	113
Baptism and the Old and the New Covenants	113
The Baptismal Covenant	118
The Unity of Inner and Outer Baptism	120
A Threefold Baptism: Spirit, Water, and Blood	127
Arguments Against Infant Baptism	129
The Dedication of Infants	132
Baptism and Marpeck's Use of Scriptural Texts	132
The Administration of Baptism	133
CHAPTER VI. CONCLUSION	135
The Doctrine of Regeneration: A Key to Anabaptism	135
The Covenant of the Regenerate	138
The Objective Power of Baptism	139
The Baptized Life	140
APPENDIX. BALTHASAR HUBMAIER'S BAPTISMAL ORDER AS FOLLOWED AT NICOLSBURG	143
BIBLIOGRAPHY	187
INDEX	195

Introduction

Much has been done in historical scholarship within recent years to bring sixteenth-century Anabaptism into a light that is both new and more accurate than heretofore. However, little has been done to reconstruct the Anabaptist theology of baptism. That baptism should not have been treated first is no error, for, as is well recognized, the center of Anabaptism is not to be found at that point. Nonetheless, as the name itself suggests, the sacrament assumed a prominence in the Anabaptist movement that it had perhaps nowhere else. This study, therefore, is an attempt to uncover the theological meaning that baptism had in the minds of several representative Anabaptists.

Rather than survey the whole of Anabaptism, it was decided to base the study on a few major representatives in the belief that a view in depth at several key points might be of more value than a general survey. The subjects were chosen according to three criteria. First, each was to represent a different point of view on baptism, preferably an original one or at least one which brought a set of ideas to fulfillment. Second, more than one strand of Anabaptism was to be represented, and all the major areas or branches if possible. Finally, each writer should have authored or sponsored an important statement on baptism, preferably a tract or series of tracts which gave a clear and thoughtful interpretation of the ordinance.

These requirements were admirably met by four writers: Balthasar Hubmaier, Hans Hut, Melchior Hofmann, and Pilgram Marpeck.[1] Hubmaier, of course, was the first to give a detailed defense of Anabaptist baptism, and the many tracts he authored on the topic stand as the classical statement of the basic Anabaptist position. But others enlarged the meaning of Anabaptist baptism. Hans Hut's *Von dem geheimnus der tauf* provided much more depth of interpretation, as did, in its own way, Melchior Hofmann's *Die Ordonnantie Godts*. Probably the most developed was the *Vermanung* signed by Marpeck and his "Christ-believing comrades of the covenant and afflictions in Christ." Latest of the works here considered, it could be expected to be the most advanced and most satisfactory of the group; it fulfills this expectation well.

Our study will seek to expand the topic of baptism to include other areas to which it is related; e.g., the doctrine of regeneration (which will prove to be a pivotal matter), the view of the church and the Christian life, and, of particular interest in Hut and Hofmann, ideas on eschatology. In doing this we are following their lead, for in Anabaptist minds, baptism had a significance that reached into many areas. In a sense, then, this work is intended as a contribution to the general study of Anabaptist theology.

Finally, consideration will be given to the question of the relation of these Anabaptists to the other branches of sixteenth-century Christianity. The question is a difficult one and it can be answered definitively only in terms much larger than baptism. But just as a view through a small window can sometimes lend perspective on a scene, so perhaps can an examination of one sacrament reveal factors that give depth to issues more central to the theological understanding. At least we believe it to be so in this case.

CHAPTER I

Balthasar Hubmaier

On Easter Day, April 16, 1525, and the three days following, Balthasar Hubmaier baptized three hundred adults of Waldshut using water from a milk pail which had been placed on the baptismal font in his church.[1] He had been baptized himself along with some sixty others by Wilhelm Reublin just the day before.[2] With this deliberate flouting of the traditional baptismal ceremony, the Anabaptist reform was introduced into the little town of Waldshut. The town was already under criticism for its part in the Reformation and the Peasants' Revolt, but it was to be all the more pressed now that a sizable portion of its citizens had taken this radical step.[3]

So extreme a move did not develop overnight, of course. Hubmaier, for some four years beginning with his arrival in Waldshut, had been thinking about issues raised by Erasmus and Luther, and from 1522 on he had devoted considerable study to Reformation ideas. In 1523 he made contact with the Zwinglian reform in Zurich, and in the succeeding two years his theological development took place largely in relation to the movements there.[4] However, he soon found himself torn between the emerging factions within the Swiss city. For a time he attempted to find a *via media* between the opposing views, but once the group led by Conrad Grebel had taken decisive action and initiated an open schism, Hubmaier realized that he too must break with the conservative reform, and thus he entered into his brief but important Anabaptist career.

The Movement Away from Infant Baptism

Although Hubmaier indicated that his doubts concerning infant baptism may have begun as early as 1520,[5] the first clear evidence of his views on baptism during his pre-Anabaptist period is the report given by both him and Zwingli of a conversation between them beside the Zurich moat in early May, 1523. According to Hubmaier they discussed infant baptism and agreed that children should not be baptized until instructed in the faith. He says they agreed that this had been the practice of the early church.[6] Zwingli is less specific and says only that they discussed repentance and the great commission in Mark 16.[7] As it happens, this is the same text which had provided the Zwickau prophets with their argument against infant baptism.[8] Hubmaier and Zwingli both say that they were pleased with the conversation.

The accuracy of Hubmaier's report has been challenged, for some have questioned whether either Zwingli or Hubmaier made such radical statements about infant baptism at that time.[9] However, Zwingli himself lends support to the report's credibility when he says: "for some time I myself was deceived by the [Anabaptist] error and thought it better not to baptize children until they came to the age of discretion."[10]

It would also seem that Hubmaier is accurate in recounting that he himself questioned infant baptism at the time. Baptism was certainly discussed in the conversation; and even if, as Bergsten suggests, this may not have been the foremost topic in Hubmaier's mind,[11] there is no identifiable reason for doubting the substance of his claim. As early then as the spring of 1523, Hubmaier was entertaining questions about the validity of infant baptism.

By fall of the same year, the Zurich debate over the method of reform to be followed in that city was brought to a public platform in the well-known Second Disputation.[12] Two topics were discussed: the use of images in the churches, which was the topic on the first two days, and the meaning of the Eucharist, debated on the third and final day. The principal difference which emerged related to how strictly the Scriptures should be interpreted, on which point Grebel took a narrower approach than Zwingli.[13]

Hubmaier sided with the Grebel group on the last day and was in fact their principal spokesman in advocating an early and radical reform of the Mass.[14] However, on the preceding day, when the use of images was under discussion, Hubmaier spoke for the Zwinglian side, counseling that care be taken in correcting this abuse, "so that no one be made to stumble nor the fraternal and Christian peace be disturbed.[15] And in a manner exactly parallel to Zwingli's view in his 1522 *Von Klarheit und Gewissheit des Wortes Gottes*, he made this statement:

> [If the] clear and holy Word of God against the images and idols in the Old and New Testaments is earnestly and regularly proclaimed to the people, . . . its strength and power will be put to use and in time will pull down all the images. It is impossible that the Word of God be preached and bring forth no fruit or works in those who hear, for God Himself has sent it forth.[16]

According to this, the moderate view, the church was to bear with weak

Christians while the power of the Word of God was allowed its way to strengthen and reform. The radical view, on the other hand, counseled no tarrying and claimed that such could be only disobedience to the commands of God.

When in December following, the tension was increased by Zwingli's agreement to allow the Zurich Council to decide the nature and extent of the reforms to be introduced at that time—a decision partially anticipated in his statement at the October Disputation[17]—the controversy between the two factions became more serious.[18] Hubmaier was back in Waldshut then, however, and thus somewhat removed from the growing dispute. But when he soon stepped wholly onto the radical side, he took as his principal text the warning that "every tree which my heavenly Father has not planted will be rooted up."[19] However, at the time of the October Disputation he was still, in part at least, a supporter of the more conservative view.

When Hubmaier began to introduce Reformation ideas into Waldshut and urge their implementation, he encountered opposition from some of his fellow priests. In order to consolidate support for his reformatory program, he advocated that a disputation be held in Waldshut, and as a basis for the proposed debate he issued in early 1524 his first published work, the *Achtzehn Schlussreden*. Whether the disputation was actually held has been a question, but Bergsten, with good evidence, believes that it was.[20]

The articles contain two references to baptism, but unfortunately neither offers anything precise on the matter. Article Eight, based on the Reformation doctrine of the priesthood of all believers, reads thus:

> Just as each Christian believes and is baptized *(getaufft wirt)* for himself, so should each examine and judge by Scripture whether he is being given right food and drink by his pastor.[21]

The succeeding article was pointed toward a refutation of invoking the saints in prayer, but it also mentions baptism:

> Just as Christ alone died for our sins and we are baptized in His name, His name alone, so should He alone be called on as intercessor and mediator.[22]

Wilhelm Mau, assuming that the article implies approval of the baptism already received, maintained that the latter statement could not have been made by an advocate of believer's baptism,[23] but the article appears too general to justify the claim. Thus, Hubmaier's first work supplies little direct evidence for our topic beyond revealing that he recognized a connection between baptism and the priesthood of the believer, a point which can be reserved for treatment in the context of baptism and church order.

On May 26, 1524, shortly after the *Achtzehn Schlussreden* were published, Hubmaier introduced his first reforms of the Mass into Waldshut, reading the Gospel lesson in German and removing the candles and other liturgical appointments. Perhaps it was the tension with the Austrian authorities that precluded his carrying the reforms further, or perhaps he was waiting for the weak to be instructed through the preaching of the Word.[24] In either event, he was still pondering the question of infant baptism, and by late fall of that year he wrote Zwingli about the matter and may even have visited Zurich to discuss baptism with him.[25]

By early 1525 Hubmaier had reached a partial resolution of the matter: he would renounce the practice of infant baptism and encourage his parishioners to postpone the baptism of their children until the latter could make their own request for baptism. Exactly when his decision was made we do not know, but it would seem to have been before January 14 when Conrad Grebel wrote to Joachim Vadian that Hubmaier would soon "write against" Zwingli's view of baptism.[26] Certainly it was by January 16, for on that day—it was the day before the dramatic First Baptismal Disputation in Zurich—Hubmaier wrote to Oecolampadius to inform him of his decision to suspend infant baptism.[27] This letter is the first express denial of infant baptism from Hubmaier's hand.

That Hubmaier should have chosen the Basel reformer as the one with whom to communicate about the new practice in Waldshut is not entirely a surprise. Not only had the two pastors already exchanged correspondence over similar matters,[28] but, of the three principal reformatory figures of the southern region of German-speaking Europe—Zwingli, Martin Bucer, and Oecolampadius—only Oecolampadius was still open to a reconsideration of infant baptism. Both Zwingli and Bucer, only a few weeks prior to Hubmaier's letter, had published strong statements in defense of the traditional practice.[29]

The arguments of Bucer and Zwingli are worth noting. They were quite similar; in fact, Bucer had requested aid from Zwingli in selecting Biblical texts for his defense of infant baptism, which request Zwingli met.[30] At least four Biblical evidences are common to both in their support of infant baptism: (1) the precedent of the "house" baptisms of the Primitive Church; (2) the fact of Christ's blessing the children and His affirmation that they belonged to the kingdom of God; (3) the statement of Paul that children are made holy in their parents (I Corinthians 7:14); and (4) the argument of the unity of circumcision and baptism, an argument only mentioned by Bucer but developed at considerable length by Zwingli.[31] Bucer was alone in maintaining the specifically theological argument that outer baptism by man and inner baptism by the Spirit of God are two distinct and separate actions, although Zwingli already held the view and shortly thereafter made it an important part of his major defense of infant baptism.³² Thus, in Zurich and Strassburg the two leading spokesmen had publicly and resolutely defended the inherited practice of baptizing infants. They would hardly have been receptive to the news of Hubmaier's suspension of the practice.

Oecolampadius, however, was still unsettled about infant baptism. Even as late as 1527 he was of the opinion that the manner and time of administering baptism were *adiaphora* and that if parents were unwilling to have their child baptized at birth the baptism could wait until the child reached the age of three.³³ Evidently he had expressed similar views to Hubmaier and now Hubmaier was reporting the actual introduction of such a practice.

Hubmaier's letter reasoned that the nature of baptism is such that infants are unfitted for it. Baptism is, he said, a pledge "by which one pledges himself to God in faith even unto death," a vow that infants cannot take. Nor, Hubmaier said, should there be any contention over the matter, since the external action is regarded even by Zwingli as a "mere sign," and since all agree that the true inner action is the heartfelt confession of Christ and the renunciation of the devil.³⁴ Perhaps aware of Bucer's interpretation in *Grund und Ursache* of Jesus' promise to the children in Matthew 19:14, he inquired of Oecolampadius about the passage, saying that he himself was inclined to believe that it does not refer to infants, since Christ said "of *such* is the kingdom of heaven," not "of *them*" (italics ours).³⁵

Notable in Hubmaier's letter is his description of the dedication service for infants which he had instituted in lieu of baptism. He related that, after the infant was brought before the assembled congregation, the minister would explain in the vernacular the Gospel passage, "let the children come to me" (which text, curiously enough, he had just doubted as referring to children and which text the magisterial reformers were using to support infant baptism!). Then the child would be named, and while the church knelt in prayer he would be given over into the care of Christ with the plea that Christ would be gracious to him and intercede for him. Hubmaier was still concerned for the "weak in the faith" and told Oecolampadius that he would baptize the children of any whose faith would be upset by the omission of baptism, noting that it is better to bear with the weak until they are more adequately instructed.

Oecolampadius responded to Hubmaier's letter by saying that he still judged infant baptism to be proper, for through the prayers of the faithful the children could be saved from the punishment of original sin.³⁶ However, in a second letter two weeks later, presumably written after Oecolampadius had received Zwingli's opinion of Hubmaier's innovation—doubtless condemning it—the Basel reformer confessed his agreement with Hubmaier that Scripture does not explicitly support infant baptism; he added that it also did not expressly deny it.[37] But more importantly, he informed Hubmaier of his own pleasure with the new practice in Waldshut and even expressed the hope that it might find acceptance everywhere.[38]

Hubmaier's letter to Oecolampadius stands as a significant document in the sixteenth century, since it records perhaps the only attempt to move from infant baptism to adult baptism without breaking wholly with the *Volkskirche* and without totally disavowing infant baptism. But Hubmaier's desire to accommodate the traditional church to the new radicalism was to be short-lived, for soon he would receive a new baptism himself and then he would move completely into sectarianism.

By early February, 1525, Hubmaier, now emboldened by the recent baptisms in Zurich and the visit of Wilhelm Reublin to Waldshut, was ready to publish his view of infant baptism and did so in a brief piece entitled *Oeffentliche Erbietung an alle christgläubigen Menschen*. The little tract proposed a public disputation on the topic and announced that Hubmaier was prepared "to prove that the baptism of infants is a work with no ground in the divine Word." The Scriptures were to be the sole arbiter in the debate.[39] Dubious of the recent translations in Wittenberg and Zurich, he specified that the Bible to be used should be "fifty or a hundred years old."

But even though some members of the Waldshut community accepted rebaptism from Reublin at the end of January, he was not ready to speak out for the new practice. Indeed, he probably had not yet become convinced it was right.

Influences upon Hubmaier

Although Hubmaier's final views came only after considerable thought and his own investigation of Scripture, several factors may be identified as having played a role in their development. He himself claimed that the first direct stimulus toward a reexamination of baptism came from Luther, specifically from Luther's 1520 *Ein Sermon von dem neuen Testament, das ist von der Heiligen Messe,* in which Hubmaier found Luther stressing the importance of faith for the sacraments.[40] According to Hubmaier's statement this would have been in 1521, which was, as we know from other sources, about when Hubmaier was becoming introduced to Luther.[41] Although Luther did not intend what Hubmaier attributed to him, it is probably true that Hubmaier's first questions about baptism did arise from Luther's doctrine of *sola fide,* just as that doctrine, interpreted in Hubmaier's own way, served as his principal defense of "believer's" baptism.

Whether the Zwickau Radicals and Thomas Müntzer were a significant influence in Hubmaier's rejection of infant baptism is difficult to say; earlier scholarship is divided on the question. Loserth claimed that Müntzer was of decisive influence on Hubmaier;[42] Sachsse[43] and Bergsten[44] admit the possibility of indirect influence from the Spiritualists of Saxony and Müntzer respectively; Mau[45] and Vedder[46] tended to see Hubmaier principally in relation to developments in Zurich. It is notable that at their meeting in the spring of 1523, Hubmaier and Zwingli discussed the text from the Marcan form of the great commission, the same text that had been used by Nicholas Storch and his followers as the proof text for their criticism of infant baptism in late 1521.[47] The passage became one of the principal ones for Hubmaier too, indeed for all Anabaptists, and it could well be that he had heard of the Storchite interpretation at that early date.

That the Grebel group, in their letter of September, 1524, announced to Müntzer their qualified pleasure with his writings is already well known,[48] and Hubmaier could have shared the same feeling, learning of Müntzer's views either from them or directly by himself. Whether Hubmaier met Müntzer while the latter was visiting in Klettgau during the late fall of 1524 is not known. Bergsten observes that it is possible that Müntzer appeared in Waldshut, but nothing more can be said with certainty.[49] It does seem certain that Hubmaier had read Müntzer—the *Protestation oder Entbietung* in particular—for he reproduces a figure from Müntzer's tract.[50] This being so, Müntzer's arguments against infant baptism, and particularly his strong claim that the source of churchly corruption lay in the misunderstanding of baptism,[51] are likely to have influenced Hubmaier's questions of the practice and to have prompted him to move toward believer's baptism.

There may have been two further sources of influence upon Hubmaier and the emerging radical party to which he belonged. Erasmus may have contributed to Hubmaier's distinction between external and internal baptism (important for both Zwingli and the Anabaptists), for Erasmus said that baptism, in order to be valid, must be accompanied by true discipleship.[52] In addition, Andreas Karlstadt was probably influential in Hubmaier's rejection of infant baptism. He was certainly admired by the Grebel circle in Zurich,[53] and it is known that Hubmaier not only read and approved his communion tracts of 1524[54] but also adopted his interpretation of "this is my body."[55] Although Karlstadt did not himself proceed to the advocacy of believer's baptism, his strong criticisms of infant baptism plus his insistence upon individual commitment of life doubtless provided further impetus to Hubmaier's movement in the direction of adult baptism, and this was equally true for the Grebel circle.[56]

However, the most important influence of all was probably the Zurich reformation, Zwingli first and then the Grebel faction. As the discussion of Hubmaier's views proceeds, we shall see in greater detail how he both resembled Zwingli and differed from him. For the present we need only point out that Zwingli's own thought on baptism had within it some of the seeds which grew into Anabaptism.

First, Zwingli held to a moderate spiritualism whereby the inner spiritual action of cleansing and regeneration was sharply distinguished, indeed separated, from outer baptism. "How could an incorporeal substance be cleansed by a physical element?" he asked of Fridolin Lindauer in 1524.[57] This view that "Spirit" acts directly upon "spirit" was soon to be developed into the distinction between inner and outer baptism, one of the pivotal concepts in Zwingli's 1525 treatise on baptism, and one which Hubmaier himself adopted, virtually quoting Zwingli in summation of the view on one occasion.[58]

Then, Zwingli, like the other reformers, emphasized the role of faith in the sacraments. Earlier he had said to Thomas Wyttenbach: "You may wash a person in baptism a thousand times, but if he does not believe, it is in vain."[59]

By late 1524 and early 1525, Zwingli and Hubmaier were describing baptism in similar terms, even though with a different meaning. Hubmaier wrote to Oecolampadius in these words:

> Baptism is a sign and symbol signifying a pledge by which one pledges himself to God in faith even unto death in the hope of resurrection to the life to come. This meaning ought to receive more consideration than the sign itself.[60]

Just a few weeks earlier Zwingli had written similarly in his *De vera et falsa religione*, published shortly after Hubmaier's letter: "These ceremonies are external signs which demonstrate to others that the recipient has pledged himself to a new life and will confess Christ even unto death."[61]

It is, therefore, no surprise to find Hubmaier arguing in several places that Zwingli had once held "Anabaptist" views. And even though Hubmaier unfortunately weakened his argument by making inaccurate citations and drawing unwarranted inferences from Zwingli's statements,[62] it is true that Zwingli had unwittingly contributed to the views which were finally to cause him so much difficulty.

Finally, the crucial influence was the Grebel group. Hubmaier spoke as their representative on the third day of the October Disputation in 1523; he was probably in communication with them on occasions late in 1524;[63] and, most important of all, he was baptized by one of their number, Wilhelm Reublin, who had already baptized others of the Waldshut community. Having been led into Anabaptism through their direct efforts, he then became their foremost spokesman—as Heinrich

Bullinger said, "their literary leader and standard bearer."[64] This leadership was expressed principally in his writings on baptism, to which we now turn.

The Case for Believer's Baptism

With the introduction of believer's baptism into Zurich through the baptism of Jörg Blaurock by Conrad Grebel and its subsequent acceptance by Hubmaier and many of his congregation, the long developing differences between Zwingli on the one hand and the Grebel party and Hubmaier on the other became hardened into irreconcilable positions. Zwingli, who had already entered into literary attack against the developing radicals with his *Wer Ursache gebe zu Aufruhr* of December, 1524, now wrote specifically on baptism in *Von der Taufe, von der Wiedertaufe und von der Kindertaufe*, which appeared the following May.[65]

The Anabaptist side of the debate was taken up by Hubmaier. At the first of the year Conrad Grebel had reported to Joachim Vadian that Hubmaier would soon write against Zwingli on baptism, but no work was begun until after Zwingli's treatise appeared.[66] Then, on July 10, Hubmaier wrote in a letter to the Town Council of Zurich: "Last Friday I began a work which I shall finish today or tomorrow, God willing, in which I demonstrate that infants should not be baptized."[67] This treatise, *Von der christlichen Taufe der Gläubigen*, was published in Strassburg; the preface bore the date of July 11, 1525.* Hubmaier's most important work on baptism, it was conceived and executed as a reply to Zwingli, although Zwingli's name is not mentioned in it.[68] He incorporated into the work, as the last chapter, his little *Eine Summe eines ganzen christlichen Lebens*, which had been published on July 1, making only a few minor textual changes in the new form of the material.[69] The debate continued with further tracts, the most important of which were Zwingli's *Antwort über Balthasar Hubmaiers Taufbüchlein* of November of the same year, and Hubmaier's *Ein Gespräch Hubmaiers auf Zwinglis Taufbüchlein*, written in late 1525 and published in 1526.[70]

Hubmaier's fundamental concern was the defense of believer's baptism. Although this raised many theological problems, the discussion in its most narrow focus centered on the question of the dominical command and the apostolic pattern and precedent. Thus Hubmaier, like many Anabaptists after him, combed the New Testament for evidence to support his belief that the early Christian Church knew only believer's or adult baptism. This was a historical question to be decided, according to Hubmaier's methodology, by the literal command of Christ and the baptismal practices specifically reported in the New Testament.

*To distinguish the two similarly named tracts, Hubmaier's work will hereafter be called **Von der Taufe der Gläubigen** and Zwingli's work, **Taufe und Wiedertaufe**.

The Witness of the New Testament

When encountered at the Second Zurich Disputation of October, 1523, Hubmaier was found to stand with Zwingli on the question of the Scriptures and against Grebel, who claimed that the doctrine and practice of the true church must conform in a narrow way to the express mandates of the New Testament. The Waldshut reformer gradually changed in his thinking, however, and in his *Schlussreden gegen Eck* of the autumn of 1524, he maintained that the church was subject to the strict rule of Scripture in every area of its faith and life and that it had an inherent right of independent judgment only in cases of personal disputes within its body—all else was clearly set down in Scripture.[71] And finally, in *Von der Kindertaufe* of late 1525 or early 1526 he announced explicitly the view which was already assumed in *Von der Taufe der Gläubigen:* what is not explicitly commanded in Scripture is forbidden. The divine law is revealed in the Bible and one disobeys it in either subtracting from it or adding to it, both of which are idolatry in that the true God is set aside.[72]

With this view of Scripture in mind, Hubmaier turned in his first baptismal treatise to the question of infant baptism and argued that the practice is unchristian, since there is no explicit New Testament injunction favoring it. No text can be found, he says, which states, "Go into all the world and baptize the young infants, teaching them some years later."[73]

The Matthaean Commission, which Hubmaier thus parodied, had already been treated by Zwingli in *Taufe und Wiedertaufe* where he cited the Anabaptist argument that the Commission contains a three-stage progression—first, make disciples of all nations; second, baptize; and, third, instruct those further who have been baptized. Against this interpretation, Zwingli argued that the two concluding elements ("baptize" and "teach") are not part of a series but are appositive to the command to make disciples. He asserted then that if the argument is to be based on word order, the text actually supports infant baptism: one is to "make disciples" by first baptizing and then teaching.[74]

Hubmaier adhered to the common Anabaptist interpretation of the Commission, supporting his argument by saying that John's baptism followed the same order.[75] Quoting all the New Testament passages dealing with John's baptism and exegeting them, often in detail, he said further that Zwingli was wrong in speculating that John may have baptized the children of some adults who came to him.[76] Upon finishing the texts relating to John's baptism, Hubmaier then turned to the accounts of Christian baptisms and asserted that none of them said anything about the baptism of infants.[77]

Pushing his argument to its limits, Hubmaier rejected Zwingli's suggestion that infants may be baptized on the basis of their future faith in Christ and contended that Jesus said, "teach [i.e., make disciples of] all nations and *thereafter* baptize them in the name of the Father, of the Son, and of the Holy Spirit [italics ours]."[78] Nor would he allow the argument that infant baptism is supported by baptism's being an initiatory sign.[79] "A beginning of what?" he asked. It could not be a beginning of the Spirit of God, for, as he reminded Zwingli, the Zurich reformer himself denied that baptism conveyed the Spirit. Nor was it a beginning of faith, for that comes only through the hearing of the Word; nor the beginning of a new life, for infants do not know good from evil.

Beyond pursuing the negative argument that the New Testament witness would not support infant baptism, Hubmaier devoted himself to the positive argument that the New Testament teaching and practice require believer's baptism. In chapter five of *Von der Taufe der Gläubigen* he brought together all the major New Testament passages relating to Christian baptism, i.e., baptism following the resurrection of Christ, and sought to demonstrate that all of them either explicitly or implicitly describe faith as prior to water baptism.

Zwingli had heard this argument before, of course, and had challenged it in *Taufe und Wiedertaufe*, claiming that if everyone waited to be baptized until his faith were perfect there would be no baptisms. He recognized that the Anabaptists were not contemplating a "perfect" faith and raised the point principally to strengthen his view that baptism was an initiation into the Christian life.[80] Nonetheless, Hubmaier took his point seriously:

> You ask, "what or how much must I know if I want to be baptized?" The answer is that you must know this much of the Word of God before you receive baptism: you must confess yourself a miserable sinner and consider yourself guilty; you must believe in the forgiveness of your sins through Jesus Christ and begin a new life with the good resolution to improve your life and to order it according to the will of Christ in the power of God the Father, the Son, and the Holy Ghost; and, if you err therein, you must be willing to accept discipline according to the rule of Christ in Matthew 18: [15-20], so that you may grow in faith from day to day like a mustard seed, even up into the clouds of heaven. That much you must know. To know and to believe this is to believe that Jesus is the Christ, which belief is necessary before baptism.[81]

Hubmaier's final defense of believer's baptism was simply that Jesus commanded His disciples to administer it in this fashion and His followers to receive it, and, therefore, this must be done. Ten variations on the theme are given, but each reduces to the principle that Christ requires it.[82] Noting that other seemingly unimportant things have been com-

30 / *Anabaptist Baptism*

manded—Naaman's washing in the Jordan, for instance—he says that each had its purpose, and more importantly, each was commanded by God. Since baptism was commissioned in the name of the full Trinity, it ought to be honored above all things. He concludes: "Whoever does it not shall be punished with many blows as a servant who knows his master's will [but does not do it]."[83]

Inner and Outer Baptism

Behind this debate regarding the Lord's command and the apostles' practice rested theological issues. Probably the most important of them was the moderate spiritualism espoused by Zwingli and adopted by Hubmaier and the Conrad Grebel group. Specifically, the problem was the relation of the inner baptism of the Spirit to the outer baptism of water.

In speaking of Zwingli's influence on Hubmaier's early views of baptism, we observed that in Zwingli's letter to Fridolin Lindauer in October, 1524, the Zurich reformer had distinguished the internal cleansing of the Spirit from the external washing in water, asserting that the Spirit acted directly, not mediately, as through the water.[84] Zwingli developed the theme further in *Taufe und Wiedertaufe* and used it to solve the problem of John's baptism, saying that John, like the disciples of Christ after him, could confer only the outer washing in water, since the inner cleansing through the Spirit was the act of God alone.[85] Bucer had used the same argument against Clement Ziegler and his followers in Strassburg only a short time before.[86]

Hubmaier was not converted to Zwingli's view on John's baptism, but he did continue to share the latter's conception of inner and outer baptism. When he wrote his second polemic on baptism against Zwingli, he included a six-point summary of his views analogous to the six points Zwingli had enumerated at the end of *Taufe und Wiedertaufe*, taking the first of them almost verbatim from Zwingli.

Zwingli	*Hubmaier*
No physical element or external thing in this world can cleanse the soul; but the cleansing of the soul is the property of the unique grace of God alone.	No physical element or external thing in this world can cleanse the soul; but faith cleanses the hearts of men.
Thus it follows that baptism can wash away no sin.	Thus it follows that baptism can wash away no sin.[87]

The comparison of Hubmaier and Zwingli on the matter has already been treated by Bergsten, who has shown that Zwingli's views in *Taufe und Wiedertaufe* were echoed by Hubmaier in *Von der Taufe der Gläubigen* and *Ein Gespräch*.[88] Both held, as the above two quotations indicate, that the inner cleansing by the Spirit is separate from the outer baptism in water. This inner baptism is identified with faith by both, although Zwingli stresses the action of grace creating faith, whereas Hubmaier speaks only of faith without describing its source.

This difference in emphasis might be expected, for Hubmaier understood faith to be the individual's spontaneous inner commitment to Christ, and as such it was the precondition for spiritual regeneration through grace. Without that brief moment of personal commitment following the hearing of the Gospel and preceding the full regenerating gift of grace, there could be, in Hubmaier's view, neither personal conversion nor objective grounds for baptism. Zwingli, because he placed more stress on the divine action in the creation of faith, felt no need of requiring the presence of faith within the baptizand prior to baptism and finally moved all the way to the doctrine of election as his basis for infant baptism.[89] In fact, he was very near to this in *Taufe und Wiedertaufe* when he said, "God baptizes with His Spirit how, whom, and when He will."[90] Hubmaier's voluntarism precluded such action by God.

Nonetheless, Zwingli had an unsolved problem in his defense of infant baptism, for, as Hubmaier constantly reminded him, faith and baptism are kept in close relation in the New Testament. Zwingli had held that the faith of the parents was adequate for the infant, but Hubmaier had objected, inquiring how one could be certain of the parents' faith. He asked whether God would damn an infant if his parents professed to a faith they did not actually possess.[91] Zwingli finally solved the problem by moving to a conception of objective rather than subjective faith, saying that the term "faith" as related to infant baptism stands "for the sum of the whole covenant which we have with God, and not for the trust and faith that an individual has in his heart."[92] With that clarification, the cleavage between Zwingli and Hubmaier was complete: for the former, baptism was an act of the church corporately dedicating the infant to the Christian life; for the latter, it was an act of the individual personally pledging himself to God.

Hubmaier argued further that, if self-conscious faith had to come before water baptism, then Spirit baptism had to precede it also, for water baptism is "an outward and public testimony (*zeugnuss*) of the inner baptism of the Spirit."[93] Water baptism signified that the baptizand knew his sins to be forgiven, or as Hubmaier quoted from I Peter 3:21, that he possessed "the certain knowledge of a good conscience with God."[94]

The statement in I Peter had already been used by Zwingli with a similar interpretation, although not to the same purpose (i.e., believer's baptism), for he found in it further confirmation of his belief that the Spirit of God, not the sacrament itself, cleanses the soul. The conscience is not made clean by water, he said, but by the "promise" (*erforschen: Angelobung*) of the good conscience.[95]

Hubmaier used the text to describe the same inner conversion but also to defend believer's baptism, understanding it to mean that the "yes" of the good conscience had to precede baptism.[96] So it was with Noah and his family, he says, for their faith preceded the ark, the "type" of baptism.[97] It was the same in the ancient baptismal liturgies, which asked the baptizand if he believed in God the Father, the Son, and the Holy Spirit, a practice surviving in the baptismal orders to his own day, Hubmaier observed.[98]

But this inner knowledge must be testified to openly, Hubmaier said: one "must, must, must" have the outer washing of the body along with the inner washing of the spirit.[99] Not that the external act is in itself necessary to salvation—it is not, he says. Many thousands have been saved without it, as the Ethiopian eunuch would have been, had there been no water available for his baptism.[100] Similarly, Zwingli admitted that water baptism could be omitted with no threat to one's salvation, for "baptism is given and received for the sake of fellow believers, not for a supposed effect in those who receive it."[101]

Hubmaier did not, like Zwingli before him and Marpeck after him, defend water baptism on the grounds that the whole man, inner and outer, was to be cared for.[102] And yet, he was near to them in claiming that the inner reality must be matched by an outer reality, even if he differed by saying that the outer side was only the revealing of the inner rather than a supportive or confirming act in apposition to the inner.

The Problem of Free Will

As already observed, Hubmaier's conception of the relation of inner and outer baptism included a voluntaristic element: the individual had to "believe" before he could be baptized. The discussion of baptism thus turned into the problem of human free will.

Hubmaier's early tracts devoted little attention to the problem, since they concentrated on more limited aspects of baptismal theology. But it was discussed in detail by two later books, *Von der Freiheit des Willens* and *Das andere Büchlein von der Freiwilligkeit des Menschen*.

The key to Hubmaier's opinion is found in his conception and interpretation of the tripartite nature of man. When the first man elected to disobey God, he did so with the wills of his flesh and soul which parts of his nature were thereby corrupted. But the will of the spirit, man's highest will, was not a party to rebellion, and the spirit of man hence survives not only uncorrupted but also in possession of its original righteousness.[103] However, the Fall destroyed man's knowledge of good and evil, and thus his spirit does not know how to guide the soul and body, even if they were able to follow.[104] As to the *imago Dei*, it was not lost but only covered over with the ashes of evil. The breath of the Holy Spirit, given through the preaching of the Word, can bring the image back to full vigor, although man's actions will still be hindered by his corrupt body.[105]

But this regeneration of the soul requires the prior action of the individual's will. At this point Hubmaier distinguished between the external calling of God through the preaching of His Word and the internal drawing of the Spirit who illumines man's soul. The former comes without one's choosing it, as the church, established by Christ for this purpose, proclaims the Word which reveals the opportunity of salvation. But the latter, the calling of God that regenerates, comes only to those who have responded to the first call in faith and have pleaded for God's Spirit.

> They must pray and like Solomon beseech God in faith for wisdom. Doubting nothing they must cry, "Father, give us this day our daily bread." Like David, they must call, "Lord, give me understanding that I may learn thy way of making righteous and thy law."[106]

> God gives power and capacity to all men in so far as they themselves desire it. . . . But whoever refuses to come—like Jerusalem and those who buy oxen and villages and marry wives—these He will leave outside as unworthy of His supper. He wants guests and givers that are uncompelled, willing and joyful. These He cherishes, for God compels no one, save by the sending and calling of His Word.[107]

> As soon as God turns to us, calls us and admonishes us to follow after Him, and we abandon wife and child, ship and cargo—everything that hinders our journey toward Him—as soon as this happens our help has already come to us, namely, His converting, drawing will. By it He wills and draws all men unto salvation. Yet, choice is still left to men, for God wants them [to come] without pressure or constraint, and under no compulsion.[108]

Upon hearing the pleas of the believer, God acts through His lifegiving Spirit to regenerate the person so that the soul has restored to it both its lost freedom and the knowledge of good and evil and thus is once again able to choose between committing and refraining from sin. Thus, Hubmaier believed in a limited free will in unregenerate man—limited, in that man is incapable of choosing and doing good until aided by the regenerating Spirit of God; free, in that man can accept or reject God's offer of His Spirit. In regenerate man the will is completely free.[109]

The significance of this for believer's baptism is perfectly clear: baptism manifests one's faith, a faith attained by one's voluntary response to God and now confessed with the aid of the Spirit. This view would be standard for the Anabaptist movement.

Not so obvious is the fact that Hubmaier here perpetuates elements of the Catholic tradition. This is true at three points. In the first place, he believed that the gift of salvation is contingent upon the proper preparation of man's will for the reception of the gift. He did not use the Scholastic vocabulary of *dispositio arbitrii* or *meritum de congruo*—these he rejected as unbiblical and hence unchristian—but he nonetheless agreed in principle with the view those terms were coined to express, namely, that saving grace is given only to those whose will is receptive to it. In part, his position departed from the Catholic view, for he said that the initial overture from God was effected by an outer "drawing" through the Gospel rather than by an inner action of the Spirit in moving man's will. To that extent, he also drew a step closer to Pelagianism, for he meant by this that the human will is inherently capable of electing to believe the Gospel. This removed him even further from the Protestant *sola gratia* and the corollary doctrine of predestination.

Second, Hubmaier's understanding of justification was nearer to the Catholic view than the Protestant view. Justification, he said, is an inner regeneration and transformation which restores to man's soul and spirit (as distinguished from flesh) the innocence possessed before the Fall and the full power of doing good. The import of this is that man's acceptance before God is renewed by a righteousness present within man rather than by a forensic announcement by God.

Finally, Hubmaier believed that the Christian could attain a relative perfection. The only limitation he admitted was that of man's flesh, which, like a faulty plane in a carpenter's hand, will mar the work, but the work can still be built.[110] This, it hardly need be said, is radically different from Luther's *sola fide* and his *simul justus ac peccator*. It is also very near the Catholic conception of grace as that gift of God which makes man acceptable in His sight and capable of living above sin.[111]

At the same time, it must be admitted that it is to a degree illegitimate to call Hubmaier's thought "Catholic," for he wholly repudiated the Catholic sacramental theology which was interwoven with all other aspects of Catholic thought, anthropology included. On the other hand, Hubmaier was not "Protestant" in the classical and normative sense either, for he understood faith to be a human action of belief which brought divine grace rather than, as in Luther and Zwingli, a more passive trust created within man's heart *sola gratia*.

The significance of this for the Anabaptist movement can be analyzed only after further evidence is adduced, much of it evidence which will come from the other subjects of this study. But for now it should be observed that this would suggest two things: that the origins of Hubmaier's thought did not lie wholly within Zwinglian Protestantism, and that he and those who agreed with him might best be classified as belonging to a third party, neither Protestant nor Catholic.

At the time of Zwingli's and Hubmaier's first baptismal works in 1525, the issue of free will was not clearly drawn, but the bases for their difference were laid in the early tracts when Hubmaier adopted a decidedly voluntaristic view as part of his apologetic for believer's baptism. Then, in the tracts of 1526 and 1527 his free will doctrine became clear. And in the latter year Zwingli put forth the counter view by defending infant baptism with an appeal to election.[112]

Original Sin and the Status of Infants

The espousal of believer's baptism also opened the question of the status of infants. Hubmaier had no answer here; he simply pleaded ignorance. In contrast to this, Zwingli had developed a completely revised doctrine of original sin as part of his attempt to undermine Catholic sacramentalism. He had treated the topic at considerable length in *Taufe und Wiedertaufe*, explaining that original sin is an "inherited defect" *(Erbpräst)* or tendency toward sin which derives from the Fall.[113] He claimed that no guilt is attached to this until the inclination manifests itself overtly in conscious sin.[114]

> Original sin is a defect which is not of itself sinful for him who has it. This defect cannot condemn one—no matter what the theologians say—until he acts out of that defect against the law of God, and one can do that only if he knows the law.[115]

In this way Zwingli was able to admit that he thought it likely that even the children of unbelievers may be saved, although he concluded that one could not be certain of this.[116] He expressed no doubt about the children of believers, however: "The soul of the child is no less God's than the soul of the [believing] father."[117]

Hubmaier's treatment was not so thorough as Zwingli's nor were his ideas so pronounced. His principal answer to the question was to plead ignorance, stating crisply:

> I am not ashamed to be ignorant of that which God has not chosen to reveal to us with a clear and explicit word. He has said to me as to Peter, "What is it to you what I wish to do with the young children? Follow thou me!"

He then concluded that one could only leave them in the hands of God. If justice were to prevail, they would be damned, but he believed himself that in God's mercy they would be saved.[118]

From this vantage point one can say that there would seem to have been no reason why Hubmaier could not have successfully and profitably taken Zwingli's views and adapted them to his own framework as, e.g., Pilgram Marpeck would later do—no inherent reason, that is. However, the debate was doubtless sharp enough to keep Hubmaier from looking to the opponent's camp to find the solution to his own problems.

Zwingli, Hubmaier, and the Idea of the Covenant

Although this was all that Hubmaier could say on the question of infants, it was not all for Zwingli, for in addition to reworking the doctrine of original sin, the pressure from the emerging Anabaptists also prompted him to find a new foundation for infant baptism: he found this in the idea of the covenant. This was one of the more successful things Zwingli did, for it provided a new basis for the practice and at the same time lent further support to his developing covenant theology.

Hubmaier's development of the covenant idea was not as extensive or as successful as Zwingli's, but limited though it was, it was still of major importance for his baptismal theology and would become even more important for succeeding Anabaptists. On both sides, Reformed and Anabaptist, the idea of the covenant became one of the major formative elements for the theology and practice of baptism.

Old Covenant Circumcision and New Covenant Baptism

In defending infant baptism Zwingli reasoned that if the children of Christians were included within the covenant and its promises—and he believed them so to be—they should be granted the sign of the covenant. Under the old covenant this sign was circumcision; under the new it is baptism, he said. If the children of Israel received the former, should not, he asked, the children of Christians receive the latter? Of all Zwingli's arguments for infant baptism this was the strongest, for it found support in the very structural principles of the Reformed covenant theology already taking shape in his own hands.

Although, in a strict sense, Zwingli's conception of the unity of circumcision and baptism may be said to have been a new development within Christian theology, there were precedents for the view. Philip Melanchthon had discussed the two ordinances in his *Loci communes* of 1521 and had described them in such a way as to leave the impression that circumcision and baptism were very closely related. Positively, both were "seals" (*sigilla*, σφραγίδες) confirming to men the truth of their justification before God. Negatively, neither effected the justification of the recipient, for the *vis justificandi* belonged to faith alone, not to the sacraments (an argument Melanchthon used against the Scholastic view that baptism was superior to circumcision by virtue of such power).[119]

There was also Catholic precedent for equating the two ordinances. Gabriel Biel had said that circumcision, like baptism, was efficacious *ex opere operato* against original sin in infants and therefore could be called a sacrament (the only Old Testament ceremony so valued by Biel).[120] Similarly, the *Decretum Gratiani*, citing Gregory the Great and Augustine, had said that circumcision removed original sin.[121] If Catholic theology, which usually spoke of the redemptive power of the sacraments as deriving from the incarnation, could produce a minority wing capable of identifying circumcision and baptism, it was relatively easy for Zwingli to make such an identification, particularly when pressure from the Anabaptists gave him added need for Biblically supported bases for infant baptism.[122]

Zwingli's first public statement of his view was in *Wer Ursache gebe zu Aufruhr*.[123] In matters of dispute the church must always follow the Word of God, he said, and if the New Testament does not provide a clear answer to every question, one must turn to the Old Testament.[124] Infant baptism is such a question, and when the Old Testament is consulted, the precedent of infant circumcision readily presents itself. As New Testament support for his view, Zwingli cited Colossians 2:11, 12 and said that the text indicates that baptism is the Christian counterpart to old covenant circumcision.[125]

In *Taufe und Wiedertaufe* Zwingli expanded the argument to say that circumcision as originally instituted was not a sign confirming Abraham's faith (as Melanchthon had said[126]) but was "a covenant *(pundt)* that [Abraham and his descendants] would by their teaching lead their children and heirs to no other God."[127] That being true, the comparable Christian sign should be given to the children of Christians, for not only do they deserve to be dedicated to an upbringing within the worship of the true God, but by virtue of being born within the covenant people they are to be considered as numbered among the children of God.[128]

Hubmaier's answer to Zwingli's view was twofold. On the basis of I Peter 3:20, 21 he said that the true Old Testament "type" of Christian baptism was the ark of Noah, not circumcision; and the ark was entered only by adult believers, not by children.[129] The second argument, and the stronger of the two, challenged Zwingli's interpretation of Colossians 2:11, 12 and denied that it suggested that water baptism succeeded old covenant circumcision. The text, he reminded Zwingli, describes this circumcision as "a circumcision made without hands." "This concerns inner baptism, not outer, water baptism," Hubmaier said.[130] Zwingli's position was not demolished thereby, but it was considerably weakened by the withdrawal of the principal text upon which the Zurich reformer had based his views.

Curiously, Hubmaier did not carry his argument further—either positively, by working out the relation between water baptism and circumcision, or negatively, by pressing against Zwingli's views (which he ordinarily did in great detail). In fact, the matter is mentioned in only two works—*Von der Taufe der Gläubigen* and the *Gespräch*—and the Colossians text is discussed only in the latter and then in brief terms. Evidently, Hubmaier felt himself unable to come to grips with the covenant theology that was the key to Zwingli's argument.[131] It was an unfortunate gap in

Hubmaier's thought, for it meant that he had failed to deal directly and constructively with Zwingli's principal defense of infant baptism. The gap was not to remain long, however, for Pilgram Marpeck, with the aid of Hans Denck and others, soon developed a successful alternative to the position Hubmaier encountered in Zwingli.

The Baptism of John and the Baptism of Jesus

At one point, however, Hubmaier replied effectively to Zwingli's view of the covenant, namely, at the problem of relating the baptism of John the Baptist to that of Christ. Notably, Hubmaier's answer drew upon Luther. He summarized the relation between the two baptisms in these words:

> Now you must confess that the external water baptism of John signified an inner chilling of the conscience because of the knowledge of sin. But the external water baptism of Christ signifies an inner solace which precedes the water, [a solace present] in the [baptizand's] faith through his knowledge of the forgiveness of sins. The water baptism of John, in its signification, chills, freezes, frightens, kills, and leads into hell, for it gives only knowledge of sin. But the water baptism of Christ, in its signification, enkindles, quickens, comforts, and makes alive, leading one out of hell, for it gives only knowledge of the forgiveness of sin through the blood of Christ. You see, these two baptisms are as far apart as cold and heat, fear and consolation, Spirit and the devil, hell and heaven, death and life. How then can you so unashamedly speak of one baptism.[132]

John's baptism was the baptism of the law; Christ's was the baptism of the Gospel.

The issue had first been raised by the Zurich Anabaptists, who differentiated the two baptisms as part of the further-reaching distinction of the two covenants, old and new. The surviving Anabaptist documents from Zurich do not provide a good illustration of their view, but Zwingli partially supplies the lack at this point, for he devoted a whole section of *Taufe und Wiedertaufe* to the question.[133] He argued against them that the baptisms were identical since the preaching of John which accompanied his baptism and provided its meaning was the same as that of Jesus and His apostles.

> John pointed to Jesus with his finger and testified that He was the Son of God, saying, "Whoever believes in him shall have everlasting life. . . ." Is that not the whole Gospel, clear and plain? Away then you who divide baptism. . . ! For the Gospel began with the preaching of John.[134]

Further, John, like the disciples of Christ, could give only outer baptism in water, for the inner baptism of the Spirit was given by God alone.

Hubmaier accepted the distinction between inner and outer baptism, but he argued against Zwingli on the role of John. He contended that John's message was incomplete and preparatory. It provided knowledge of sin but not of forgiveness, for the latter was given through Christ alone. John proclaimed "the harsh and terrifying law, . . . and sin and death, just like the other prophets and preachers of the law" and did so because his role was only to prepare persons for Christ from whom alone they could receive forgiveness.[135] John was under the law, not under the Gospel.[136]

Thus, Hubmaier said, the Gospel began with the announcement of the forgiveness of sins following the death and resurrection of Christ. It was, therefore, not truly preached by Christ's disciples until after the resurrection, and, by the same token, Christian baptism did not begin until then, specifically until its institution in the great commission. The preceding baptism by John the Baptist was like the preaching that accompanied it and served only to reveal repentance, not to speak of forgiveness.[137] With the resurrection and the announcement of the Gospel of forgiveness, a new baptism was instituted as a sign testifying to the forgiveness now possessed by the believer, a reality heretofore not present.[138]

In saying these things Hubmaier at once continued and departed from Catholic tradition. He continued it in that he distinguished Christian baptism from that of John the Baptist and found in the great commission a crucial text for the institution of the ordinance; he departed from it in that he formally limited the institution of the ordinance to the great commission alone, rather than locating it in a series of events as the later Catholic theologians had done.[139]

Hubmaier's distinction between the two baptisms was compromised, however, for he found in John's baptism of Jesus a pattern which all Christians must follow in their walk of discipleship, and in this way, he partially reunited the baptism of John with Christian baptism.[140] Nonetheless, he claimed that all those baptized by John had to be rebaptized in the name of Christ. He called this the only case of a true "rebaptism."[141]

With this distinction in the historical roles of the law and the Gospel, and the related distinction between John and Jesus, Hubmaier had all the material necessary for interpreting redemptive history in terms of the two covenants, as later Anabaptism did so effectively. This could also have helped him to describe the relation between circumcision and baptism. He did not move in the direction of two covenants, however, but preferred to speak of a single covenant available to the Old Testament faithful in promise and to believers in reality.[142]

Beyond being a preparation for the revelation of the Messiah on the stage of history, John's preaching of the law—or more properly speaking, the law itself—has in Hubmaier's view a continuing function after Christ in that it reveals sin and convicts of it. That is, the law earlier prepared a race for the Gospel; now it prepares each individual. Conflating the image of Jesus as the Great Physician with the figure of the Good Samaritan, Hubmaier said that Christ can heal the wounds of a sinner only by first administering the wine of the law with its knowledge of sin and repentance, after which He gives the oil of the Gospel to comfort and heal.[143]

Hubmaier here reflects Luther's view of law and Gospel, a view he perhaps learned from reading Melanchthon.[144] The view became an important one for him, for its stress on the experience of repentance provided him a further argument in favor of believer's baptism.

The Baptismal Covenant

The debate over John's baptism, though laden with many implications, was only a minor element of the discussions about the covenant and baptism. Fundamentally, the issue between Hubmaier and Zwingli was one of two rationales of the baptismal covenant which differed in both theory and practice.

On the one hand, Zwingli believed that the baptismal covenant was the corporate act of the church which dedicated the baptizand, adult or infant, into the divine covenant. In the case of the infant, this was already his spiritual possession by virtue of the promise of God given to believers and their offspring. On the other hand, Hubmaier viewed baptism as the individual's own pledge of faithfulness and obedience to Christ, a pledge given within the Christian *Gemeinde* but made by the individual.

That baptism pledged one to the Christian life had earlier been stressed by Erasmus, who was perhaps the first Reformation figure to emphasize the point. A statement in his *Enchiridion militis Christiani* of 1502 virtually sounds like the later Anabaptists:

> Perhaps you do not know, O Christian soldier, when you were already being initiated into the mysteries of the life-giving bath, that you gave yourself by name to Christ as your leader (*Duci*). . . ? If you should too little stand by your covenant, does it not occur to you that you pledged yourself to such a kindly leader, that you dedicated your head, bound by His sacraments as if by a votive offering, to His fateful purposes? To what purpose was He delaying to impress the sign of the cross upon your brow, unless while yet alive, you might fight under His banner?[145]

Luther adopted the same theme in his *Ein Sermon von dem heiligen hochwürdigen Sakrament der Taufe* of 1519, describing Christ as the Christian's *Herzog* under whose banner of the cross the Christian "constantly fights."[146] But for Luther the divine side of the baptismal covenant was of the greater importance. Baptism, he said, was principally a sign to the baptizand of God's covenant not to reckon sin against him. "There is no greater comfort on earth than baptism," Luther said, "for through it we are judged in grace and mercy which reckons no sin [against us]."[147] Somewhat like the Franciscan idea of the *pactio Dei* in the sacraments, baptism for Luther was God's *Bund* assuring the baptizand of salvation.[148]

Zwingli's view was nearer Erasmus than Luther, for his early statements emphasized baptism as the Christian's "pledge" to Christ. "Baptism is the sign of a pledge," he said, "which indicates that whoever receives it is committed to amend his life and follow after Christ."[149] In words which seemed to speak of adult baptism and were thereby all the more a catalyst for his debate with the Anabaptists, Zwingli said: "The man who receives the sign of baptism designates himself as one who wants to hear what God says to him, learn His precepts, and live according to them."[150]

This did not mean, Zwingli said, that baptism was unsuitable for infants. It is only the "initiation to new life" and does not require the prior possession of that new life, as he understood the Anabaptists to say. Were such a requirement established, it would mean, he believed, that one could not receive baptism until he could live above sin. Nor did one have to understand all the implications and responsibilities of Christian living before being baptized. This sacrament, Zwingli said, is much like the cowl that introduces initiates into a monastic order: "The initiates do not know the rules and statutes when the cowls are made, but they learn them in their cowls."[151]

Military imagery appears in Zwingli too. He illustrated baptism with the analogy of the white cross that a Swiss Confederate wore on his uniform as a symbol of his loyalty to his people and suggested that Christian baptism was like the covenant-pledge of the *Eidgenossen*.[152] He did not consolidate the two vows as, e.g., Johann Eberlin von Günzburg had;[153] nonetheless, his concern for the New Israel in both its civic and ecclesiastical aspects was clearly reflected in his struggle to keep infant baptism, for he was well aware that the compact between church and *Obrigkeit* would be severely weakened were the practice discontinued.

However, it was not Zwingli's desire to accommodate the responsibilities of the civic *Eid* and the ecclesiastical *Bund* that drew Hubmaier's strongest criticisms. Rather, it was the Zurich reformer's assumption that one may be given the baptismal vow without voluntarily seeking it, or, more specifically, that unwitting infants may be enrolled through baptism into the duties of the Christian life. To make his point, Hubmaier happily quoted Zwingli's statement that baptism is a sign that one "is committed to amend his life and follow after Christ."[154] His rejoinder followed:

> Deo gratias! The truth finally comes to light! But if baptism is the sign of a pledge (*pflichtzeichen*), the pledge must precede the sign; and if a pledge is to be made, one must be instructed by word or Scripture beforehand.[155]

Then, having asked whether Zwingli's view truly represented early Christian baptism, Hubmaier continued:

> [The priest] mumbles over the infant in Latin (it could as well be German, for infants know one as well as the other; it is an error either way). Then the priest asks: "Credis in deum patrem omnipotentem, creatorem celi et terre? Say 'I believe.' " Now if it is in the Word of God that the godparents are to answer for the infant, "I believe," prove it with clear Scripture. But if it were in Scripture, why would the priest not say to the godmother and godfather: "You godparents, say 'we believe' "? . . . What they say should be said by the infant.[156]

As to Zwingli's objection that Hubmaier's interpretation of the baptismal pledge implied that whoever affirms the vow must be able to live without sin, Hubmaier's answer was a simple denial: he was fully aware, he said, that no one lived without sin.[157]

In his own development of the pledge concept, Hubmaier proceeded in two directions, the first relating to the individual, the second relating to the church. In a manner reminiscent of Luther and Erasmus, he applied the *miles Christi* theme to baptism and described it as a pledge to Christ under whose banner the Christian would fight, striving against sin the whole of his life.[158] It will be a difficult struggle, Hubmaier says, for the Christian, like Christ, will be beset with "fear, temptation, tribulation, the cross, and all manner of trouble in the world because of the faith and the name of Christ."[159] Finally, he will be isolated with no comfort but that of the Word of God; but with it he will be able "to quench all the fiery darts of this world, Satan, and sin."[160] This suffering will be partially inward as the Christian struggles with temptation and fear, but it will come largely from the affliction imposed from without by the unregenerate world which is hostile toward the church of Christ. The Grebel group had earlier described the Christian's lot in similar terms, calling this suffering a "baptism": "True Christian believers are sheep among wolves, sheep for the slaughter; they must be baptized in anguish and affliction, tribulation, persecution, suffering, and death."[161] As we shall see in greater detail, Hubmaier called this the baptism of blood which every Christian may expect, since Christ Himself underwent it before ascending to glory. Hubmaier agreed with Luther that this suffering may aid in the fulfillment of one's salvation, for it works along with the baptisms of Spirit and water to heal and purify of sin.[162]

The theme was to be developed much further by Hans Hut and his followers in their conception of the "baptism of all suffering"; indeed, the general idea of baptismal suffering was prominent in the whole Radical movement,[163] a point to which each of our subjects will testify, but it was not developed any further by Hubmaier. Even so, it is of note that with his more traditional attitude toward society and the civil powers, and with his general lack of mystical orientation, Humaier should make important use of a view that would play a great part in the thought of the mystical and pacifistic strands of Anabaptism.

In addition to this "private" aspect of the baptismal pledge, Hubmaier recognized a "public" or corporate side related to the church—this receives the greater attention. He said that baptism does two things in relation to the congregation: first, it identifies the baptizand as having turned in repentance from his sin and offered himself to Christ in faith; and second, as the vow pledging the baptizand to the Christian life, it enrolls him in the church whose supportive and corrective discipline he thenceforth shares. Reminding the reader that every church requires these two things—that the members be identified and that they be disciplined—he moves on to argue for believer's baptism as a *sine qua non* of the church: "Where there is no water baptism there is no church, no minister, neither brother nor sister, no fraternal discipline, excommunication or readmission—we speak here of the external church of which Christ spoke in Matthew 18:[15-20]."[164]

The first of these elements is the more straightforward: baptism is "an external confession or witness whereby the brethren and sisters can know one another in an open way, for faith is in the heart alone."[165] Little more need be said of this aspect of the baptismal vow, except to note the important point that in this instance the baptismal action is directed toward the congregation, for it announces the faith of the baptizand to the church.

The second element is more complex. Hubmaier continues his description:

> In receiving water baptism, the baptizand confesses publicly that he has yielded himself to live henceforth according to the rule of Christ. In the power of this confession he has submitted himself to the sisters, the brethren, and the church, so that they now have the authority to admonish him if he errs, to discipline, to ban, and to readmit him.... Whence comes this authority if not from the baptismal vow?[166]

The authority to bind and loose—the authority of the keys—is here tied with the baptismal pledge, so that the congregation is understood as able to exercise its disciplinary power over the individual, power ultimately derived from Christ, by virtue of the individual's having yielded himself to the church through baptism.

In part, Hubmaier was building on Luther before him, who, in denying the doctrine of the papal *plenitudo potestatis*, had claimed that no member or officer of the church had any separately derived power over the others but that "all Christians are truly of the 'spiritual estate,' . . . because we have one baptism, one Gospel, one faith, and are all Christians alike."[167] Even the power of ordaining and consecrating was, Luther said, derived through baptism, which, of course, all Christians have in common.[168] Zwingli too had grounded the disciplinary authority of the church in the doctrine of the universal priesthood of believers[169] and had treated the ban as a power of the local congregation (*kilchöre: Gemeinde*), without making explicit reference to baptism or the baptismal vow.[170]

Hubmaier went a step further than Luther and Zwingli, however, and described the power of the ban in terms of the vow given at baptism, thereby understanding both baptism and the ban in covenantal terms, even though he did not employ the term *Bund* which would become standard for other Anabaptists.[171] The effect was the same as with the later Anabaptist covenanters, however, for the congregation was conceived to be a band of the faithful, pledged together in discipleship and relying on each other for both supportive and corrective discipline. Christian baptism with its "knowledge of a good conscience" was here broadened by the penitential baptism of John, so that the believer, now redeemed within, pledged himself through baptism to the demands of the Christian life. When several joined together in this, a Christian congregation was formed, at once penitential and pure.

Again we encounter the Anabaptist doctrine of regeneration, now in terms of church order, rather than just in terms of individual life and the power of the will as before. Since, in Hubmaier's view, the renovated soul "may or may not sin," and since the church was to be kept pure, the baptismal vow became crucial, for it was the point at which the believer obligated himself to the Christian life and was thus the point at which he publicly and formally recognized the church's disciplinary power over him. Following Luther and Zwingli, Hubmaier understood the congregational actions of baptism and ban to rest on the Reformation doctrine of the universal priesthood of believers, but he differed from the classical reformers in an important regard: the "believers" who were to receive baptism had been, in his view, renewed and restored to health in soul and spirit, not merely justified forensically.[172] These reborn persons were capable of both pledging themselves to the Christian life and living it. In this way both baptism and ban were grounded in the Anabaptist doctrine of regeneration.

Baptism and the Church

Although Hubmaier and Zwingli agreed that Christian discipline was the responsibility of the local congregation, not of the universal church,[173] they did not agree on baptism's role in respect to these two forms of the church. Zwingli, believing that the infants already belonged to the church universal and invisible (Zwingli did not speak of a visible, universal church[174]), maintained that they should be admitted into the local congregation through baptism and that the sacrament served only to enroll them in the *ecclesia particularis*.[175] Hubmaier, perhaps once again reflecting his Catholic background, held that baptism enrolled one in the *ecclesia universalis*, believing that this is visible, not invisible.[176] Since, in his view, the local congregation was the "daughter" of the universal church, and since both (local and universal) are the church on earth, a believer entered the one when he entered the other.

If, however, baptism enrolls one in the *ecclesia universalis*, it must be closely related to salvation; and Hubmaier, in fact, said that it is. Not all of his statements reveal this, for many speak of the relation between baptism and the church in terms of Anabaptist voluntarism, whereby baptism, as a profession of faith, is the foundation upon which the church takes its rise: "This outward profession makes a church and not faith alone."[177] But the congregation of believers gathered through baptism was, in his view, more than the fellowship of the faithful: it was also the earthly successor to the incarnate Christ, and as such it had the power of forgiving sin:

> After the resurrection, Jesus gave His disciples, as His emissaries and servants, the power of forgiveness of sin, saying: "Receive the Holy Spirit. Whosoever sins you remit, to them they shall be remitted; whosoever sins you bind, to them they shall be bound. . . ." Before the resurrection, Christ's disciples pointed to Him all who had confessed their sins, that He might forgive them, announcing forgiveness of sins to them with an evangelical word, as He often did. But *after the resurrection they received that same office* [italics ours], so that they themselves were to announce the forgiveness of sins through Christ, who, no longer here bodily, is present in His Word and through His disciples, and will abide with us so to the end of the world.[178]

Here Hubmaier is speaking of the powers of the Word and the Spirit which the church has by virtue of Christ's having given them to His disciples before His ascension. But the power of these keys is a high office, for, as he said later in *Von dem christlichen Bann*, after the resurrection Christ gave "all his power" to the church, the same power which He had received from the Father.[179] The disciples, once they possessed this power, pointed the sinner to the church for forgiveness, not to Christ, as had been done by John and the disciples before Christ's death and resurrection.

The relating of the power of the keys to baptism was done chiefly in Hubmaier's *Grund und Ursache,* a portion of *Von der Taufe der Gläubigen* revised and enlarged about the same time he was writing *Von dem christlichen Bann.* His statement is as follows:

> Whatever importance one attributes to fellowship with God the Father, the Son, and the Holy Spirit, to communion with all the heavenly hosts and the whole Christian church, even to the forgiveness of sins, so much ought he to attribute to water baptism. For through this baptism one enters and is incorporated into the universal Christian church, outside of which there is no salvation.
>
> Not that remission of sins is to be attributed to the water, but rather to the power of the keys, which Christ in the power of His Word gave to His Spouse and unspotted Bride, the Christian church for the time of His physical absence, hanging these keys at her side when He said to her, "receive the Holy Spirit. . . ."
>
> Here one should note carefully that the universal church now has the power on earth to loose or bind sins, which power Christ had when formerly a man bodily present here. Whoever believes the Word of God now enters the ark of Noah which is a true type of water baptism, and thus he will not drown in the flood of sins outside the ark.[180]

When one receives baptism, Hubmaier says, he enters the true ship of salvation by which alone one can escape the floods of sin. Since the church can be entered only through water baptism, the ordinance is, thus, raised from the level of a simple confession of faith to the level of redemptive necessity, cases of emergency being the only exception. Not wanting to appear a sacramentalist, however, Hubmaier attempted to qualify this by saying that the actual power of the keys is found in the Word, not in water baptism itself.

Two conclusions may be drawn from this. First, Hubmaier has preserved, in attenuated form, the Catholic doctrine of the keys by insisting that one must belong to the visible, universal church in order to receive salvation. Thus, his final position on the necessity of baptism was that the external testimony of the good conscience is as necessary as the inner testimony. Earlier statements had said that baptism was necessary because Christ had commanded it; but now there is another side to the matter—water baptism is necessary for the forgiveness of sins, in that it introduces the believer into the church of Christ within which alone forgiveness is found. And even though Hubmaier said that outer baptism did not save, in his view it certainly admitted one to salvation and thus was virtually as essential as inner baptism, though not as powerful nor in itself redemptive.

The second conclusion is partly an anticipation of things to come with the other subjects of our study, but it is related to Hubmaier also. Hubmaier was very near to having baptism speak *to* the baptizand as well as *for* him. Most of his treatment stressed the confessional aspect of the ordinance, of course, according to which the inner experience of grace is turned into outer testimony to gain the recognition of the other believers. But baptism enrolled the believer in the church of Christ, the fellowship of the redeemed, and it was only among this fellowship that one could find salvation, he said.[181] Baptism, then, was a sign to the baptizand that he belonged to the house of salvation, to the company of the saints—perhaps not a sure sign in the sense of a sacrament, but a strong sign nonetheless. Thus, just as Hubmaier thought of an inner witness of the Spirit which testified to one's salvation, he also thought of an outer witness, water baptism, which signified to the baptizand that he belonged to the company of the true believers. Hubmaier's statements were not this explicit, but his position said this implicitly. We shall see that Hut, Hofmann, and Marpeck will be explicit about this objective element in baptism. Meanwhile it is notable that Hubmaier, who stressed the confessional side of baptism so earnestly and persistently, should articulate a position which had latent within it much more than confessional baptism.

The New Testament

The discussion of Hubmaier's debate with Zwingli over the relation of John's baptism to that of Jesus treated the major theological issues but did not examine their views on the principal New Testament text involved. This is the account in Acts 19:1-7 of Paul's baptizing in Ephesus a group which had already received John's baptism. The passage, a *locus classicus* for this question, had been discussed earlier by Martin Bucer in his *Grund und Ursache* in which he argued for the unity of Jesus' and John's baptisms. Bucer said that the Ephesians were baptized "in" (*auff*) or "into" (*zu*) the baptism of John, not "with" (*mit*) it; that is, they had not received even John's baptism but had only been baptized in anticipation of it.[182]

Zwingli took a different turn and said that the text should be translated "into what were you baptized," i.e., on what grounds, or to what end.[183] The same distinction had been made only a few paragraphs earlier where Zwingli said that the Matthaean form of the commission should be translated, "baptizing them into the name" (*in den namen*), not "in the name" (*im namen*) of the Trinity.[184] Further, he argued that the word "baptism" may be understood in the New Testament to mean "teaching" and should be read thus in this passage. His conclusion was that the Ephesians were baptized by John on the grounds of their faith in the Messiah to come, and that Paul needed only to administer the baptism of teaching, introducing them into the full knowledge of Christ.

Hubmaier took issue with Zwingli—"that light-headed man" as he called him—on the matter of the prepositions and cited against him the 1524 Zurich New Testament which preserved the Vulgate reading, *in quo* (*worinn*).[185] Hubmaier took great delight in reminding Zwingli (in the *Gespräch* where he dealt with him by name) that the latter had praised the Zurich translation with "high words."[186]

Using the distinction between law and Gospel as the key to his interpretation, Hubmaier claimed that Acts 19 tells of a true rebaptism. Hubmaier described the sequence of events as follows:

> First, John led his hearers into the knowledge of their sins. Second, he baptized those who confessed their sins and made them his disciples. Third, he pointed them to Christ. Fourth, Christ forgave their sins. Fifth, all who believed in the forgiveness of their sins had to be rebaptized by Christ's apostles. Thus, one may call this a true "rebaptism."

But not wanting to prove too much, he added:

> But this baby bath, which we previously held as baptism, is not baptism at all, and is not worthy of the name "baptism." Therefore, there are no grounds for saying that we receive "rebaptism."[187]

The reverse side of Hubmaier's view that John's baptism was only a preparation for Christian baptism was that the latter was instituted by the resurrected Christ through the great commission. It is of note that Hubmaier, and the Anabaptists in general, stood with Catholic tradition on the question of John's baptism. The Schoolmen had held, following the Fathers, that John's baptism was not the same as that instituted by Christ, a position confirmed by the Council of Trent.[188] Hubmaier marked out what was to be the standard Anabaptist position on the matter, namely, that John's baptism had been only a preparation for true Christian baptism, for since baptism is a sign testifying to the baptizand's experience of forgiveness, it could have been instituted only after that forgiveness was present, i.e., only after the resurrection of Christ.[189]

Although Hubmaier did not understand I Peter 3:20, 21 in the covenantal signification so important for many other Anabaptists, he did build an important part of his argument on the text, claiming that the "good conscience" saves, since it is the inner assurance by faith of the gracious forgiveness of God.[190] Further, the reference of the text to Noah's "baptism" in the flood served Hubmaier as a defense against Zwingli's argument that circumcision was the Old Testament counterpart to Christian baptism.[191] Zwingli had used Colossians 2:10-12 as his principal New Testament support for the argument. Hubmaier dealt with this too, maintaining that the passage refers to an inner circumcision or baptism, not an outer baptism.[192]

In Hubmaier's letter to Oecolampadius of January 16, 1525, he had asked the Basel reformer to give his view on the promise of Christ to the children,[193] inquiring whether Christ's saying "of such" instead of "of them" was the key to the interpretation. Hubmaier himself thought it was and interpreted the verse to mean that Jesus was giving a lesson in humility.[194] Oecolampadius' reply of *ca.* January 18 did not answer the query, but his next letter adopted the view already put forth by Zwingli and Bucer. Even though the text said "of such," the fact that Jesus proceeded to bless the children was support enough for infant baptism.[195] Hubmaier retained his own view, although other Anabaptists were to use the text as an argument against infant baptism by claiming that, if the children were already holy, they needed no baptism.[196]

In addition to these, Hubmaier collected virtually all the New Testament texts which record actual baptisms and commented on them. Adducing evidence from each of them, he argued that preaching and faith preceded every recorded baptism given by both John and the disciples of Jesus.[197]

Other passages, like Hebrews 10:22 and Romans 6:3, 4, also appear in Hubmaier's writings but were not employed as major supports for his arguments. Hebrews 10:22, which speaks of "our hearts sprinkled clean from an evil conscience and our bodies washed with pure water," provided an excellent proof text for his conception of inner and outer baptism, and he used it on occasion, although less often than one might expect.[198] Romans 6:3, 4, a natural text for the Anabaptists who stressed the idea of dying to sin and rising to new life, was, surprisingly, not commented on in *Von der Taufe der Gläubigen* but was only referred to.[199] It was employed in the *Gespräch,* however, where Hubmaier chided Zwingli for having used it in *Taufe und Wiedertaufe* to support infant baptism. Hubmaier claimed that this text was the strongest one on the Anabaptists' side since it emphasized the inner death and resurrection which, Hubmaier said, had to precede water baptism.[200]

Tradition and the Church Fathers

More than any other Anabaptist in our study, Hubmaier, drawing on his training as *doctor theologiae,* enlisted the aid of ancient patristic and conciliar statements to support his advocacy of believer's baptism. He did not intend to provide added authority for his belief—Scripture was all-sufficient for that, he said—but he did hope to prove to his opponents that believer's baptism had been the early practice of the church.[201]

The studies of Sachsse and Bergsten have already explored this area of Hubmaier to profitable result. The former located most of the references cited in Hubmaier's *Der uralten und gar neuen Lehrer Urteil*,[202] which contains the bulk of his citations, and the latter has provided a brief overview of the area, devoting particular attention to Hubmaier's use of Jerome and Augustine.[203] The contribution of the present study will be to survey Hubmaier's references and classify them according to the purpose to which he put them and the source from which they were derived.

The Defense of Believer's Baptism

Oecolampadius, in his 1525 tract against the Anabaptists (*Ein Gespräch etlicher Predicanten zu Basel*), had cited Origen as a witness that infant baptism had been the practice of the church since apostolic times.[204] Hubmaier also had read Origen and replied with references of his own, attempting to use them as a rebuttal against Oecolampadius.[205] The quotations were not entirely apt, however. In the first place, Hubmaier cited no passage referring directly to believer's baptism but used only references that spoke of general matters like repentance, hearing the Gospel, and faith—all of which Hubmaier understood to represent believer's baptism, even though they do not do so in the original text.[206] Second, the citations are near the three principal passages in Origen which testify to infant baptism, and one of them is even in the same paragraph.[207] Hubmaier's use of Origen, therefore, is considerably less than successful in building his case for the ancient practice of believer's baptism.

Bulking large over the Origen quotations is the series of citations from the *Corpus juris canonici*, first referred to in *Von der Taufe der Gläubigen* and later quoted in the *Urteil*.[208] The *Corpus* was quoted first as further evidence that the early church employed a catechumenate period in preparation for baptism and then was also cited for its approval of rebaptisms in cases where the original baptism was invalid.[209] Hubmaier took especial delight in this evidence, of course, since he felt he was using the pope's own weapons against him.[210]

In addition to the heretical Origen and papal canon law, Hubmaier adduced evidence from several Fathers to demonstrate the early church's practice. Tertullian's description of the baptismal ceremony in *De corona militis* was cited,[211] as was Cyril's mention of faith before baptism,[212] and the case of the youths baptized by young Athanasius, which baptisms were declared valid since the lads were believers and desired baptism.[213] Hubmaier also referred to Athanasius directly, noting that he spoke of repentance as prior to baptism.[214]

In this way Hubmaier attempted to demonstrate that the early church knew and followed the custom of baptizing adult believers. But his argument was at best a weak one, for not only is his evidence poorly chosen at times (the case of Origen is the notable instance of failure here), but the argument tends toward a *non sequitur*, as follows: since the early church baptized believers, it did not baptize infants. Hubmaier's argument was not so strong as he thought.

In addition to using the Fathers as evidence of the baptismal practice of the early church, Hubmaier also enlisted their theological views in support of his own. Ambrose and Theophylact were called on to testify that faith is necessary to a valid and efficacious sacrament, the former saying that a sacrament is grounded on the Word and faith together, the latter saying that faith without baptism cannot save, a point which Hubmaier read in reverse.[215] But for stronger support Hubmaier turned to Jerome and Basil the Great, whom he could quote directly—in words which Hubmaier himself might have written—to the effect that faith preceded baptism.[216]

Hubmaier also found patristic support for making a sharp distinction between the Old and the New Testaments and between the baptisms of John and Jesus. On the former he recalled Cyril of Jerusalem who spoke of the "figures" of baptism in the Old and the New Testaments,[217] and Basil the Great who saw the Flood as prefiguring Christian baptism.[218] To show the difference between the baptisms of John and Jesus, at least five Fathers were cited: Origen, Cyril of Alexandria, Jerome, John Chrysostom, and, mistaking him for a Father, Theophylact, the eleventh-century Archbishop of Ochrida in southern Yugoslavia—all of whom understood John's baptism to have been preparatory and incomplete, and understood true Christian baptism to have been instituted with Jesus.[219]

One additional view found support in the traditionally heretical figure, Origen. This was the interpretation that Jesus' statement, "of such is the kingdom of heaven," is to be understood as a lesson in humility.[220]

Taken together these passages comprise a relatively large collection of patristic evidence. It is very likely that Hubmaier had examined the Fathers from very early in his questionings about baptism, for his conversation with Zwingli in 1523 included the point of early Christian baptismal practice. However, when he began to advocate believer's baptism in writing, he made only gradual use of the evidence, for his first purpose was the exegesis of Scripture, whose teaching must be followed, he said, no matter what the early practice had been. He remained suspicious of the Schoolmen, just as he had been when he wrote the *Achtzehn Schlussreden* in which he claimed that Aquinas, Bonaventure, Scotus, and Occam had built on human reason, not on God and His Word.[221] For a time, he cited Augustine with nothing but criticism and blamed him more than anyone else for the development of infant baptism, and particularly for the view that infants would not see God if they died unbaptized. But later he found support in Augustine and cited him in arguing that repentance must precede baptism and that baptism must be accompanied by faith.[222] Hubmaier's treatment of these early writers came to its conclusion in late 1525 or early 1526, when, after being released from his confinement in Zurich, he composed the *Der uralten and gar neuen Lehrer Urteil,* perhaps with the aid of books to which he had access in Augsburg, or elsewhere between Zurich and Nicolsburg. And even though the work contained numerous errors, both bibliographical and theological, it did serve to call attention to one aspect of the early Christian practice, and, perhaps more importantly, to show Hubmaier's desire to stand in continuity with the church of early times.

The Three Baptisms: Spirit, Water, and Blood

Catholic tradition, beginning with the early Fathers, had spoken of a threefold baptism, a conception based specifically on I John 5:6-8: "There are three witnesses, the Spirit, the water, and the blood" (verse 8). The New Testament, of course, has much to say about the baptisms of Spirit and water, and these were certain to find elaboration through the development of the church. The idea of a baptism of blood did not have an explicit basis in Scripture, however, and may be said to have been developed out of the historical situation of the early church, when it faced the problem of the martyrdom of believers who died as unbaptized catechumens. Tertullian and Cyprian, recognizing the devotion and true faithfulness of these unbaptized martyrs, and recalling Jesus' comments about His own martyrdom, said they had received a baptism of blood. Tertullian said: "This is the baptism which both stands in lieu of the fontal bathing when that has not been received, and restores it when lost."[223] Cyprian, recognizing the great meaning of such a death, spoke of it as "greater in grace, more lofty in power, more precious in honor" than the first baptism in water, having the distinct advantage of taking one beyond the possibility of sin.[224]

The deficiency of water baptism was also a problem in the case of any who were converted but through an emergency or unusual circumstance died before they could receive water baptism. The Fathers reasoned that God would surely supply their lack. Ambrose, speaking at the funeral of Emperor Valentinian II who died while yet a catechumen, gave voice to the view:

> Did he not obtain the grace which he desired? Did he not obtain what he asked for? Certainly he obtained it because he asked for it.[225]

Thus in addition to the *baptismus sanguinis,* the church came to think of a baptism of desire, or a *baptismus flaminis.* As the epistle had said, "There are three witnesses, the Spirit, the water, and the blood; and these three agree."

Thus, Hubmaier had a long tradition before him when he began to speak of the three baptisms. But as an Anabaptist he could not describe them in the traditional way. In Catholic theology the baptisms of blood and Spirit (when separate as the baptism of desire) were necessary articles of faith, for, since water baptism was essential to salvation, they served to replace that baptism when water could not be legitimately obtained. Hubmaier considered water baptism necessary, of course, but largely because of the Lord's command and baptism's power to introduce one into the church, not because of any action it performed within the baptizand. Thus, its omission in cases of emergency was no threat to the individual's salvation. Yet, the text in I John stood awaiting interpretation, and since it already had a traditional relation to baptism, Hubmaier treated it with baptism in mind.

While Catholic theology envisioned an individual as ordinarily receiving only one of the three baptisms, Hubmaier considered all three to be necessary. We have already seen the sense in which this was true of Spirit and water baptisms. Since Spirit baptism was the action of regeneration, it was the reality of salvation itself, but water baptism was necessary too, unless one was absolutely prevented from receiving it. Following these, the Christian would enter the baptism of blood. The three baptisms are summarized in this passage:

> I confess three types of baptism: that of the Spirit given internally in faith; that of water given externally through the oral confession of faith before the church; and that of blood in martyrdom or on the deathbed. Christ spoke of the latter in Luke 12[:50-53], and He also told of the spiritual wine and oil which the Samaritan poured into the wounds of the injured man (Luke 10[:34]). John names these three baptisms with which all Christians must be baptized "the three witnesses on earth" ([I] John 5[:8]). Whoever will cry to God with Christ, "Abba Father, dear Father," must do so in faith and must also be baptized with Christ in water and suffer with Him in blood.[226] Then he will be a son and heir of God, a coheir with Christ, and will be glorified with Christ (Romans 8[:15-17]). Thus, no one should be surprised at persecution or suffering, for Christ had to suffer to enter into His glory (Luke 24[:46]). And Paul writes that all who want to live godly lives in Christ Jesus will suffer persecution (II Timothy 3[:12]). This is the third or last baptism in which one is to be anointed with the oil of the holy and comforting Gospel by which we are made pliable and ready for suffering. Thus is our sickness healed and we receive forgiveness of sins (James 5[:13-15]).[227]

Blood baptism is described here as both martyrdom and the deathbed. The first, which recalls the discussion of baptism as a dedication to suffering, serves to place Hubmaier within the "theology of martyrdom" often characteristic of evangelical Anabaptism from the Grebel group onward. In Hubmaier's view, suffering is first encountered when the law creates anguish and guilt within the soul, as indeed is mentioned in this passage. But following the regenerative work of the Holy Spirit this affliction subsides, and the suffering of temptation and persecution begins. As with Christ, this starts soon after baptism.[228] The Christian should glory in this suffering, for it shows that he has been made worthy to follow in Christ's way, and if so, he will be sustained in it by God's grace.[229] Thus, like Jesus, he has a baptism yet to be accomplished, perhaps martyrdom itself in which he shall give his final witness of a good conscience.[230]

The second sense in which Hubmaier spoke of a baptism of blood related to the deathbed, whereby he seems to have been recalling Luther's view that baptism is a lifelong death to sin, and resurrection to new life in Christ. "What is the baptism of blood?" Hubmaier asked: "It is a daily mortification of the flesh continuing unto death."[231] Thus, Lutheran and Anabaptist elements were combined, so that Hubmaier understood the baptism of blood to begin with the inner suffering of guilt brought on by the law, to continue through the daily struggle of learning to conform unto Christ, and to be concluded in death. Whether a violent death on the martyr's pyre in the final testimony of a good conscience, or a more peaceful and natural expiration, the result would be that the Christian would thereby die his final death to sin and the flesh, and enter the final resurrection to righteousness and the spirit.

The Administration of Baptism: "Eine Form zu Taufen"

The first baptisms performed by Hubmaier in Waldshut have already been briefly described. A milk pail served as the receptacle for the water, the baptisms were by affusion, and, according to the St. Gall reformer and chronicler, Johannes Kessler, the Waldshut Anabaptists threw the old baptismal font out of the church.[232] One account says they threw it into the Rhine.[233] The informality matches, perhaps exceeds, the descriptions of other early Anabaptist baptisms. What words were used in the baptisms we do not know; but we may presume that Hubmaier's later *Eine Form zu Taufen*, which gives "the form we use at Nicolsburg and elsewhere," preserves at least the general structure of the later, more formal baptismal services at Waldshut, even if it does not reveal the method of the first baptisms.[234]

According to the Nicolsburg order, the believer would present himself to the bishop of the congregation who would examine him to determine whether he was ready for baptism. The *Form* says that, at a minimum, the candidate should understand the articles of faith (presumably the Apostles' Creed) and the doctrines that pertain to the Christian life, and he should be able to pray, a reference evidently to the use of the Lord's Prayer.[235] Once it was established that the person was ready for baptism, the bishop would present him to the church, which would kneel in prayer as the baptism was begun. Following the bishop's prayer for the gift of the Holy Spirit upon the baptizand, the bishop would administer the baptismal vow, which began with a modified form of the Apostles' Creed. Following the Creed, there was a statement of the baptizand's desire to "enroll in the visible Christian Church unto the remission of your sins," and then the affirmation of his willingness to submit, if necessary, to the three steps of the dominically instituted fraternal discipline. The baptizand would reply to the questions of the Creed with "I believe" and to the questions of intent with "I will."[236]

Upon the completion of the vow, baptism was administered in the name of the Trinity. Then followed the imposition of hands of the bishop who therewith pronounced to the baptizand that he now shared in the power of the church's "keys" and in the breaking of bread and prayer.[237] No mention is made of the mode to be used, but the fact that the baptisms were evidently to take place within the church building suggests that the mode was pouring.

The most notable thing about Hubmaier's order is that baptism was placed in the context of the congregation; in fact, Hubmaier's *Form* presented a rather formal ceremony, in contrast to the baptisms in kitchens or by the roadside often encountered in accounts of the Anabaptists. It seems that Hubmaier practiced baptism in this general fashion from the beginning of his Anabaptist career, for, in spite of the alleged indignity of his first baptisms, they were performed within the church building and, presumably, with the approval of the congregation present for the occasion. Further, Hubmaier's *Eine Summe eines ganzen christlichen Lebens,* his first specifically Anabaptist tract, later incorporated into the *Von der Taufe der Gläubigen,* described the procedure for baptism in virtually the same way as the more detailed *Eine Form zu Taufen:* the candidate was to present himself to the church and testify publicly to them of his faith before accepting the baptismal vow and receiving baptism.[238]

Only two further things were said by Hubmaier about the administration of baptism. The first pertained to the minimum age for receiving the ordinance. In reply to Zwingli's statement that baptism signified one's desire to hear the Word of God, Hubmaier said that this was true and that therefore baptism must wait until the will is developed, something that takes place in about the seventh year.[239] The second was that there should be no rebaptism in cases of an unworthy administrator, for the validity of baptism depended upon the baptismal vow of the one receiving baptism, not upon the character of the person administering it.[240]

The *Form* concludes with three criticisms of the received practice of baptism and the Eucharist: the church has forsaken God's law in adopting infant baptism; it has been more concerned for "the weak" than for true Christian doctrine and practice; and it has allowed water, bread, and wine to be called "sacraments," when the true "sacraments" are the baptismal vow of faithfulness and the Eucharistic pledge of love. Thus, like Hubmaier's tracts on the theology of baptism, his tract on its practice also presents a polemic for baptism as a voluntary pledge to Christ, a pledge which Hubmaier observes, in the original sense of *sacramentum*, can be properly called a "sacrament."[241]

The "Rechenschaft"

Hubmaier's final statement on baptism was the confession in his *Eine Rechenschaft des Glaubens* before the imperial authorities in Vienna. Unlike his earlier recantations in Zurich under the pressure of Zwingli,[242] his final statement contained no essential departure from his Anabaptist position.

> I have taught nothing about baptism except that it is a public and oral confession of Christian faith and a necessary renunciation of the devil and his works. By this, one yields himself by the power of God the Father, and Son, and Holy Spirit in such self-surrender (*gelassenhait*) that he will suffer, die, and be buried with Christ in the faith that he will also rise with Him to eternal life.[243]

Summary

As the first written defense of Anabaptist baptism, Hubmaier's baptismal tracts were an excellent statement of the Anabaptist position. Grounding his arguments principally on a close exegesis of the New Testament, he provided his brethren with a comprehensive collection of Biblical texts and theological arguments in defense of believer's baptism. And even though his attempts to find support for their view in patristic and contemporary authors were considerably less than successful, they did serve to demonstrate to his like-minded readers that infant baptism was not the universal practice of the early church, and that the new movement in favor of believer's baptism owed a degree of its inspiration to the more conservative reformers of Hubmaier's own time.

Hubmaier also developed two important theological corollaries to the doctrine of believer's baptism: freedom of the human will, and regeneration of the soul. In both of these he marked out positions which became common to Anabaptism. According to the first, salvation comes to man only after he himself has freely responded to God's offer. Since no infant is capable of this, infant baptism is improper. But the first also leads to the second: the will that is capable of choosing to receive God's grace is reborn by that grace and thereby receives the power to obey the will of God in all things. This being true, baptism serves as the formal means through which the reborn believer commits himself to this life of obedience in fellowship with other believers. Part of the significance of this was that baptism was the public profession of faith and commitment of life. But the other part was that baptism rests, in this view, on the doctrine of regeneration—regeneration conceived as inner renewal, a metaphysical change within the person giving him once again the power of living righteously.

In addition to these "subjective" elements, Hubmaier also recognized an aspect of baptism which might be called "objective": it enrolled one in the visible community of salvation. While regeneration came to the believer as a direct act of God received on the condition of faith, this alone was not enough for full salvation, for the Holy Spirit ordinarily performed His full operation within the church. Since baptism was the official introduction into the church, it was the sign of entering the place of salvation. To the faithful, this was surely a heartening thing, for baptism and the Lord's Supper were, apart from character and daily actions, the only visible marks of the saints—marks by which the faithful could recognize each other, and, by the same token, find assurance that they themselves were among the redeemed. This objective element was perhaps not clearly recognized as such by Hubmaier and it was not explicitly developed; but it was latent in his view. Later Anabaptists would make it explicit, although in a different way, as the next subject of the study will illustrate.

Finally, Hubmaier described baptism in a way that included the whole of the Christian life, for not only did it witness to the regeneration already wrought within the heart of the believer, but it signified the struggle with sin that lay ahead of him. Although Hubmaier did not stress the possibility of martyrdom as much as other Anabaptists would, he was sure that the Christian's fight with sin would be difficult and perhaps painful. At that point he contributed an important concept to Anabaptist baptismal thought: the baptisms of water and Spirit would be completed through the baptism of blood in the lifelong battle to conquer evil by the power of the Spirit.

CHAPTER II

Hans Hut: Backgrounds in Thomas Muentzer and Hans Denck

The figure of Hans Hut stands in sharp contrast to Balthasar Hubmaier, not only in education and profession, but even more in outlook and thinking, particularly in the intense eschatology that was foreign to the Waldshut Anabaptist. According to Hut's testimony during his trial in Augsburg, he first came to doubt infant baptism after engaging in a discussion of the topic with three radicals at Weissenfels in Saxony; the date was probably early 1524.[1] Visits to Wittenberg failed to convince him of any New Testament authority for the custom, and upon returning to his home in Bibra (near Meiningen in Thuringia[2]) he put his new convictions into practice by refusing to permit the baptism of his new child. The local authorities refused to countenance his obstinate views and ordered Hut's expulsion which was effected after a brief imprisonment. But he was not converted to Anabaptism *per se* until the spring of 1526 when, on Pentecost Day, May 26, Hans Denck baptized him into the new brotherhood.[3] From then until his death in the Augsburg jail on December 6, 1527, he devoted himself to perhaps as industrious a missionary apostolate as is known among the Anabaptists.

As compared to the first subject of this study, Hut's literary output was very small. Only two tracts survive (and the authorship of one of them has been questioned[4]), along with a devotional piece (largely a concordance),[5] perhaps two letters,[6] and his confessions to the Augsburg authorities.[7] The last is the principal source for reconstructing Hut's life and is also of value for his thought at several points.

The most important of these documents for Hut's views on baptism is his interesting homily on the topic entitled *Von dem geheimnus der tauf*. It has been long recognized that Hut was influenced by Thomas Müntzer, but recently this issue has been revealed in a new light with Gordon Rupp's suggestion that the homily may be a reworked form of a piece originally written by Müntzer.[8] Our investigation has tended to confirm Rupp's suggestion. But before the details of the argument can be undertaken, it is necessary first to sketch Müntzer's own ideas as well as those of Hans Denck, whose influence can also be traced in the homily. This will also lay the basis for an analysis of Hut's own ideas.

Baptism According to Thomas Müntzer

Müntzer's early writings had little to say about baptism. The *Angebliche Propositionen des Egranus*[9] of 1521 contains no reference to baptism and the *Anschlag zu Prag* of the same year describes it only negatively.[10] In the latter, Müntzer criticized those who said that salvation comes through faith and outer baptism; he claimed that salvation is given only through the inner baptism of the Holy Spirit. The same view was represented a month later by the Zwickau prophets who reported they had gotten their ideas from Nicholas Storch and Müntzer.[11]

Müntzer's next statement on baptism, his most thorough one, appeared in the 1524 *Protestation oder Entbietung* which he wrote as an attack upon infant baptism and an apology for his own view of baptism.[12] "True baptism is not understood," he said, and therefore Christendom had opened its doors to the "beastly monkey-business" of the *Schriftgelehrten* with their fictitious faith and false, infant baptism.[13] No infant baptism was known in the early church, Müntzer said, for all candidates for baptism were prepared through a catechumenate period which served to separate the tares from the wheat, something infant baptism cannot possibly do, he insisted. Challenging the *Buchstabengelehrten* to produce even one text showing that Christ and His disciples baptized infants or ordered others to do so, he argued that the church had erred greatly in allowing the outer sign to become of more value than the "inner essence," for the latter is the true baptism. Neither Mary nor the apostles received water baptism, he said, and yet they were saved, because they had the true spiritual baptism within.[14]

Having stated his opinion of the contemporary baptismal practice, Müntzer then returned to the Fourth Gospel for a series of Biblical texts to support his view that true baptism is the inner baptism of the Spirit. His defense rested largely on a symbolic interpretation of John's usage of the term "water," an interpretation Müntzer based principally on two texts. The first passage is John 3:5: "Unless one is born of water and the Spirit, he cannot enter the kingdom of God." This text has not been understood by the reformers, Müntzer says, because they have neglected to compare it with John 7:38, 39, which reads:[15]

> "He who believes in me, as the scripture has said, 'Out of his heart shall flow rivers of living water [an allusion to Isaiah 44:3; 55:1, and 58:11].'" Now this [Jesus] said about the Spirit, which those who believed in him were about to receive.

When these two texts are compared, their meaning is clear, Müntzer says, for they reveal that "water," when used this way in Scripture, means "spirit," and spirit in two senses. First, the term means the movement of the spirit of man in the troubles of doubt and despair preceding the gift of faith. Second, it means the movement of the Spirit of God as it fills the void of man's soul with true spiritual baptism. Merging these two aspects of inner baptism—as he believed them to be merged in practice—Müntzer says that "water" should be understood here to mean "the movement of our spirit in the Spirit of God." It is not to be understood as signifying a literal baptism in water.[16]

To develop his point, Müntzer carries the reader through the first six chapters of John, finding the term "water" in each chapter, each time interpreting it to mean the inner baptism of the soul through human doubt and the Spirit's power. His discussion proceeds as follows: the water that would flow forth in the wilderness according to Isaiah's prophecy[17] is the Spirit given to Christ at the Jordan.[18] The water changed to wine is spirit also, this time man's spirit, striving for salvation and life.[19] John baptized where there was "much water,"[20] or much movement of the Spirit, as in the spring of living water[21] and the Pool of Bethzatha.[22] And, Müntzer observes, Christ appeared to the apostles on the Sea of Galilee after the storm on the water.[23] All of these events speak of inner baptism, he said, for all symbolize the inner movement of the spirit of man and the complementary action of the Spirit of God in the struggle of faith and salvation.[24]

To be born of "water and the Spirit" is no light thing, Müntzer says, for such a birth is effected only through the agonies of the inner cross. This commences with the first *Ankunft* of faith which is brought upon the soul by the Spirit through the sufferings of doubt and despair, *Anfechtung* and inner trial. By this the soul is readied for the reception of the Holy Spirit and the reconception of the Christ within.[25] In this fearful trial the soul is cut loose from all creaturely ties, even from Scripture which also is of the creaturely order. As the Holy Spirit descends into the deepest abyss of the soul, the person is left bare before the awesome power of God who alone can give him new life.[26] As Meister Eckhardt had earlier said,[27] in this experience one hears the voice of John the Baptist crying in the wilderness of one's heart for repentance. But within that wilderness there springs up a new fountain of life, the waters of divine wisdom, i.e., the waters of inner baptism.[28] At first these waters flood the soul bringing despair and fright like that of the psalmist of old.[29] But then they also cleanse and heal and bring new birth and new life to the soul.[30] They create a new covenant within, whereby, like Abraham, the person swears to walk before the Lord in holiness.[31] This inner suffering, the descent of the soul into the spiritual hell of doubt and *Anfechtung*, is the true sign of Jonah, the only sign given to the elect to assure them of their salvation and their inclusion within the covenant.[32]

At this point we are introduced to a different conception of the covenant from those seen in the preceding chapter, for Müntzer's covenant was basically a covenant created within by the Spirit of God through the experience of inner baptism. Alongside this inner covenant, however, he adopted an external covenant related to the religio-political ends of his revolutionary movement. Perhaps utilizing ideas of *Bund* and *Bundsgenossen* from Johann Eberlin von Günzburg,[33] and probably drawing on the *Bundschuh* movement as well, Müntzer gathered his followers into a covenant "to stand by the Word of God"[34] and to implement this through social and even military action. Like the burghers of the time, who annually reaffirmed the covenant of their town by having their names entered in the official roll at the *Rathaus*,[35] the Müntzerites of Allstedt had their names publicly inscribed in the list of the covenanting elect and affirmed this "by the upraised hand."[36] In this fashion they entered into the covenant of the elect which was to renew the church and Christian society.

However, water baptism seems to have played no part in the entrance into this covenant. For even though Müntzer denied the validity of infant baptism, claiming that children should be old enough at baptism to have "a fresh recollection of it all their life," he seems to have adopted no adult baptism in its place.[37] It is true that he considered a child's baptism at the age of perhaps six or seven as a replacement for "infant" baptism,[38] but he could hardly have interpreted this child baptism in terms of the covenant of the militant elect. Further, his only recorded statement on the relation of baptism to the peasants' covenant denied external baptism any role in this covenant. The statement appears in a letter to the castellan, Hans Zeiss, written in July, 1524, just as Müntzer's movement was about to enter its more revolutionary phase:

> There must be a definite covenant *(bund)* made in such form that the common man will bind *(vorpinde)* himself to the faithful magistrates for the Gospel's sake.... The untested will want to say, "What need have we of such a covenant? We have already covenanted *(verbunden)* in baptism that a Christian should and must suffer!" My answer is: first learn what baptism is. Learn, and search whether the witness of God may be found in you.... For the whole counsel and knowledge of God must be known and felt in its length, height, breadth, and depth.[39]

That is, one must have the inner baptism of the fiery trial of the cross—an external baptism is no help. Admittedly, the outer baptism to which Müntzer here refers is infant baptism, specifically (according to the context) infant baptism as understood by Luther—one which pledged the person to a daily death and resurrection in anticipation of the final resurrection.[40] And, in point of fact, the adult covenantal baptism of the Anabaptists had not yet been developed. Even so, the force of Müntzer's statement is plain: the covenant is formed within by the baptism of the Spirit.

At this point, Müntzer's concern to revitalize Christian society through a select group of Christians was very near to the aim of Conrad Grebel and Felix Mantz in early 1524, when the two Zurich radicals approached Zwingli with a proposal to call on the believers of the town to elect a Town Council wholly of men disposed to Zwingli's (and their) views.[41] In both cases there was a desire to reform both the church and society through a group specifically dedicated to religio-political ends—in Müntzer's case, a group formally organized and banded together through a covenant with each other and with God; in the case of Grebel and Mantz, a Town Council officially elected by the informally organized "believers" of the town. In neither case was a new water baptism originally contemplated as a badge of membership within the reform party. But when the two reform movements failed in their aim of renewing "Christendom," each turned away from the great church and proceeded to refound a church of the faithful—Grebel, Mantz, and their company doing this in Zurich, while Hans Hut and Melchior Rinck did the same within the Müntzerite movement in Germany. It was this decision to renounce the reformation of the traditional church in favor of reestablishing what they believed to be the church of the New Testament that prompted the introduction to the new baptism in Zurich and its later adoption in southern Germany.[42]

Hans Hut was the first follower of Müntzer to advocate the new baptism. He did so, partly at least, under the influence of Hans Denck.

Baptism According to Hans Denck

Whereas Müntzer turned his spiritualism into revolutionary channels, supporting and even briefly leading the peasants of Frankenhausen in their uprising against the authorities, Hans Denck adopted a more conservative posture in regard to both the established *Obrigkeit* and the two principal sacraments. But at the same time he was strongly influenced by Müntzer. Whether Denck and Müntzer met when the latter came to Nürnberg to have his *Hochverursachte Schutzrede* printed is uncertain,[43] but Denck knew of Müntzer's writings and probably obtained some of them from Hut who had stayed in Denck's home at Nürnberg.[44]

The sixth point of Denck's confession to the Nürnberg authorities in January, 1525, is his first recorded statement on baptism.[45] Like Müntzer he thought principally of the inner baptism of the Spirit. This commences, Denck said, with doubt and anxiety and is accomplished through the descent of the Holy Spirit into the abyss of the soul. Quoting the same verse from the Psalms as Müntzer, he like Müntzer used the figure of "water" for the experience of being overwhelmed by the divine.[46] Also, he spoke of this baptism as a covenant wrought within the heart.[47] To describe this, Denck adopted Luther's translation of I Peter 3:21, "the covenant of a good conscience with God."[48] In this covenant the old life is put away and the person rises to new life with Christ, all through the transforming action of God in the soul through the Word of God and the Spirit. Only this "water" can save, Denck says. But external water is not to be despised on that account. John the Baptist and the disciples of Christ administered baptism in physical water, since "whatever cannot stand water is all the less able to suffer fire," the latter being the full baptism given by Christ which consumes the dross of the soul and completes Christ's work. Outer baptism is not necessary to salvation—only inner baptism effects that, he says—but "wherever outer baptism is performed in terms of this [inner] covenant, it is good."[49]

In *Von der wahren Liebe* Denck carried the covenant idea one step further. Contrasting the voluntary character of sonship in the new covenant against the birthright sonship under the old, he described baptism as a *bundzeychen*. In doing this he united the inner experience of salvation—already called a covenant by Müntzer—and the outer action of public commitment in baptism and thereby gave to Anabaptism a key term and concept for both baptism and ecclesiology.[50] What was only a *Pflichtzeichen* for Hubmaier was now a *Bundzeichen* and the way was clear for Denck's successors, Hans Hut and Pilgram Marpeck, to develop a covenantal ecclesiology that would take Hubmaier's view of the disciplined congregation and enlarge it in terms of the covenant wrought by God within the heart. This also opened the way for Marpeck to interpret the two Testaments in covenantal terms.

Since baptism assumes a voluntary entrance into the covenant with God, there is no justification for giving it to infants, Denck said. Further, teaching must precede baptism, else one makes baptism more necessary than teaching. Christ's command makes the matter clear, he said:

> "Go and teach," or "make disciples of all nations,[51] baptizing them" (i.e., those whom you have made to be disciples), "in the name of the Father," who has begotten them, "of the Son," under whose yoke they are committing themselves, "and of the Holy Spirit," through whose power they shall persevere to the fulfilling of the Father's will.[52]

Finally, as he said in his *Widerruf* at Basel, baptism cannot be given to infants, for one cannot discern which is a Jacob and which an Esau.[53]

Like Hubmaier, Denck argued that the inner spiritual baptism which creates the good conscience is the true successor to Old Testament circumcision. The old covenant ordinance was an external command given to the fleshly children of Abraham, Denck said, but true baptism is an inner reality given to the patriarch's spiritual progeny.[54]

Denck also stood very near to Müntzer in his conception of inner baptism. But he went a step beyond him in uniting the inner baptismal covenant of the Spirit and the outer covenant in water, thereby formulating a specifically Anabaptist interpretation of baptism. Denck did not put his new ideas into practice until over a year after the Nürnberg confession, when, in May, 1526, he received baptism from Hubmaier in Augsburg.[55] He immediately proceeded to baptize others, and within a few days he had converted and baptized Hans Hut, his friend from earlier days in Nürnberg.[56]

In baptizing Hut, Denck introduced a new missionary-apostle into the Anabaptist movement. The ideas of the former Nürnberg humanist were to have considerable influence on him. It seems also that the views of Denck's baptizer, Balthasar Hubmaier, affected Hut, for the latter spoke of the same three baptisms of Spirit, water, and blood which were seen in Hubmaier. Hut's principal mentor would, however, continue to be Thomas Müntzer. To see the extent to which this is true requires examining the problem of the authorship of *Von dem geheimnus der tauf*.

The Authorship of "Von dem geheimnus der tauf"

Gordon Rupp, Professor of Ecclesiastical History in the University of Manchester, has recently challenged the traditional view that Hut authored the very imaginative *Von dem geheimnus der tauf, baide des zaichens und des wesens: ein anfang eines rechten warhaftigen christlichen lebens*.[57] After describing the tract's concept of the "Gospel of all creatures," and tracing it back through Thomas Müntzer to Raymond of Sebonde, a Spanish Franciscan who taught at the University of Toulouse in the early fifteenth century, Rupp concludes his statement of the problem with these words:

> Either this tract was written by Huth, who in that case emerges as one who was thoroughly soaked in Müntzer's doctrines, or this writing is by Thomas Müntzer himself, trimmed, edited and even interpolated perhaps, but bearing the imprint of Müntzer's originality upon it.[58]

Our method of treating the problem will be, first, to review the evidence and arguments presented by Rupp's article relating to possible authorship by Müntzer. We shall then introduce evidence to show that it is improbable that the tract in its present form is from Müntzer's hand. The investigation will conclude with arguments for Hut's having rewritten a Müntzer tract.

The Evidence for Müntzer

Professor Rupp, adding to the work of Lydia Müller and Grete Mecenseffy,[59] compiled an impressive collection of important terms and expressions in the tract which are especially characteristic of Müntzer (at least thirty-eight of them by our count).[60] Many of these are the familiar and colorful criticisms of Luther and his followers: they deny that Christ must suffer in members as well as in head; they preach a "false faith" leading common men astray through using the Scriptures as a "cloak," all the while espousing *Bruder Sanftleben* and ignoring the "bitter Christ." Taulerian terms like *Gelassenheit*, *Langenweil*, the "friend of God" (notably as in Müntzer, "the elect friend of God") are employed, as well as the more general mystical terms, "beginning" and "movement" of the Spirit of God, and *Anfechtung*. The subtitle is Müntzerian,[61] and the list would continue: *Geheimnis*, *Urteil* (virtually a *terminus technicus* for both Müntzer and the tract), *Ordnung*, "work of God," and many others—more than enough to make it clear that Müntzer's vocabulary abounds in the tract.[62]

Rupp also points to the theological conceptions common to Müntzer and the *Geheimnus*. First, the *Geheimnus* and Müntzer share the same natural theology. Engrained into the very nature of things, they say, is the principle of suffering through which alone the creature comes to its fulfillment. This is the Gospel itself, "the Gospel of the crucified Christ." Müntzer says:

> All of Holy Scripture speaks of nothing else—as all creatures testify—than the crucified Son of God.[63]

The *Geheimnus* agrees:

> The whole Scripture and all creatures show nothing else than the suffering Christ in all His members.[64]

Second, both Müntzer and the *Geheimnus* say that one enters into the redemption of Christ only through the inner baptism of spiritual suffering. Through the "movement" of the Spirit, the soul is led into the "anguish" and inner "hell" through which it is purged of creaturely desires and lusts. Emerging from this suffering, the soul is then granted the gift of God's Spirit and "true faith" in Christ. This is the "bitter Christ," not the "sweet Christ" of the Lutherans who have only the "false faith" of the *Schriftgelehrten*.[65]

In speaking of this baptism Müntzer and the *Geheimnus* use the same terms: "the true baptism" and "the essence" (*Wesen*) of baptism.[66] It is described symbolically as "water," meaning the inner movement of the Spirit which pours over one like the waves and billows that passed over Jonah.[67] And both take the "sign of Jonah" to refer to this inner baptism.[68]

These similarities in word and idea are all important, but Rupp's strongest evidence for Müntzer's authorship is the seeming dependence of the tract on the *Theologia naturalis sive liber creaturarum* by Raymond of Sebonde. At several points the *Geheimnus* is close enough to Raymond to suggest direct knowledge of his work. The most important of these is the tract's doctrine of the "Gospel of all creatures," a bold natural theology, whereby the mystery of the crucified Christ is found in nature as well as in Scripture.[69]

That Christian truth was to be found in the natural world was no innovation, of course, for the *liber naturae* had been the source of medieval symbolic art[70] as well as the inspiration for Catholic mystics—Bernard, Meister Eckhardt, and others.[71] However, perhaps none but Raymond of Sebonde—significantly a Franciscan—had valued this natural knowledge so highly as to say that the "Book of the Creatures," as he termed it, was superior to written Scripture—superior because the former could not be interpreted erroneously (he said), as could the latter.[72]

At three specific points Rupp finds the *Geheimnus* echoing Raymond's *Theologia naturalis*. The first is in Raymond's concept of the "Book of all Creatures." The principal passage about it in the *Geheimnus* runs thus:

> The whole world with all creatures is a book in which one sees *in work* all that is read in the written book. All the elect from the beginning of the world to Moses studied in the *Book of All Creatures* and have understood it by their reason, for it is written by nature through the Spirit of God in the heart, because the whole law is expressed in terms of the works of the creatures [italics ours].[73]

The same expression had been used by Raymond who distinguished two books which taught of God: "the 'Book of Every Creature' or the 'Book of Nature,' and the 'Book of Holy Scripture.' "[74] The knowledge in nature has been available to all men since the beginning, Raymond says, and is a necessary prerequisite for understanding Scripture.[75] Although the *Geheimnus* introduces a new expression, the "Gospel of all creatures," the idea is the same, with one important modification: the knowledge conveyed through the creatures is of redemptive suffering, as Müntzer held, not of creaturely joy, as the Franciscan Raymond understood it.[76]

A second point is that both Raymond and the *Geheimnus* distinguish between the "works of God" in nature and the "words of God in Scripture."[77] Although Müntzer did not use these particular terms, he certainly shared the anti-academic viewpoint contained in the idea, for he often criticized the "book scholars" who know letters but not the Spirit.

The third point of similarity between Raymond and the *Geheimnus* is that both see an analogous relation between man's dominion over creation and God's reign over man. In both cases the lower order reaches fulfillment only through submission to the higher.[78] It is an important theme in Raymond and a crucial one in the *Geheimnus*. Müntzer had already anticipated it with his analogy of the soil in his *Von dem gedichteten Glauben* according to which man, like the soil, must suffer being weeded and plowed by the Word of God before he is capable of producing good fruit.[79] And he gave brief formulation to it in a letter of December 11, 1523.[80] But it is only with the *Geheimnus* that the Müntzerian interpretation of Raymond's idea is presented in its most developed form.

Rupp concludes then that the author of the tract knew Raymond's book and knew it well, for he chose important themes from it and handled them with understanding. This would, he says, preclude Hut from the authorship, since, as Rupp assumes, it is unlikely that Hut knew Latin.[81] (This assumption can be questioned as we shall observe below.[82]) The knowledge of Raymond would make Müntzer all the more probable as the author, for he was not only an avid reader but is known to have read other things also circulated by the Lefèvre circle in Paris.[83] Further, Rupp argues that since the ideas of the *Geheimnus* are found in germ in Müntzer's known writings, it would seem entirely probable that Müntzer found occasion to work them out in greater detail, as in fact is found in the *Geheimnus*.

To lend further support to his case, Rupp points out that the unusual paraphrase in the *Geheimnus* of two verses from the ninety-third Psalm almost certainly derives from Müntzer. He had used the verses in his Allstedt liturgy, interpreting them to speak in mystical language of the *Langeweil* of man's awaiting the coming of God who would make the heart of the elect to be His throne. The *Geheimnus* has a paraphrase of the translation, which F. W. Ratcliffe of the Manchester University Library says is different from every translation he has seen in pre-Reformation Bibles.[84] Rupp admits the possibility of Hut's having seen the Allstedt liturgy (Hut very possibly carried the liturgy among the Müntzer articles he had for sale)[85] but believes it is more likely that this is a case of Müntzer's recalling his own translation.

These are the principal points of evidence that Rupp introduces. In addition, he mentions lesser points: for instance, the tract's employment of an Aristotelian teleology, which suggests a relatively learned mind behind the tract.[86] (However, he also notes that Hut can speak of the "highest good.")

There also seems to be evidence of the author's direct use of Latin. For instance, the use of *Urteile* for *judicia*—translated as *Rechte* by Luther and as *Ordnungen* by the Zurich Bible—suggests this.[87] Rupp recognizes that an argument for the author's knowledge of Latin seems to face a contradiction at the outset, for he says that the conversion of "preach the Gospel *to* every creature" into "preach the Gospel *of* every creature" is possible only in the German and not in the Latin or the Greek, unless violence is done to the grammar.[88] He observes, however, that the concept itself rests even more on Colossians 1:23, which in the tract reads, "the Gospel which has been preached to you in all creatures."[89] The Vulgate reading, *"evangelii . . . quod praedicatum est in universa creatura,"* would seem to be the likely source for this, even though it is a forced translation. It is certainly a more probable source than, for example, Luther's *"unter alle creatur."*

We can note beyond Rupp that the author of the tract had evidently been challenged on the translation, for he expands the point and says that one should not understand *"in allen creaturen"* to mean that "the Gospel is preached to dogs and cats, cows and calves, hay and grass, but, as Paul says, 'the Gospel that is preached *to you in* all creatures' " (italics ours).[90] The "to you" is added with the support of Romans 1:19, 20, to which the author immediately refers, saying that Paul there speaks of how God's power and divinity are seen "through the creatures" (*"bei den creaturen oder werken"*).[91]

There are then four classes of evidence which Rupp sees as pointing toward authorship by Müntzer: first, the terms and expressions of Müntzer which abound in the tract; second, the doctrines which are common to both, particularly the concept of inner, spiritual suffering as both the *Wesen* of baptism and the ever-present affliction of the "members" of Christ; third, the concept of the Gospel of all creatures, the developed, highly original statement of ideas partially present in Müntzer, but here amplified in direct reliance on Raymond of Sebonde; and fourth, lesser matters including the probable use of Latin and the adoption of Müntzer's translation of Psalm 93:2 and 5. This amounts to an impressive array of evidence and one can only conclude that the origins of the tract lie with Müntzer, either directly or indirectly. Three of these facts suggest that the relationship was probably direct: the knowledgeable use of Raymond's *Theologia naturalis*, the presence in expanded form of ideas present in Müntzer's writings, and, to a lesser extent, the wide use of Müntzer's vocabulary.

The Evidence for Hut

We have seen that the internal evidence for authorship by Müntzer is weighty. However, the tract is attributed to Hans Hut.[92] Is there evidence to indicate that Hut contributed to its composition?

It is known that Hut and his disciples used the concept of the Gospel of all creatures in their preaching. Hut himself included the theme in his *Ein christlicher underricht*,[93] and Ambrosius Spittelmaier told at his trial how Hut "led him into the knowledge of God through his preaching of the creatures."[94] But this provides no direct aid in solving the authorship question, for Hut could simply have taken these ideas from the *Geheimnus*.

However, there are at least two elements within the tract which indicate the hand of Hut: the conception of baptism as a covenant through which a disciplined church is constituted; and the use of the literal argument from Mark 16:15, 16 for believer's baptism. In addition, the internal structure of the tract yields evidence that the present form of the piece is the result of work by two persons. We shall examine these points in turn.

In Rupp's opinion one of the strongest evidences for Hut's authorship of the *Geheimnus* is the use of the term *Verwilligung*, a key term in the tract but one unknown in Müntzer.[95] We can add that not only the term but the concept with which it is associated speaks for Hut and against Müntzer, for *Verwilligung* as the *Geheimnus* speaks of it is a baptismal dedication whereby the baptizand commits himself to the life and fellowship of the disciplined church. Such a view was foreign to Müntzer. The *Geheimnus* describes this covenant in these words:

> One receives the sign of baptism as a covenant *(bund)* of dedication *(verwilligung)* before a Christian church which itself received the covenant from God in His name and has the power and authority to share it with all those who have a heartfelt desire for it. As the Lord said, "what you shall bind on earth shall also be bound in heaven." ... This covenant is a dedication to the obedience of Christ with a rendering of divine love toward all the brethren and sisters with body, life, goods, and honor, irrespective of what evil the world may say to him.[96]

The emphasis upon the church and the power of the keys reveals this as a statement of Anabaptist covenantal ecclesiology and baptism in the tradition of Hubmaier; its concept of the *Bundsgenossen* is in the tradition of Hans Denck. As we saw above, Müntzer did not hold such a view of baptism, and on one occasion, even repudiated the idea of a covenant in water baptism.

Hut, on the other hand, did believe in a baptismal covenant. In his trial at Augsburg he testified in these words:

> God gave water for a sign of the preceding covenant [in the Spirit] whereby one declares and confesses that he wants to live in true obedience toward God and all Christians, and that he wants to lead such a life as to be without blame. Whoever trespasses, living unrightly, acting against God and love, should be punished by the others with words, [not the sword], for this is the ban which God announced. Such [a sign] is to be a witness before the whole church.[97]

* * * *

One who desires rebaptism accepts no other covenant than ... that he will live as the word of the Lord shows him and will expect the cross daily.[98]

In these statements one sees both the inner covenant wrought in the heart through the Spirit as understood by Müntzer and Denck, and the outer ecclesiological covenant made through water baptism as anticipated by Hubmaier and in a way also by Denck.[99]

Even though the *Geheimnus* does not explicitly describe inner baptism as a "covenant" as Hut did at his trial, it places the same stress on the inner dying and rising which must precede water baptism. But more important is the conception of the covenant in water as the constitutive element of the church and as the means whereby the individual submits to the church's disciplinary powers. This conception, deriving from Hubmaier (and obliquely from Denck), brings the viewpoint of the tract into full agreement with Hans Hut. We judge this to be the strongest evidence for Hut's authorship.

Next in importance is the tract's interesting use of the Marcan great commission. The text was widely used within the Radical Reformation in support of believer's baptism. The Zwickau prophets, Clement Ziegler, Hans Denck, and Hubmaier—these and others had employed it earlier. Its use in this tract gives an important clue for the question of authorship.

First of all, the tract gives the literalistic argument for believer's baptism often found in Anabaptist sources; whoever believes and is *then* baptized will be saved.[100] But this would not seem to be Müntzer, for he ordinarily employed a more imaginative hermeneutic. Further, Müntzer once cited this text in ridicule of the view that faith plus baptism will save, contending that salvation comes only through the inner baptism of the Spirit.[101]

Hut, on the other hand, used both the text and the Anabaptist argument based on it. In fact, during the Augsburg trial he said that this was the text which converted him to Anabaptism.

> He was moved to rebaptism by the words of Mark 16:[15, 16], namely, that preaching is first, faith second, and baptism third. One must abide by the word of the Lord, adding nothing thereto, neither turning to the right or the left.[102]

The *Geheimnus* speaks in a similar vein, although he could have learned from the tract instead of contributing to it.

The tract not only employs the Marcan text to defend believer's baptism, but it does so in a curious way, and this is the important clue. Following the lengthy introduction which bewails the loss of knowledge concerning the true *Ordnungen* of God, the author, sounding like Hut in his Augsburg statement, announces that the true "order" of salvation is comprehended in the three steps of the Marcan great commission.

First, Christ said, "Go into the whole world and preach the gospel to every creature." Second, He said "whoever believes," and third, "shall be saved." This order must be preserved. . . . Where it is not preserved there is no Christian church of God but only [one] of the devil.[103]

This sounds Anabaptist enough to be Hubmaier himself. What follows, however, is not an exposition of the argument for believer's baptism, but a discussion of the Gospel of all creatures. Indeed, most of the tract is an exposition of what may be termed Müntzer's three stages in redemption: hear the Gospel of all creatures ("preach"), suffer the action of the Spirit who creates faith through *Angst* and *Anfechtung* ("believe"), and lead the life of redemptive suffering in Christ ("be baptized"). There are three steps well enough, but not the three steps of the Anabaptist argument for believer's baptism.

And yet, upon looking closely, one finds the Anabaptist argument there after all. The merging of the two themes becomes noticeable when the author introduces the second point in the homily. Having first discussed the Gospel of all creatures ("preach"), he introduces the second point of the commission: "believe." The transition from point one to point two is as follows:

> Out of such hearing [of the Gospel] comes the second part of the divine order spoken by Christ: "Whoever believes." However, even if a man clearly understands the simile of the Gospel in all things or creatures, hearing and believing it and that it must be the same with him, that is not enough, for he must show and testify this to all men. Therefore, the third part of the divine order must follow: "and is baptized, he shall be saved."[104]

Curiously, point two has turned into point three and that of the Anabaptist order, not of the Müntzerian order. The tract, in good Anabaptist fashion, promptly moves into a discussion of believer's baptism, with the related themes of confession of faith, the covenant, and the power of the keys. However, following this Anabaptist section, the topic of faith ("believe") is then reintroduced and is treated in straight Müntzerian terms. The discussion is then carried through in the Müntzerian order and is brought to a conclusion with the important final section on the *Wesen* of baptism (point three: "be baptized").

Thus, when the tract is examined closely, it is seen to be a statement on the Müntzerian theme of salvation through baptismal suffering into which the topic of the Anabaptist baptismal covenant and the argument for believer's baptism have been interjected. And both discussions are based on Mark 16. However, the result is not a loose conjunction of words and ideas, even though the tract's organization may be puzzling at first; but instead, it is an effective synthesis of Anabaptist covenantal baptism, like that of Hubmaier and Denck, and spiritual baptism, like that of Müntzer and Denck.[105]

72 / *Anabaptist Baptism*

In the tract's view, the *Ordnung* is clear, as Hubmaier, Denck, and Hut expressly said: baptism is given only when preceded by preaching and faith, in that order. The content of the preaching, however, is not just the words of the Bible but the more mystical Gospel of all creatures. And faith is not the "faith which comes by hearing," but the "faith of God" achieved before baptism through sinking into the "water of all tribulation" and being loosed from reliance on creaturely things, and then after baptism by accepting the life of meaningful, redemptive suffering.

The theological synthesis is more successful than the textual synthesis, however, for the latter would seem to read more smoothly without the section on covenantal baptism and its companion paragraph in the introduction. This fact suggests that the text of the *Geheimnus*, like its theology, originated with Thomas Müntzer, but that it has now been revised and transformed by having been put through the hands and mind of one committed to a covenantal baptism, namely, Hans Hut.

It was noted above that Rupp assumes, with Lydia Müller, that Hut did not know Latin, and that he, therefore, could not have had access to Raymond's *Theologia naturalis*.[106] The point is not a crucial one for Rupp's argument; however, if Hut knew no Latin, the case for Müntzer's authorship of a part or a stage of the *Geheimnus* would obviously be thereby improved.

There is evidence, however, that Hut may have known some Latin. Although he had worked for some years at the unlearned occupations of wine distiller and sexton, he was a book salesman at the time of his conversion to Anabaptism, and he also testified to having worked as a bookbinder.[107] This would suggest that he had probably had some association with Latin. Further, he testified that he had visited Wittenberg during the time of his early doubts about infant baptism and while there had "heard sermons and also lectures in the schools."[108] We know that he was referring to theology lectures, for his point was that the lectures did not provide an adequate defense for infant baptism. If this statement is true, he must have been able to understand some Latin.

If he did know Latin, one could say that he could have read Raymond's *Theologia naturalis* himself and that by putting this with ideas he had learned from Müntzer, he could very possibly have written the *Geheimnus*. Three arguments would tend to deny this. First, although it would have been possible for Hut to have known of Raymond and to have possessed a copy of his book, it is certainly more probable that Müntzer would have been the one who read and made use of him. Raymond's book is large and technical and hardly the kind of reading that would engage a traveling book salesman. Second, the *Geheimnus* gives enough evidence of Müntzer's hand, both in style and ideas, to make it likely on these grounds alone that Müntzer was behind the tract. Finally, the tract itself, when broken open, gives clear evidence of being edited and revised in order to interweave Hut's three stages of baptism within a discussion of Müntzer's three levels of baptism. For these reasons we judge Rupp's argument for Müntzer to be sound.

We find, thus, that the baptismal theology of the *Geheimnus* reveals that the tract could not be by Thomas Müntzer and yet it gives evidence of having originated with him. Further, the tract seems to have come from two hands, not from one. Finally, the tract is the best statement we possess of the double meaning Hut and his followers drew from the great commission. We conclude, therefore, that the *Geheimnus*, in its present form, is a composite work which stems from Thomas Müntzer and Hans Hut, the latter of whom completed it by revising an earlier piece of Müntzer's—which piece we can call the *Ur-Geheimnus*—so that the onetime Spiritualist tract now conformed to Hut's own strain of Anabaptism.

Further Details

There are several final details related to the question of the authorship of the *Geheimnus*. First is the question of identifying the person who coined the expression, the "Gospel of all creatures." The expression derives from Mark 16:15, of course, in which *"das Evangelion aller Kreatur"* is transformed from a dative singular to a genitive singular and thence to a genitive plural. The transition was more than a linguistic accident, for it was clearly prompted by theological concerns. Nonetheless, Rupp's point that this was accomplished through the German form of the text, rather than through the Latin or the Greek, is surely valid. Thus, neither Müntzer nor Hut can be excluded on linguistic grounds from having coined the expression.

As to the Marcan text itself, it was important to Hut as a proof text for Anabaptist baptism; and, since his mystical natural theology was related to inner baptism, he could easily have seen that the text was susceptible to a modification that would join baptism and this natural theology. Müntzer did not have the same attachment to the Marcan text; in fact, he was probably averse to it, since he considered much of the misunderstanding of baptism to be due to its having been misinterpreted.[109] However, that fact itself might have motivated him to give a "true" interpretation of the passage. He changed other Scriptural texts rather abruptly; he could have changed this one also.[110]

As to the Colossians text, the modification would seem to be by Müntzer, for he would doubtless have been familiar with Vulgate reading which stood behind it. Since he gave considerable thought to the revelation of God in creation, he may well be the one who first conceived of the change.

Rupp has also noted the "rather banal reiteration of 'Darum,' 'Derhalben,' 'Alhie' which suggests an untutored style" (and he adds parenthetically, "or one who thought in Latin?—Etiam, Quaemadmodum, etc."). Rupp suggests that this may point toward Hut.[111] The reference to the possible influence of Latin is, of course, related to the question of Müntzer's hand in the *Geheimnus*, but an examination of Müntzer's writings reveals that even his Latin has fewer conjunctions and linking-words than the *Geheimnus*.[112] The other alternative seems the more likely: the words are the result of an "untutored style." Again the evidence points to Hut as the final hand.

Finally, was the editor Hut or could it have been one of his disciples?[113] Several factors would indicate that it was Hut. For one thing the *Geheimnus* is the *locus classicus* for the appropriation of Müntzerian themes by the Hut wing of Anabaptism. The merging of the Anabaptist three-step process of baptism (hear, believe, be baptized) with the Müntzerian Gospel of all creatures is nowhere so clearly done as here.[114] That this conversion of Müntzer into an Anabaptist version of the Gospel of all creatures was first done by Hut himself is well attested to. Disciples like Ambrosius Spittelmaier and Veit and Martin Weischenfelder commonly report that it was to this type of Anabaptism that Hut converted them.[115] Further, it is of note that the three points which Martin Weischenfelder, one of Hut's early converts, used to describe Hut's teaching exactly summarize the *Geheimnus*: the Gospel of all creatures, the Anabaptist view of the great commission, and the doctrine of baptismal suffering.[116] Also, if it is true that a Müntzer tract lies behind the *Geheimnus*, Hut is the logical one to have possessed the Müntzer material in the first place. It is certain that he is the author of the specific combination of ideas in the *Geheimnus*; and he was preaching these ideas before the other writers of the movement were converted. It would seem, therefore, that the ascription of the *Geheimnus* to Hut is correct and that it was he who recast the Müntzer material to form this important Anabaptist tract on baptism.

Exactly when Müntzer would have given the *Ur-Geheimnus* to Hut is uncertain. Rupp, assuming that the piece moved directly from Müntzer to Hut, notes two possible occasions: Müntzer's visit with Hut in Bibra when he gave Hut his work on Luke 1 for publication, and the eve of the Battle of Frankenhausen, after Müntzer ordered Hut's release from confinement.[117] In either event, the transfer to Hut would have been easily accomplished.

It seems, therefore, that the *Geheimnus* came into being in the following way. First, Müntzer formulated a developed statement of his once fragmentary natural theology, describing it in terms of the levels of experience involved in redemption. The theme of the work was baptism, principally the inner baptism of suffering through the transforming Spirit of God, partially described earlier in the *Protestation*. Hut, already subscribing to Müntzer's views but now converted by Denck to Anabaptism, rewrote the *Ur-Geheimnus*, enlarging it with his new Anabaptist ecclesiology and the Hubmaier-Denckian conception of covenantal baptism. The Marcan commission served as the text in both cases. When modified to speak of the Gospel of all creatures, it was very Müntzerian, and when read straight it supported the Anabaptist argument for believer's baptism.

It seems, then, that the *Geheimnus* is a unique illustration of the confluence of these two streams of Radical Reformation baptismal theologies. As has already been suggested by earlier writers, Hans Hut, his disciples, and the Hutterites after them, all found in water baptism an outer action which corresponded to and undergirded the inner baptism of the cross as they had learned it from Müntzer.[118] Further, Hut and his followers merged the more individualistic and mystical conception of redemption held by Müntzer and Denck with the congregational emphasis found in Grebel and Hubmaier. It was Denck who first began this synthesis and provided in his concept of the covenant the appropriate tool for uniting the inner experience, the outer public testimony, and the formation of the *Gemeinde*. But it was the *Geheimnus* with its unusual natural theology that carried the Müntzerian ideas a stage further and brought them into logical and practical relation to covenantal baptism and the doctrine of the church. The material basis for this was Müntzer's natural theology of the *Ur-Geheimnus*. But the formal development was due to Hans Hut, who, it may be said, thereby converted Müntzer posthumously to evangelical Anabaptism.

CHAPTER III

Hans Hut's Baptismal Theology

Hans Hut used the term "baptism" to comprehend three distinct but interrelated elements: the outer covenant which announced the baptizand's faith to the church and enrolled him in its disciplined fellowship; the inner baptism of redemptive suffering through the cross of Christ; and the eschatological sign or seal which was to prepare his converts for a victorious role in the events of the imminently expected Last Day. The baptism of inner suffering had logical priority among the three, for it was the experience and appropriation of salvation; however, since the baptismal action itself is presented largely in terms of the covenant in water baptism, and since it is more readily described than the process of inner baptism, our discussion will begin with it. The eschatological significance of baptism will be discussed last.

The Baptismal Sign and Covenant

As we observed in the preceding chapter, Hut continued Müntzer's aim of creating a new society through the covenant. However, he modified Müntzer's view radically by conceiving of the new society as a church of the elect separate from the world rather than as an armed brotherhood that would renew Christendom by the sword. Hut's reversal in aim was due directly to his conversion to Anabaptism by Hans Denck.

Hut had already learned from Müntzer that inner baptism of the Spirit was a *Bund*, but now he learned from Denck that the outer manifestation of this in the action of water baptism was also a covenant. Specifically, it was a covenant pledging one's faithfulness to God. Hut may also have heard of Hubmaier's view that baptism was a covenant with the congregation of believers, for this too became an important element in his view of the covenant in baptism.

One of the principal passages in the *Geheimnus* on the outer covenant in baptism reads thus:

Baptism must be added to the first two elements [preaching and faith] and be carried out thus: the candidate must be willing to bear and suffer all that the Father will impose upon him through Christ, and he must resolve in his heart to renounce the world and abide in the Lord. He then receives the sign *(zaichen)* of baptism as a covenant *(bund)* of dedication before a Christian church, which itself received the covenant from God in His name and has the power and authority to share it with all who have a heartfelt desire for it. As the Lord said, "what you shall bind *(binden)* on earth shall also be bound *(gebunden)* in heaven." No man shall be received and covenanted *(verbunden)* into such a fellowship unless he has already heard and learned the Gospel and, believing what he has heard, has dedicated himself therein.

This covenant is a dedication to the obedience of Christ with a rendering of divine love toward all the brethren and sisters with body, life, goods, and honor, irrespective of what evil the world may say to him.[1]

The passage recalls Hubmaier's three steps in baptism—preaching, faith, and water baptism—although Hut has in mind the preaching of the Gospel of all creatures with its pronounced emphasis on redemptive inner suffering. As in Hubmaier, the baptismal vow serves both to dedicate the baptizand to the Christian life with its concomitant responsibilities to the Christian brethren, and to enroll him within the church's discipline under the power of the keys.

The use of the term "covenant" is an addition, which came to Hut from Hans Denck. Hut went beyond Denck, however, for the latter's extant writings provide no instance of his relating the baptismal covenant to the disciplinary powers of the church, as Hubmaier had done with his idea of the baptismal pledge. It was an important addition, for it meant that the inner reality of salvation, the outer confession of it, and the formal union of the believers as the church could all be combined under one rubric. We are anticipating at this point, however, for this synthesis did not take place fully until Pilgram Marpeck.

Interestingly, Hut has altered the traditional meaning of the terms "bind" and "loose" in Matthew 18:18. Instead of understanding "binding" as the use of the ban, as was true in the Catholic Church, Hut interpreted it as the "binding" together of the Christians in the baptismal *Bund*. By implication, the "loosing" would then be performed through the ban, as the congregation let the offender loose to fall once again into the world. This alteration was evidently first made by Hut, for Hubmaier, who spoke of a baptismal *Pflicht* instead of *Bund*, used the terms in their traditional way.[2]

For Hut the baptismal covenant was also a pledge to suffering—the suffering borne by Christ in His members from the foundation of the world. As in Hubmaier, this is the affliction Christ Himself knew in the

78 / Anabaptist Baptism

days of His flesh. Hut reveals this element most clearly in his Augsburg confessions:

> When a person desires baptism, no other pledge *(verpflichtung)* is required than this . . . . : that he desire to live as is revealed to him by the word of the Lord; that he desire to manifest love toward everyone; and that he will expect the cross each day. If he does not do this, the others have the power to discipline him verbally.[3]

Again, he says that they taught:

> The Gospel of Christ crucified, how He suffered for our sake and was obedient to the Father even unto death. In the same way we should walk after Christ, suffering for His sake all that is laid upon us, even unto death.[4]

And in the summary of baptism which he gave to the authorities he describes this as a baptism of blood:

> This is the true baptism which Christ announced to His disciples when He said, "Are you able to be baptized with the baptism with which I am baptized?"[5] This is the baptism that witnesses over the whole world wherever any such blood is spilled.[6]

As Christ covenanted in John's baptism at the Jordan "to fulfill all righteousness," so the Christian pledges himself to suffer martyrdom if necessary, and certainly to accept persecution from those who stand against Christ.

Water baptism, as well as pointing one forward to the baptism of blood, is also a sign of the prior baptism of the Spirit, Hut says, for it testifies to the church that the baptizand has known the inner redemptive operation of the Spirit. In fully developed form, the idea of Spirit baptism in Hut included the descent of the Spirit into the *Abgrund* of the soul, which action would shake the soul free of its comfortable ties to creaturely supports and cast it onto the great and tossing sea of God's power and grace.[7] But his confession at Augsburg gives a simpler statement relating it to the outer baptism in water.

> The baptism of the Spirit is the assurance and dedication in the divine word that the person desires to live as it is announced to him through that word. This is the covenant *(bund)* of God which God makes with him in his heart through the Spirit. In addition, God gave water [baptism] as a sign of this preceding covenant. In this baptism, one announces and confesses that he desires to live in true obedience towards God and all Christians in such a way as to require no disciplinary punishment. . . . God stated that this sign should be a testimony before the church.[8]

As with Hubmaier, the outer baptism in water was a testimony of the inner experience of grace, but in Hut this was expanded to include the process of redemptive, inner suffering as manifested in the Gospel of all creatures.

Inner Baptism: "Das Wesen der Taufe"

Hut's outer baptism was a "sign" of the spiritual baptism within. This inner baptism was the true baptism; he called it the *Wesen* of baptism.[9] It was also the *Wesen* of salvation, for it included the whole process of regeneration.

As in Müntzer, this process took place in three stages according to which one gradually moved more deeply into the successive levels of salvation. It began with the knowledge of God gained through creation; it deepened in the experience of inner suffering and doubt as one was weaned from self-love and love of the creatures; it was fulfilled in the attainment of sanctification (called "justification" by Hut) through the work of the Spirit. Hut's understanding of the process was not identical with that of Müntzer, but he seems to have drawn heavily on Müntzer as well as Denck.

Hut's clearest formulation of this three-stage process is found in *Ein christlicher underricht*. Each level of the process is identified with a member of the Trinity. In a statement similar to one by Hans Denck, he said:

> First, God is known through His omnipotence and power in all creatures. Second, He is known through the sternness and righteousness of His Son. Third, He is known through the goodness and mercy of the Holy Spirit.[10]

Our discussion will follow the same Trinitarian order.

The First Step: Knowledge of the Father

In Müntzer, the first level (as we may term it) of redemption comes as one learns the Word of God from creation, a Word which includes both the glory of God and the redemptive suffering of man. Hut agreed that one learned of the glory of God from creation, but one learned nothing of redemptive suffering here—that came only with the second level. Further, this was, in Hut's view, largely an intellectual knowledge, not a mystical knowledge that convulses the soul. All "rational men" know this much of God, Hut says: namely, that the invisible things of God are revealed through the visible things He made. But to know this alone is to lack the true saving knowledge of God; that comes only through the crucified Christ.[11]

The Second Step: Knowledge of Christ

According to *Ein christlicher underricht*, knowledge of Christ is gained only at the second level of religious experience.[12] At this level one learns of Christ, His obedience to the Father, His suffering, death, and resurrection. One also hears the Gospel of all creatures with its message of fulfillment through obedience and suffering. Here one enters the true baptism of "the water of all tribulation and the bath of rebirth" through which regeneration is found. Hut and Müntzer are insistent that this is no knowledge "by hearing alone" and no "fictitious faith"; rather, this involves a true participation in the sufferings of the body of Christ, and thus it involves anguish and affliction.

In Hut's view, this level is attained only through experiencing the mystical cross within, the redemptive cross of *Gelassenheit* before God. Like Müntzer and Denck before him, Hut built on Jesus' statement about the "baptism with which I am baptized,"[13] and on the second chapter of I Peter with its stress on suffering and discipleship. He said that there is no other way to know the Son than by walking in His footsteps and bearing His cross.[14] In part this would involve the "outer" suffering of persecution imposed upon the righteous by the worldly; but it would be principally an inner spiritual anguish and affliction which would purge the soul of creaturely lusts and, in time, make the person righteous through suffering the work of God within. Like Christ, the Christian would be despised, imprisoned, threatened with death, but most of all he would be driven to the desperate state of isolation and alienation known by Jonah and Christ, both of whom found themselves utterly bereft of help in heaven or earth.[15]

Hut says that this process begins when one first realizes from Scripture and creature that this is the way of salvation. However, it comes into full expression only when the Spirit of God moves the soul, cuts it off from creaturely help, and leads it into the hell of despair where no comfort avails but that of God.[16] When this happens, "believed" faith becomes "known" faith and Christ is born within:

> Each person must suffer every article [of faith] within, for there is no other way to come to the knowledge of the highest good. The Word must be conceived within us, with a pure heart and through the Holy Spirit, and thus become flesh within us. This happens through great fear and trembling, as with Mary when she heard the will of God from the angel. The Word must be born in us also and this takes place only through pain, poverty, and distress, both within and without. When the Word is born and becomes flesh within us, so that we praise God for such a blessing and our hearts stand in peace, then do we become the mother, sister, and brother of Christ.[17]

Hut says that when this despair descends as the Spirit works on the soul, all creaturely support falls away and, more, even God's help is removed for a time so that the person becomes truly conformed to the crucified Christ and cries with Him, "My God, my God, why hast thou forsaken me?" But, if God leads into hell, He also leads out again; if He kills, He makes alive,[18] and the person is raised from this death to share the new life with Christ.

The Gospel of All Creatures

The pattern of the crucified Christ is not confined to Scripture, Hut said. In fact, it is found more immediately, perhaps more clearly, in the world of nature where the principle of fulfillment through suffering is revealed in every creature. This is "the Gospel of all creatures" which Hut had derived from Thomas Müntzer.

As we saw above, behind this lay the figure of Raymond of Sebonde, the Franciscan philosopher who found the "book of the creatures" to be superior to the book of Scripture. "The book of nature cannot be falsified, blotted out, or falsely interpreted," Raymond said, but the book of Scripture can be "interpreted falsely and understood wrongly."[19] When Raymond read this "book of the creatures," he found the lessons of obedience and faithfulness by which man should order his life toward God in emulation of the attitude of the creatures toward man.[20]

However, when Müntzer and Hut read the book of nature, they found a different order of lessons. These told of the suffering and anguish which every creature undergoes in fulfilling its intended nature and destiny. As early as 1523, Müntzer recognized the analogy between creation's obedience to man and man's obedience to God,[21] and the following year he stated that the Gospel itself is found in creation: "All of Holy Scripture speaks of nothing else than the crucified Son of God, as all creatures testify."[22]

It was only with the *Ur-Geheimnus*, however, that Müntzer carried the idea to its fullest development. He said that every creature has its own cross through which its full nature is realized: the tree must be hewed and planed to become a plank suitable for a house; the animal is killed, cleaned, and cooked to become food for man's table; etc.--the examples are numerous. Everywhere it is the same, he says: the lower order must submit to the higher order which alone can bring the former to its full development. As with the creatures, so it is with man:

> From parables like these man should closely observe how all creatures must suffer the work of man [upon them] and how they come to the end for which they were made only through pain. He will see that man, in the same way, comes to salvation only through the suffering and affliction which God works within him. Indeed, both the whole of Scripture and all creatures point to nothing other than Christ suffering in all His members.[23]

As in Raymond, the lower level finds fulfillment only in obedience. But unlike Raymond, Müntzer (whom we believe to have been responsible for this portion of the *Geheimnus*) and Hut understood this obedience to involve suffering, whereby the weeds of creaturely lust would be rooted out and the field of the heart would be made ready for the fertile seeds of the Gospel.[24]

Hut and his followers drew repeatedly upon this natural theology. Often it was used to chide the *Schriftgelehrten*, who send their hearers to books and not to nature which the common man can more readily understand. The false teachers depart from Jesus who sent the gardener to his trees, the fisherman to his fish, and the carpenter to his wood, each to learn in his own place how the world lives through redemptive suffering.[25] At other times they claimed that even the Turks and Jews have this book, and that many have read it and learned of Christ far better than some leaders of the church.[26] But most of all, the term was used simply to reinforce their belief that redemption comes only through suffering: "By the Gospel of all creatures nothing is said or preached but Christ crucified—not Christ the head alone, but the whole Christ with all His members, the Christ which all creatures preach and teach."[27]

This suffering is inner baptism, like that which Jesus knew in the baptism of the cross and, Hut says, that which Israel knew at the Red Sea.[28] Baptismal images abound: it is the waves of doubt and despair suffered by Jonah and the psalmist;[29] it is the washing away of sin,[30] and the knowledge of the deep.[31] Often it is called the "water of all tribulation" or the "baptism of all suffering," two very common terms in the *Geheimnus*.[32]

Most of all it is "true baptism":

> Whoever finds Pharaoh behind him, i.e., all persecution, tribulation, anguish, and distress, and the sea before him, i.e., the helplessness of all creatures, and believes that he is bereft of God, finding nothing but death, he it is who stands and is in the right baptism to which he dedicated himself towards God and his brethren under the sign [of water baptism].[33]

Müntzer had used the same expression earlier in his *Protestation oder Entbietung* in a discussion of "the true faith" which faith, he said, was achieved only through the waters of anguish and doubt in the "movement" of the Spirit.[34] The *Geheimnus*, carrying the idea further, describes how one is then cast into the depths of despair and torn from the help and comforts of the creatures.

> [In this baptism] one can find comfort nowhere, not in any creature. As David said, "My soul refuses to be comforted." Psalm 77[:2]. And again, "I am driven far from thy sight." Psalm 31[:22]. Man is thus thrown into the abyss *(abgrund)* of hell. Jesus called this the sign of Jonah. No one can bring you joy there except He that led you in, and it is He whom you must await. When He comes with His comfort in the Holy Spirit, then man rejoices that he has left all worldly lust, pleasure, and glory and has counted all as dung.[35]

Hans Denck had expressed himself similarly in his *Bekenntnis für den Rat zu Nürnberg*.[36] And the idea of being torn loose from the creatures through the mystical descent into hell was an important element of the *Deutsche Theologie*.[37]

The Inner and Outer Covenants

We have already seen how Hut united Hubmaier's view of the baptismal pledge and the power of the keys with Denck's concept of the covenant. He also extended the covenant idea by more closely relating the inner and outer covenants. The relationship he drew was not as close as that which Pilgram Marpeck was to develop, but it was the beginning of the union of the inner and outer aspects of the baptismal action.

Although Denck saw the covenant of a good conscience principally as an inner covenant of the Spirit, whereby the new law was written on the heart in fulfillment of Jeremiah's prophecy,[38] he also recognized an outer aspect, as one testified to this covenant publicly through water baptism.[39] This testimony looked toward the past in that it recalled the work already performed within the believer, but it also looked forward by pledging the baptizand to the life of discipleship.[40]

It is this future aspect which the *Geheimnus* develops, for it describes the water covenant as a dedication to the "true baptism" in suffering. In its inner aspect, this was the water of all tribulation; in its outer form, it was, as Hut later said, the baptism of blood. Müntzer had envisioned a baptism of mystical suffering wholly separate from water baptism, and Denck had placed baptismal suffering before water baptism, understanding the latter to be the public manifestation of the inner experience. Hut, differing from his mentors, saw another line of relationship, whereby the water covenant was not only a public announcement of the prior inner covenant, but was also a dedication to the fulfillment of that covenant in suffering, principally spiritual suffering, but perhaps persecution and martyrdom as well.

It was in this way that he arrived at the distinction between the "sign" of baptism and the "essence" of baptism. The principal passage reads thus:

> The [outer] baptism which follows preaching and faith is not the true reality *(wesen)* by which man is made righteous, but is only a sign, a covenant, a likeness, and a memorial of one's dedication, which [sign] reminds one daily to expect the true baptism, called by Christ "the water of all tribulation." It is through this baptism that the Lord makes one clean, washing and justifying him of all fleshly lusts, sins, and impure works and life.
> Man knows that no creature can justify *(rechtfertigen)*[41] itself and achieve its final nature *(wesen)* without man to whom it is subject. In the same way, no man can justify himself and reach his end *(end)*,

> i.e., come to salvation, except through the work of God in the baptism of all tribulation. . . .
>
> Thus the water of all tribulation is the true essence and power of baptism, whereby one sinks into the death of Christ. Nor was this [true] baptism first instituted at the time of Christ. It has been since the beginning, and every elect friend of God from Adam on has been baptized in it, as Paul says.[42]
>
> Christ also accepted this covenant from God at the Jordan and testified thereby that, obedient to the Father, He would manifest love toward all men for an example, even unto death. Thereafter, He found the baptism of all tribulation poured over Him by the Father in great profusion.
>
> Therefore, the sign and the essence *(wesen)* of baptism must be sharply distinguished. The Christian church gives and administers the sign or the covenant of baptism through a true minister, as Christ received it from John. Thereafter follows the true baptism which God gives, first through the water of all tribulation, and second in the comfort of the Holy Spirit. God lets no one be swallowed up in this baptism. As it is written, He leads into hell and out again, He kills and makes alive again.[43] Since even the Lord had to be baptized with this baptism, whoever wants to be His disciple must be baptized in the same way.[44]

The passage is an unusual one, for it interweaves several themes: salvation through inner suffering, the universal nature of this spiritual baptism, the discipleship of Christ, and the outer covenant. However, the principal point is clear: true baptism is mystical suffering under the tutelage of the Holy Spirit; it is signified by the water covenant, which manifests the fact that it has already begun and pledges the baptizand toward its later fulfillment; further this true baptism may someday be confirmed by outer suffering in persecution.[45] The principal emphasis is placed on the process of inner struggle that follows the covenant in water baptism. Hut says: "True baptism is nothing other than a struggle with sin one's whole life long."[46] The statement recalls Luther who said that one pledges himself in baptism "to slay your sin more and more as long as you live, even until your dying day,"[47] a thought echoed in Denck, although without the baptismal context.[48]

The sufferings involved in this baptism are not simply one's own— they belong to the whole body of Christ, a theme important in Müntzer, Denck, and Hut. The *Geheimnus* says:

> Christ the crucified has many members in His body. But there is none who does not bear the labor [of the cross], or suffer, or is [at least] dedicated to suffering after the prototype of the head [Christ Jesus].[49]

Critical of the satisfaction theory of the atonement, the tract chides the *Schriftgelehrten* who say that "Christ the head bore it all."

Hut and his followers were often challenged at this point by their opponents, who claimed that Hut denied the sufficiency of Christ's suffering for mankind's sins and that Hut, therefore, threatened the doctrine of the atonement. Hut answered in reply that "Christ did enough for the sins of the whole world" and that man could add nothing to this.[50] Nonetheless, he was certain that in walking the way of discipleship, Christ's follower would know the same sufferings Christ had known; and he insisted one could not be saved without them, even though their efficacy derived from no inherent merit of the sufferer, but from the power of Christ, the head of the body and exemplar.

The Third Step: Knowledge of the Holy Spirit

The first two levels of the knowledge of God—knowledge of His omnipotence and power, and knowledge of the crucified Christ in baptism—were to be fulfilled by the final level, knowledge of the goodness and mercy of the Holy Spirit. This may be called the resurrection side of baptism. Hut says:

> After the body of Christ [is known] then the third part is revealed, the goodness and mercy of the Holy Spirit, which one attains only through the water of tribulation and the bath of regeneration, in which one is born anew, becoming a child of God and a brother of Christ. One is now comforted in this baptism, awakened from the dead, led out of hell, and made alive in Christ. This man does not live in himself, but Christ lives in him. He is therefore full of joy and courage in the Holy Spirit.[51]

The pains of redemption would thus be left behind, and the believer, now purged of worldly lust and desire, could know the full mercy of God and have free access to the Father. In Müntzer's term, he would now be an "elect friend of God." Hut says in *Ein christlicher underricht:*

> What does one see through the Holy Spirit? He sees the Father with the power of His omnipotence by which he is made. He recognizes the Son in whom he is tested, purified, justified, and circumcised, being truly made a child of God. He now has free access to the Father and becomes one with Christ and all His members. These all are one church and one body in Christ.[52]

This level of redemption is the fulfillment of the inner baptismal action, for with the knowledge of the Holy Spirit comes full and genuine *Gerechtfertigkeit*. Hut distinguished this from forensic *Gerechtigkeit*. The latter, he said, is first given to the believer who, having heard the Gospel of all creatures, has responded in faithful dedication. But it is only preparatory to the actual regeneration that comes through the redemptive discipline of the cross.

> Faith which comes from hearing is reckoned unto justification *(gerechtigkeit)* until the person is made righteous *(gerechtfertigt)* and

cleansed under the cross. When that happens, his faith is such as to be conformed to the faith of God and [to be] at one with Christ.[53]

The two stages must be clearly distinguished, Hut says, since each has a different form of faith.[54] The initiatory faith is man's faith, weak and variable, but the faith of a *gerecht* man is God's faith, strong and unshakable. Man's faith, untested and unproved, is sufficient only to be reckoned as righteousness.[55] But once it is tested, and the rough ore is smelted and refined to pure gold in the fires of the spiritual hell of doubt and affliction, it is brought to maturity in the comfort of the Holy Spirit and the sure strength of divine faith. All worldly lusts are thereby left behind, the law of God is perfected within, and the person can now gladly assume the burden of Christ, whose yoke is easy and whose burden is light.[56]

Even though the distinction is clear, it is difficult to be precise as to when Hut believed this latter action took place. On the one hand, Hut thought of baptism as a lifelong struggle with sin; on the other, sin would be removed before life ended. For instance, he could say of this "just" man:

> Even though such a man should sin and fall, this would not happen by lust, and therefore he would not be condemned. The Lord holds him in His hand and the sin would be forgiven and not reckoned as sin.[57]

The explanation perhaps lies once again in the distinction between the inner and outer baptism of suffering. As the inner baptism progressed toward fulfillment, the person would be less and less prone to sin; and even if he were to fall for a moment, this would not, Hut said, be due to inner lust but to the temptation of the moment. Thus the inner war with sin would gradually wane as righteousness prevailed. The outer war would continue, however, and might even grow more fierce, perhaps to be climaxed in a final conflict on the martyr's pyre. The latter was a war that could not end until death or the return of the Lord. Significantly, the baptism Hut administered looked forward to both eventualities: the baptism of blood in persecution,[58] and the return of Christ, who would then claim those who had been made righteous through baptism.

Baptism and Eschatology

The relation of Hut's eschatology to his views on baptism has received less attention than other areas of his thought.[59] Perhaps it is because this related more to his baptismal practice than to his baptismal "theology." Whatever the reason, the trial testimony of both him and his followers is perfectly clear: Hut was baptizing in preparation for the soon expected second advent of Christ.

Hut's support of Müntzer and the peasants, and his presence at the Frankenhausen debacle are already well known, as is the fact that upon gaining release from the victorious authorities he returned to his former home at Bibra (which he had sworn never to revisit without official permission) and attempted to foment revolution there. Preaching to the citizenry from the town's open pulpit, he proclaimed that the time was at hand for them to accept the sword from the hand of God and, with divine help, overthrow the corrupt magistrates.[60] His pleas had little effect, however, for within a few days the whole movement of the peasants had been crushed and Hut had to flee.

It is not known exactly when Hut moved to a more moderate position on eschatology. Robert Friedmann has suggested that this may have resulted from the influence of Jörg Haug, the popular preacher of Bibra at whose invitation Hut had preached in the town.[61] Whether then or during his stay at Nürnberg later in the year, it seems certain that he modified these eager, revolutionary schemes and, during his Anabaptist period, advocated that Christians should practice obedience to the *Obrigkeit* until the Second Advent.[62] At that time, however, the elect would join Christ and assist Him in meting out punishment upon the godless.[63] His followers seem to have continued in the same view.[64]

Considerable evidence is at hand to suggest that Hut had established a date on which the end was anticipated. It is certain that he expected it to come at the conclusion of a three-and-one-half-year waiting period, but it is unclear when that period was to have begun.[65] Marx Mayer testified that Hut had claimed at the "Martyr's Synod" that it was initiated with the Peasants' War,[66] a dating that was shared by Jörg of Passau.[67] Others, calculating from various vantage points, said that the end would come in eleven months (i.e., November, 1528), eighteen months (late 1529), and twenty-two months (mid-1529).[68] Hut himself denied knowing the "time and hour."[69] Whatever the date, Hut and his followers were not only preparing themselves intensively for it but were also baptizing to that end.

The principal evidence for an "eschatological" baptism among Hut and his followers is found in the court statements of Hut's followers. Hut himself left no express statement of the matter, although he did say that all who did not live as Christ commanded would be destroyed in the approaching judgment, and that only those who did preparatory penance would be spared.[70] One would assume baptism to be implicit in this. What is only implicit there was made clearly explicit by several of his followers. Hermann Anwald[71] testified thus:

> Hut took two fingers, dipped them in water, and made the sign of the cross on his forehead. Whoever does not have this cross will find God sending His angel who will strike him dead. And all who are unbaptized will be slain by the angel.[72]
> Hut told him that those who are signed on the forehead are the rebaptized, but those without the sign will be slain by the angel.[73]

The patrician Eitelhans Langenmantel recounted the same view, relating it to the prophecies in the Apocalypse about the seven angels and the seven seals:

> The Apocalypse tells of the seven angels who are commanded by God to pour out seven plagues on the world in the last days. The Lord tells the first angel, "Do not harm the earth until I have sealed our brethren *(mitbrueder)* on their foreheads." (Rev. 7:3.) The accused understands this to refer to all Christian men who have been and shall be baptized.[74]

Hans Hübner combined Biblical and historical themes into an even more striking statement:

> The Turk will enter the land bringing great war upon all, coming from either the north or the south and from Hungary. When that happens, the Gospel will be preached loudly and clearly. When the Turk comes, the people will flee into the forests and hide themselves. But those who have bound *(verpunden)* themselves to Christ through this sign [of baptism] shall flee into the wilderness, and into Hungary. Judgment will then ensue, and those who have accepted the covenant will root out all those who survive the Turks. Immediately thereafter Christ will come and the Last Day. It is twenty-two months before the Last Day comes.[75]

This, then, was no routine baptism but, rather, an eschatological sign which would protect the recipients at the Last Day. Those with it would be saved; those without it would be judged.

The baptismal vocabulary of Hut's followers reflects the same thing, for they intentionally referred to the ordinance as a "sign" or "seal" and denied that it should be called "baptism." They were "signed," not "baptized," they said. Young Wolfgang Wüsten from Hagenmühle, a member of the conventicle at Baiersdorf, said to the court: "I was not rebaptized; rather, Jörg Volck gave me a sign of the covenant *(verpundnus)* towards God with water on the forehead in the name of the Father, the Son, and the Holy Spirit."[76] Even the authorities recognized this vocabulary, wording their questions accordingly. They asked Jörg Dorsch: "What moved you and your wife to accept rebaptism a year and a half ago, or as you term it, to receive the sign?"[77]

In part, this use of the word "sign" may have derived from Hut's distinction between the sign and the essence of baptism. One of the defendants at Baiersdorf revealed that the term could have this meaning. She said that Hut told her: "To administer the discipline of the Lord is to be an enemy of sin; therefore, as soon as I give you the sign you will suffer persecution."[78]

However, it was clearly an eschatological "sign" and "seal" too. In testimony quoted above we saw Langenmantel speaking of it as the seal

Hans Hut: Baptismal Theology / 89

of God mentioned in Revelation 7:3.[79] He gave this testimony on two occasions, both times in regard to a little collection of paraphrased Scripture verses found among his belongings at his arrest.[80] The brief piece, significantly entitled *Vom gehaimnus des tauffs,* reads thus:

> Do not harm the earth until the servants of our God are sealed for me[81] on their foreheads. Rev. 7[:3].
>
> Mark *(bezaichne)* the people for me with a sign on their foreheads. Ezek. 14[:?]. [An error for 9:4?]
>
> The angel smote those who had not the sign. Exod. 14[:19 conflated with 12:29?]
>
> Those without the sign shall be punished. Rev. 9[:4].
>
> Smite for me those without the sign—everyone, woman and child— and spare none. Ezek. 9[:4-6].[82]

It seems that this little piece came from Hut's *Buch mit den sieben Siegeln.* Hut admitted composing a book by that name which was based on the seven seals in Revelation.[83] Presumably this was the book described in another testimony as a collection of Biblical passages telling of the severity of the judgment at the Second Advent, a booklet compiled for the purpose of turning people away from sin.[84] According to Langenmantel, the little "book" we have quoted was written by Hut and was in circulation among several of the brotherhood.[85] Since the contents of the book described by Langenmantel match those of Hut's *Buch mit den sieben Siegeln,* and since Langenmantel recognized Hut as the author of this little book, it seems certain that the five brief paragraphed verses are from the presumably larger collection compiled by Hut.[86]

Thus, even if the larger material of the *Buch mit den sieben Siegeln* is lost, enough survives to establish the fact that the eschatological sign on the forehead was of great moment to Hut and his followers. When that fact is combined with earlier evidence of "signing" the elect on the forehead in baptism in preparation for Judgment Day, it is clear that eschatological baptism was a dominant theme with them. Notably, it was important enough for Hut to have compiled a book of Scripture verses to be used in convicting his hearers of sin and their need for repentance before the judgment.

However, Hut evidently said that it was not the external sign alone that would protect the baptizand at the Last Day, but baptism in its fullness, including the true baptism of suffering under the cross. Ambrosius Spittelmaier said that all who insisted on remaining in their infant baptism, refusing to follow Christ as they should, would be punished even more severely in the Day of Wrath than the Turks and Jews.[87] Like John the Baptist, Hut's followers spoke of the baptisms of water and fire, meaning baptismal suffering under the cross by the former, and by the latter, the judgment of God both on earth and in hell. The *Geheimnus* also spoke of these and said that "whoever will not hear the voice of God in water must hear it in fire," although it did not make the eschatological character of fire explicit.[88] Spittelmaier again gave best expression to the idea. The time was at hand, he said, when God would purge all things, and "whoever will not be baptized now with Christ in Spirit, water, and blood, must be baptized later in the lake of fire."[89] Echoes from beyond the Jordan are clearly heard here, and even though it seems to have been the authorities' custom to speak of an Anabaptist leader as "the Baptist," both they and Hut's followers must have sensed the unique power of the name "Johannes der Täufer" by which they referred to him.[90]

Two conclusions can be drawn from our discussion of eschatological baptism. The first, and more general one, is that Hut clearly continued the tradition of Thomas Müntzer in seeking to gather an elect people in preparation for the impending Day of the Lord. Moderating the strains of overt revolution, he seems to have proclaimed a postponed seizure of the sword, saying that it would be given to the people by Christ at His coming. Whether preaching that or a milder form of eschatological expectation, Hut was held by his followers to be "a prophet sent from God."[91] As such, he filled a role much like that of John the Baptist, for he announced both salvation and judgment.

The second conclusion relates to the effect this had on baptism. The ordinance now stood as a sign to the baptizand that he was numbered among the elect people of God. Müntzer had said that the experience of inner baptism would be the sign of one's being among the elect, but one would think that among the impatient throng at Frankenhausen that day there were few who could have laid claim to that rare experience. In fact, Müntzer himself appealed to an objective sign when he pointed to the rainbow that appeared as a seeming miracle to assure them of God's presence. However, water baptism was another matter. Anyone could know whether he had received it or not. Thus, if Hut's follower lacked the profound inner baptism desired by Müntzer, he could find assurance in the covenant of water baptism, a covenant which dedicated him to the inner baptism of the Spirit, but did not assume it had already been completed. In part, this outer action served to reveal the elect to each other, much as Hubmaier's baptism made possible the recognition of the brethren. But, in the words of the *Geheimnus*, it also served "to assure him and make him certain that he is an accepted child of God, a brother or sister of Christ, a member of the Christian church and the body of Christ."[92] Thus, it gave the baptizand evidence of his belonging to the covenant people. Hut, thus, pointed to a less dramatic form of confirmation than Müntzer's rainbow, but one more readily at hand. Whoever received this baptism could know that he had been "sealed" with a sign recognizable to the angel of God, a sign that identified him as a member of the elect.

Wolfgang Wüsten gave expression to this new aspect of the covenant sign when, after speaking of how Christ Himself needed the strength of divine power to fulfill the law, he said:

> We need the same. *Therefore the Lord has covenanted (verpunden) Himself to them and they to Him,* for if they did not bind themselves to Him, He would not bind Himself to them. We have baptism as a sign of this covenant *(verpundnus),* for, as the Scriptures say, "He will make an eternal covenant with his people." And again, "He desires for himself an elect people." For this reason the accused can well imagine that the elect must smite the world, for the world praises God only in taverns with cursings and oaths. But God does not want that, for He says that His house is a house of prayer. Therefore, they have covenanted with Him that they should no more curse or swear, and *He has covenanted with them* that He will give them strength and power. The flesh is weak and can do nothing without the grace of the Holy Spirit. *For this cause we have taken the sign of the covenant.* As the Lord says in the Gospel, "Whoever does not keep his covenant should be expelled." And again, *"Whatever you shall bind (pinden) on earth shall be bound in heaven....*[93] (Italics ours.)

This statement moves considerably beyond Hubmaier and Denck, for baptism here is not just the self-dedication of the baptizand, nor the outward manifestation of the covenant of renewal wrought within through the Spirit. It is these, but it is also a sign given to the baptizand from God assuring him of God's faithfulness and of the baptizand's inclusion within God's elect.

An important change of direction was thereby introduced into the Anabaptist understanding of the baptismal action. Baptism now spoke *to* the baptizand as well as *for* him. In Wüsten's statement this was developed to a considerable degree as he recalled Old Testament texts and even the dominical promise of the keys, interpreting both as related to baptism: the former identified the elect and the latter made the action eternally binding. Whether Wüsten represented the thinking of the group here is uncertain, since supporting evidence is lacking. In any event, it is certain that he was typical in this one important aspect: baptism was to be a supportive sign to the baptizand. Hubmaier was near to this but never expressly stated it. Now it was stated, and this can be described as a significant development in Anabaptist baptismal theology. It is an element we shall find echoed and expanded in Hofmann and Marpeck.

The Three Baptisms: Spirit, Water, and Blood

Hubmaier had distinguished three types of baptism: baptism of the Spirit in regeneration; baptism in water, as the believer pledged his life to God and the church; and baptism in blood, both in a daily death to sin and resurrection to new life, and in the recurrent persecution from the world. The same three baptisms are found in Hut's statement to the Augsburg authorities:

> There are three forms of baptism: Spirit, water, and blood. The three agree and give witness on the earth.[94] The first, Spirit baptism, is the promise *(versicherung)* and dedication in the divine Word testifying that one wants to live as it was proclaimed to him through the Word. This is the covenant of God which He makes with men through His Spirit in their hearts.
>
> In addition, God gave water for a sign of this preceding covenant. In water baptism one declares and confesses that he wants to live in right obedience toward God and all Christians, and that he wants to live above reproach. Whoever trespasses and lives unrightly, acting against God and love, should be punished by the others by words. This is the ban, which God announced, and which is to be a witness before the church.
>
> The third baptism is blood. This is the true baptism which Christ declared to His disciples when He asked, "Do you wish to be baptized with the baptism with which I am baptized?" This baptism witnesses throughout the whole world wherever such blood is spilled.[95]

The order is the same as in Hubmaier; but it has now been given a greater precision through the idea of the covenant. The only thing lacking of Hubmaier is the view that the baptism of blood includes the Christian's daily fight against sin. But, since Hut elsewhere made explicit mention of this aspect of the Christian life, one can assume it to be inferred here.[96] Since neither Müntzer nor Denck had used the same distinction, it seems certain that Hut was drawing directly upon Hubmaier at this point. In fact, in one respect, his statement is nearer to Hubmaier than to his own remarks elsewhere, for no mention is made here of the baptism of the Spirit in redemptive suffering that was to follow water baptism.[97] Perhaps the forum of the courtroom was too confining for Hut to present a statement of the more subtle spiritual baptism in inner suffering.

A more detailed description of the three baptisms is found in Leonhard Schiemer's tract, *Von dreyerley Tauf im Neuen Testament,* which, in the absence of a complete discussion by Hut, can be taken as representative of Hut's school of thought. Schiemer begins with a discussion of Spirit baptism, which he says is a pledge "of obedience to the Father" in imitation of Christ, who was obedient unto death.[98] No one is able to make this inner pledge unless he has the assistance of the Holy Spirit, Schiemer says. And, "if one can surrender himself to God wholly and completely, this is a sure sign that he has the Holy Spirit.[99] Hans Schlaffer described Spirit baptism similarly and added that only Christ can give this baptism, for no man is capable of it.[100]

In Schiemer's discussion of the second form of baptism, he too spoke of baptism as acting upon the individual. He described it as a "confirmation" or "seal" of "faith and the inner covenant with God."[101] While partly a testimony or a confirmation given by the baptizand himself, it was also the witness of the Christians to the baptizand; for baptism, like a seal on an envelope, is given only when one knows the contents. Thus it certified the presence of faith, and in doing so, served to confirm the baptizand's inner belief. He said that baptism is to be received "only from those whom Christ has elected and commissioned thereto in the office of the Gospel, that is, the Christians." Schlaffer spoke similarly, adding that it is a very weighty matter since even Jesus waited until His thirtieth year to receive it.[102]

In Schiemer's tract the baptism in blood is merged with the image of the cup, as it is in the Gospel accounts.[103] Schiemer, like Hut in his confession, described this principally in terms of persecution. He said that Judas, Herod, Pilate, and the rest who inflicted this baptism on Jesus, are ready now to give it again.[104] Schlaffer had the same idea, stressing perhaps more emphatically the theme of discipleship and *imitatio Christi*.[105]

It is of note that the emphasis of Hut, Schiemer, and Schlaffer turned more and more to the side of an imposed suffering, as distinct from inner spiritual suffering, even though some of the latter would be included. One can conclude from this that the views of Müntzer were being further modified, so that the inner suffering which dominated his thoughts so strongly was now giving way to a conception of "outer" suffering, i.e., an affliction brought on from without, specifically a persecution inflicted by the godless. It was, in fact, this latter view of suffering that was subsequently held by the Hutterites, who conceived of themselves as faithful witnesses as to Christ amid the afflictions of the wilderness.[106]

The Baptisms of John and Christ

In the face of the imposing place of the Marcan great commission and the texts on the three baptisms, all other Biblical texts used by Hut are negligible. One matter must be singled out for attention, however, since it relates directly to problems discussed in regard to Hubmaier—this is the question of John's baptism.

In his trial testimony Hut repeated the view seen in Hubmaier that the Ephesian baptisms recorded in Acts 19 were "rebaptisms," since the twelve men had been baptized earlier by John.[107] The *Geheimnus* also speaks of those baptized by John as being "baptized again," but in this

94 / *Anabaptist Baptism*

case the second baptism is not water baptism, but the "true baptism" in suffering.

> The baptism of John in water is imperfect and can free no one from sin. It is only a figure, a preparation, and a type of the true baptism in Christ. Therefore, one must be baptized a second time in Christ. Christ Himself accepted this first baptism [in water from John], but it was only a figurative thing. However, through it He entered into the true essence [of baptism].[108]

One finds, thus, a double distinction, whereby John's baptism is imperfect, first by being external and not internal, like true baptism, and, second, by being only preparatory to the water baptism instituted by Christ. Müntzer had held the first of these, as had Denck, and we saw Hubmaier expressing the second.[109] Thus, we have another indication of the merging of two baptismal traditions in Hut.

The Administration of Baptism

We have already observed that Hut's baptism was an eschatological sign or seal, and that, in accordance with Revelation 7:3, he believed himself to have been "sealing" the elect on their foreheads as the sign of their readiness for the Last Day. Several accounts of his baptizing in this fashion survive. Hermann Anwald tells how Hut "took two fingers, dipped them in water, and made the sign of the cross" on Anwald's forehead.[110] According to Martin Rothe, a town official at Neustadt near Eisleben in Thuringia, Hut used his thumb, dipping it in a dish of water and making a cross on the baptizand's forehead.[111] Often, however, Hut seems simply to have poured over the person's head.[112] Ordinarily the candidate would kneel, and evidently the others present did the same.[113]

The baptisms were often preceded by an exposition of the Gospel of all creatures. The candidate was informed that his baptism would launch him on a difficult way that could include persecution and would certainly involve "anguish, affliction, and suffering," as he submitted to the will of God.[114] Following his baptism, the convert would be welcomed into the fellowship of the faithful, who would enjoin him always to greet his new brethren in the name of God and to reply to their greeting with "amen."[115]

Hut's brotherhood seems to have confined the power of performing baptism to those whom the congregation chose. Ordinarily, of course, Hut was the baptizer and he probably acted with charismatic authority as well as formal authority. However, Augustine Bader stated that persons other than Hut gave baptisms also, but only those whom the *Versammlung* selected. He said: "Whenever the brethren send out one of the members of the congregation *(versamlung)*, they give him the authority to baptize."[116] He doubtless refers to the commissioning of

Anabaptist missioners. By the same token, Melchior Kern testified that he did not baptize, for he had not been commissioned to do so.[117]

Beyond the fact that the candidate for baptism had to be a believer and be ready for the "true baptism" of suffering, nothing is said in the accounts about necessary prerequisites for receiving the ordinance. However, Hut's followers did consider one thing to be desirable, namely, that the candidate be thirty years of age. Ambrosius Spittelmaier asserted proudly that his baptism by Hut took place when he was the same age as Christ at His baptism.[118] Hans Schlaffer observed that, since the temptations and afflictions that would follow baptism were no child's play, the candidates for baptism should not be children; he thought thirty to be the proper age.[119] And the author of the *Fünf Artikel* (perhaps Peter Walpot) said that Christ's baptism at thirty serves as an example that we should be baptized at an age of understanding.[120] Thus, the basis for the view was partly the ideal of the *imitatio Christi*, and partly the practical and theological factors that belong to the practice of believer's baptism. Their opinion was later shared by Michael Servetus, who reasoned, in a more developed theological fashion, that baptism should be delayed until the age of thirty since original sin, which faith and baptism are to destroy, does not reach its full development until then.[121] Schlaffer and Spittelmaier did not construct so elaborate a theological defense of their view as Servetus did. However, they resembled Servetus in that they too were probably dependent upon earlier Paulician practice, even if not on the anthropological speculations of Archbishop Theophylact of Orchrida which Servetus seems to have known.[122]

In summary, Hut's baptismal theology is notable for three characteristics: its merging of views from Müntzer, Hubmaier, and Denck; its understanding of baptism as an eschatological sign; and its belief that baptism could act on the baptizand. The influence of Müntzer is seen primarily in the conception of the Gospel of all creatures and the idea of the inner baptism of redemptive, spiritual suffering. Uniting this with Denck's view of the covenant, Hut understood this universal baptism of inner suffering to be an integral part of the discipleship to which one dedicates himself in the baptismal covenant.[123] But the covenant concept was given more precise formulation too, for the covenant bound the church into a disciplined unity in addition to being the inner experience and the outer manifestation of renewal. Thus Hubmaier's ecclesiology, Müntzer's mystical baptism, and Denck's covenantal baptism were united.

If Hut continued Müntzer's eschatology, he also related it to water baptism by interpreting the ordinance as the eschatological seal to be given in the last days as the sign of the elect. This meant that the universal baptism of suffering was then being brought to fulfillment in the great events of the Last Day. One was to prepare for this occasion by entering the covenant of the elect. The redeemed were to be identified by their possession of the inner and outer baptisms; whereas, in Müntzer the identification of the elect was through their inner baptism and the outer religio-political covenant.

Finally, by understanding water baptism as an eschatological seal, Hut and his followers made explicit an element only implicit in Hubmaier: namely, that outer baptism acts on the individual as well as for him. In relation to eschatology, baptism stood as a sign to the baptizand that he was enrolled among the elect. But the ordinance had a broader signification, for it assured the baptizand of being in the body of Christ, and in Schiemer it was a seal of faith confirming to the baptizand his possession of true faith.

Thus, Hut articulated a bold and striking theology of baptism. It was significant not only for its unusual nature, but for its place in the stream of developing Anabaptist theology, for Hut stood at the point where several tributaries flowed together; and, if we may press our metaphor, where each was transformed in the churning rapids of Hut's fervent preaching and ingenious mind. The stream would soon find a broader channel, however, and would become more placid as his successors, Pilgram Marpeck on the one hand and the Hutterites on the other, found less validity in Hut's radical eschatology and were, therefore, more free to develop Anabaptist ecclesiology to its full.[124]

Meanwhile, another John the Baptist appeared, or, as he thought more appropriate, Elijah, and was himself calling the elect into the center of the events of the Final Day. This was Melchior Hofmann. We now turn to him and developments in lower Germany and the Netherlands.

CHAPTER IV

Melchior Hofmann

Like Hans Hut, Melchior Hofmann combined several strains of thought. They ranged from the Lutheranism surviving from his early reformatory activity, to medieval pietism, apocalyptic chiliasm, and evangelical Anabaptism. This bold variety of thought was matched if not surpassed by his deeds: his sharp attacks against the Lutheran Reformation, his announcement of new revelations through Leonard and Ursula Jost, and his claim to be the second Elijah, the prophet of the Last Day. These eccentric views alone would be enough to ensure Hofmann a place in Reformation studies, even if he had not been the person principally responsible for taking Anabaptism to the Netherlands.

The reason for his inclusion within the present study is his tract on baptism, *Die Ordannantie Godts,* which contains one of the most colorful descriptions of baptism in Reformation literature.[1] Intended as a discussion of the ordinance of baptism as given in the great commission, the tract draws on a rich collection of Biblical texts and symbols and presents Hofmann's views on baptism in a wide context of ideas encompassing virtually all of his thought.

Regeneration and the Baptismal Covenant

Like several of the Strassburg Anabaptists, Hofmann divided the process of regeneration into two stages. The first stage, the "birth of the letter" as Hofmann called it, bestows the power to become a child of God and is followed by the true spiritual birth which makes one an elect son of God. Clement Ziegler seems to have been the first to use the distinction, though without actually speaking of two "births,"[2] and Marpeck used it as well, in his case with a vocabulary like Hofmann's.[3]

Building on John 1:12, Hofmann said that all who believe in Christ receive "power to become children of God" and are thereby made "letter servants," as distinguished from true spiritual children.[4] Like Hubmaier, Hofmann held to the restoration of the human will in Christ, according to which these servants in the letter were understood to be fully capable of choosing good and doing it, and in this way were able to become children of God.[5]

Earlier, while still a Lutheran, Hofmann had espoused the doctrine of predestination. In *Das 12. Capitel des propheten Danielis ausgelegt,* he argued from the Parable of the Great Supper that, like the earthly host, the Heavenly Host also "compels" His guests to enter the banquet, guests He had chosen from the foundation of the world. The individual had no choice in the matter and, because of God's greatness, should give only praise to God, whether saved or damned.[6]

As an Anabaptist, however, Hofmann adopted the common Anabaptist position of a universal atonement and with it the concomitant belief in the freedom of the human will. Like Denck before him, he wanted to exonerate God of responsibility for man's sin, and thus he said that God originally created all men for salvation and none for damnation, and that Christ had brought life for all men just as Adam brought death upon all.[7]

However, he attributed to man no simple free will; rather, it was a freedom given to man in stages. As a direct result of the incarnation—and perhaps an immediate result universally felt[8]—mankind first received a degree of freedom through the "light that enlighteneth every man." By its power to attract, this light draws men in the direction of God, and thus they receive a limited freedom toward good. It is essentially the freedom to accept the Gospel when fully preached to them.[9] Also, since this is the light from the "sun," i.e., the new dispensation, in contrast to light from the "moon," the old dispensation, it is strong enough to show men the way to salvation. Added to this light is the power of the Gospel itself by which an even greater portion of the light of God is shed abroad among men.

However, if the first level of light has been given to all men in all times since the incarnation, the second, the level of the Gospel itself, is given only in certain times, specifically the time of the apostles, the time of John Huss, and Hofmann's time (in which Hofmann was the principal agent).[10] Those who receive this Gospel in faith receive the birth of the letter, which birth restores to man the full power of choosing between good and evil.

> The noble and high will of God is that He should omit no one, now or in the future. As it is written in Ecclesiasticus 15[:14]: "he made man from the beginning."[11] That is, He brings man forth from the first death of Adam through His Word Christ Jesus to live again. He brings to him a true illumination and spiritual cleansing and sets him in the hand of His will, meaning that man becomes a truly free creature (John 8[:32]).[12] From then on he may himself choose his own course and way, and eat either of goodness or of evil. Whether

he chooses life or death, to walk in God's will or stay in Satan's—
whatever he selects and chooses will surely be given to him.[13]

Accordingly, Hofmann revised his earlier interpretation of the Parable of the Great Supper to say that God compels no one to enter the kingdom.[14] All men, he said, have the degree of freedom associated with the gift of God's light in the incarnation, and when they hear the Gospel they may accept or refuse its offer of life. Those who accept are born again; by this birth they receive the power to seek and to attain the level of born sons of God.[15] Those who faithfully pursue this goal will be rewarded by the birth in the Spirit, or what traditional theology had called sanctification. But those who fall by the way will die the second death. No resurrection avails to save one from that death.[16]

It is by the covenant in water baptism that those illumined through the Word pledge themselves to the struggle necessary to achieve the full spiritual birth. Hofmann understood this pledge to be at once the covenant of obedience binding the believer to the heavenly captain and a pledge of marital faithfulness to the divine bridegroom.

It was probably the Strassburg Anabaptists (who themselves converted Hofmann to Anabaptism) who supplied Hofmann with his conception of the baptismal covenant. The idea had been espoused by several figures among them since at least as early as December, 1526, when Jacob Gross described baptism to the city authorities in Denckian terms: "Baptism is a covenant of a good conscience through God; the covenant removes no uncleanness of the flesh."[17] Gross, who was baptized by Hubmaier in Waldshut, may have read Denck's writings and very probably met Denck, who was expelled from Strassburg about the time of Gross's trial.[18] Later, in January, 1529, Jacob Kautz and Wilhelm Reublin presented to the city council a confession which spoke of baptism as an act in which the Anabaptists "made a covenant with God in our hearts to serve Him henceforth in holiness all our days by His power and to make such known to the *bundtsgenossen.*"[19]

As a Biblical basis for his view, Hofmann combined ideas and images from three principal passages of Scripture: the account of the Exodus, the story of the faithful bride in the Song of Songs, and the account of Jesus' baptism. He treated these as "types" of Christian baptism. Thus, he described the Hebrews' departure from Egypt and their covenant at Sinai as the pattern to be followed in the spiritual exodus of the soul.[20] Again, like the bride of the Song of Songs, the believer was to yield himself to the heavenly Bridegroom in full willingness to go into the wilderness with Him.[21] And most of all, he pointed to the example of Christ who covenanted with God at the Jordan.[22] All three texts relate to a wilderness experience: the Exodus with the forty years of wandering, the Song of

Songs with the removal to the upland pastures, and Jesus' baptism with the forty days of temptation.

Hofmann used a dual symbolism to describe the baptismal covenant. Like Hubmaier and Denck before him (and Erasmus and Luther as well), Hofmann thought of the baptismal covenant as the baptizand's pledge of faithfulness to the heavenly Captain and King.[23] But more important for him was the symbolism of the nuptial covenant, the covenant which betrothed the believer to the heavenly Bridegroom. At this point he drew on the mystical tradition; but, notably, he modified it by identifying the nuptial covenant with baptism. The Song of Songs, long a source of symbolism for the mystics, was the principal Biblical source for this. Hut described how the preaching of the Gospel was the kiss of the heavenly Bridegroom bringing sweetness and joy. All who responded by accepting His message of forgiveness were to "wed and bind" themselves to Christ, forsaking all others. They were to become wholeheartedly obedient to Him so that His desire would be theirs and they would be able to say, "I live, yet not I, but Christ lives in me."[24] In the first instance, this was an inner action like the spiritual "covenant of a good conscience" in Denck and the inner covenant of "true baptism" in Hut. But, again like Denck and Hut, this was also manifested in an outer covenant in water baptism.[25]

As already noted, Hofmann stressed that the "baptismal" vows of Israel, of the bride of the Song of Songs, and of Jesus, were all followed by a journey into the wilderness. Hofmann here drew on the mystical tradition by interpreting these earlier events as timeless symbols of the way redemption is effected. Instead of a physical wilderness and outer conflict, this was an inner struggle within the wilderness of the soul.[26] As in Müntzer, this was the inward process of dying to the creaturely and being raised to divinity. In Hofmann's view, however, as we shall see shortly, the wilderness also referred to the trials of the elect immediately before the Last Day, and thus mystical and eschatological considerations were joined.

Following the tradition earlier represented by Richard of St. Victor, Hofmann understood the *Wüste* to be a stage in the soul's itinerary of redemption.[27] The whole journey would require forty-two days, Hofmann said. It would begin at the point where one leaves Egypt, the land of bondage, and crosses the Red Sea of spiritual and water baptism to enter into covenant with God. That is only the beginning of Spirit baptism, however, for it continues through the forty days of the wilderness itself. As in Hut's "true baptism," one here suffers the onslaughts of doubt and despair as the soul is weaned from love of the creatures and its betrothal to Christ is made complete. The forty-second and last day is the day of entrance into the Promised Land where one can rest free from the privations and terrors of the wilderness.[28] Hofmann's resemblance to Richard is striking, as this statement from Richard indicates:

> The soul is led by God into the wilderness where it is fed with milk so that it may be inebriated with inward sweetness. . . . But first we must leave Egypt behind, first we must cross the Red Sea. First the Egyptians must perish in the waves, first we must suffer famine in the land of Egypt before we can receive this spiritual nourishment and heavenly food. He who desires that food of heavenly solitude let him abandon Egypt both in body and heart, and altogether set aside the love of the world.[29]

Notably, however, Hofmann has added the baptismal covenant which appears at the point of "crossing the Red Sea."

In the experience of the wilderness, the believer dies to the old life and its power. This was true for the Hebrews at the Red Sea, Hofmann says, for they were baptized and deadened to the world there.[30] This is Paul's putting off the old man, the First Adam, and his putting on the Second Adam, Christ.[31] As in Müntzer and Hut, this is the purgative cleansing of inner baptism in which the baptizand suffers the loss of his hold on the creatures. He is tried and tested in his soul, and he is brought forth renewed within, assured of the grace of God, and inwardly reborn in the power of the new life in Christ. By the submission of his will to Christ, the believer becomes more and more at one with Christ until he is "in Christ Jesus and Christ Jesus is in [him]."[32]

The result is a complete regeneration—one may say, sanctification—in which the old Adam dies and the new Adam is raised within. Sin is no longer a viable possibility within the regenerate. Hofmann says:

> They who have once struggled through and conquered are the elect of God. They will never again leave Christ and the eternal temple of God. Nor does the second death have any more power over them, for the first death is passed away. All is made new within them. They are taught by God and He is their light and lantern through the Holy Spirit, both then and forever. Those who came to Christ can be taken from His hand and power by no one, nor ever separated from Him unto eternity. Indeed, they are conquerors; they have died in the Lord and thus can sin no more. A new, true rebirth sustains them so that they cannot and will not fall in all eternity.[33]

Nor does the law have sovereignty over them any longer, for "they live unto righteousness and no longer unto sin."[34]

All who receive water baptism dedicate themselves unto this regeneration, but Hofmann asserts that not all attain it. For those who fail, there is no second repentance. Like the Hebrews in the wilderness, they fall under the condemnation of death, this time the "second death" from which there is no resurrection.[35] Chiding those—he doubtless means the Lutherans—who say that one cannot achieve this high level of spiritual power in this life, Hofmann argues that, if the Hebrews did not complain of being unable to make the journey through the wilderness in their time,[36] neither should the Christian. God is ready to supply power adequate to everyone's need on this pilgrimage, Hofmann says, for He has not only restored to the believer the knowledge of good and evil through the illumination of the Word, but He has also given the believer full freedom of will and the power of His grace to achieve what he wills. Thus all who elect death do so at their own behest, not as a result of a divine decree.[37]

This is quickly recognized as another theology from that of Luther, to which Hofmann had adhered for a time. Further, as we saw with Hubmaier, there is a sense in which this continues Catholic theology, for Hofmann's conception of regeneration as an inner illumination through the Word runs parallel to the Catholic conception of grace as an infused transforming power *(gratia creata)*. In both cases there is a divine action which heals the individual and restores to him the power of attaining righteousness. Hofmann's position was, however, more extreme than the Catholic view, for he expected all believers to be able to attain the goal of sanctification, whereas the Catholics ordinarily reserved this for only the life of discipline and meditation.

For Hofmann, then, water baptism was a dedication toward and entrance into the wilderness experience of testing and purgation, much like that of the Exodus and of Christ's temptations. Supposing that the believer had knowledge of good and evil sufficient to his need, Hofmann recalled how the Israelites who wavered and doubted in the wilderness perished there with no hope of a second grace, while only the faithful survived. So it would be with the Christian: "no one is saved unless, according to the will of God, he carries the fight to the end, as did the disciples in Luke 22[:28],[38] and Joshua and Caleb with the survivors in the wilderness [Numbers 14:24, 30]."[39] Supporting his argument with a flood of Scripture references, Hofmann reiterated that all who fail will lose their inheritance and the gift of grace, only to receive the lake of fire as reward.[40] But those who were faithful in this spiritual testing would be born into spiritual life. Thus, like Hut's "true baptism" in trial and suffering, Hofmann's baptism in the wilderness served to carry the believer to the state of full regeneration; according to both, the covenant in water baptism launched one on this pilgrimage.

Baptism, Eschatology, and Redemptive History

Although Hofmann may not have expressly described water baptism as a comforting sign of God's certain grace, as, for instance, Luther did, he nonetheless considered it a sign of redemption. This was so in two ways: first, the ordinance was a sign standing in a succession of signs

Melchior Hofmann / 103

belonging to the line of redemptive history; second, baptism stood in an eschatological context charged with the expectation of an imminent end of the age. To isolate this aspect of Hofmann's baptismal theology, we shall have to describe his conception of *Heilsgeschichte* and the intimately related principle of hermeneutics he used, as well as his views of the *eschaton*.

In Hofmann's view, the Scriptures are composed of "figures" which point beyond themselves to the true reality or the "spirit" behind them. This may be an allegorical relationship, as in the case of the three angelic visitors to Abraham, who stand as symbols of the Trinity;[41] or it may be typological: for instance, the lamb's skin which God gave to Adam and Eve points to Christ, the Lamb of God;[42] the ark of Noah signifies Christ and His redemption to come;[43] and, in a figure often cited by Hofmann, the Exodus symbolizes the gathering of the elect out of the land of Pharaoh at the Final Day.[44] The hidden meaning of the symbols in Scripture is attainable only by those who possess the Key of David, i.e., by the spiritual men, the "apostolic teachers" as Hofmann calls them. All others see only the figures, and since they are ignorant of the Spirit, they are unaware that the images are only "figures."[45] The spiritualist center of Hofmann's thought becomes clear at this point, for it is only the power of the Spirit that unfolds to the reader the vast dimensions of spiritual depth in the Bible (through allegory) and of historical prediction (through typology).[46]

In part, Hofmann's method of allegory and typology was intended for describing elements found within the confines of Scripture itself, for it provided a way to affirm that the Bible was self-interpreting and self-consistent. Thus, he noted that the Old Testament mercy seat is plainly interpreted in the New Testament as meaning Christ Himself; the former is "figure" and the latter is spirit.[47] Hofmann's principle of the "cloven hoof" was the express manifestation of this idea. According to this, "the whole Word of God is double or twofold."[48] To get the whole meaning of two contrasting, sometimes seemingly contradictory, passages, one must collate them, often comparing them with yet another passage. For example, Hofmann found that two contrary passages—the statement in Ecclesiasticus 18:13 that God has mercy on all men, and the comment of Paul that God has mercy on some and hardens the hearts of others (Romans 9:16-18)—are reconciled in Paul's assertion that God has shut up mankind in disobedience in order finally to have mercy on all (Romans 11:32).[49] Thus, the principle of the cloven hoof was aimed at bringing unity to the Bible.

Hofmann believed, however, that the Key of David could also unlock truths which reached beyond the pages of Scripture—truths which were the charts of the events of the Final Day. In some cases, these were found in typological figures, particularly in the figure of the Exodus; in other cases, these were allegorical images. Jesus' statement about the sign in the heavens of the Son of Man is an example of the latter. Allegorizing the symbols of Matthew 24, Hofmann said that the sign of the Son of Man is the cross, i.e., suffering, which will be imposed upon the elect (the "heavens"). The stars (the preachers, pastors, and priests) will fall from the spiritual heaven, and the sun and moon (respectively Christ, and faith in the Gospel) will be darkened.[50] In this case the passage is predictive to begin with, but in others Hofmann found a predictive element when it was not already recognizable.

However, it was not just the Biblical writings which were predictive for Hofmann, but the *events* of Biblical history. The best example of this is the Exodus, which in Hofmann's view prefigured, successively, the baptism and temptation of Christ, the baptismal experience of the soul, and now the "baptism" of the church in the Last Day when it would be led into the wilderness in preparation for the end of present history and the introduction of the new kingdom.[51] Thus, in addition to containing predictive elements in its expressly prophetic passages, the Bible was held to record a series of events which stood in an inner relation to each other understandable only in terms of *Heilsgeschichte* and eschatology. For Hofmann, hermeneutics was thereby turned into soteriology and eschatology. The one who possessed the Spirit would be able not only to see these deeper levels of reality in Scripture, but, seeing them, to read the events of his own time in light of them. Finally, if one saw the expected events occurring around him, he could be sure that he stood in the center of the line of salvation, for figure and spirit would always be found together. The true prophet, Hofmann said, would be aware of these things and know the place where salvation lay in his time; for, as he often said, "The Lord does nothing without revealing His mystery to the prophets."[52]

Believing himself to be a prophet with the gift of reading both Scripture and history in this fashion, Hofmann claimed to know that the end was at hand. In his commentary on Daniel 12, written in 1526, he asserted that even though one could not name the day or hour, one could predict the "time," for God had always revealed this to His elect. Just as Abraham, Daniel, Anna, and Simeon knew what God was doing in their time, so the man of the Spirit could know in his time.[53]

Hofmann proceeded to give the details of his own "time," for he was convinced that it was the time of the end. The end period would last seven years in all, he said, or, more accurately, two periods of three and one-half years. The figure of three and one-half was arrived at through a complex merger of numerals from important Biblical events. The Flood, the Exodus, and the temptation of Christ each lasted forty days or years, and when the forty is read as months it matches the 1,260 days of Revelation 12:6—or so Hofmann reasoned. Further, Revelation 12:14 places the woman in the wilderness for "a time, and times, and half a time," which, when read as years, equals (approximately) the 1,260 days of Revelation 12:6. Daniel 12:7 also speaks of "a time, two times, and half a time." Thus, Hofmann found ample Biblical support for his numerology. But since this forty "days" would be the consummation of the age, the period would be doubled to a full seven years, the time of fulfillment.[54]

The time would begin with the appearance of the two "witnesses," Elijah and Enoch, who, like Moses and Aaron at the Exodus, would announce the impending action of God. Yet unrecognized at the time of Hofmann's writing (1526), they would soon reveal themselves, Hofmann said, and would then preach for the first three and one-half years. At the end of the period, they would, like Christ, be arrested, persecuted, and killed. Thereupon would follow the second period. It would begin as a time of peace, but as the elect gradually gathered, ruling Babylon would reveal herself and toward the end would loose her destruction on the faithful. The cross would descend on the spiritual Jerusalem and the final baptism of blood would be poured out. When the destruction reached its full, Christ would return and rescue the elect from the great tribulation.[55]

Krohn observed that, if Hofmann believed the seven-year period to be beginning at the time he wrote the commentary on Daniel 12 (as Krohn thinks he did believe[56]), the period would have ended in 1533. However, when Hofmann was charged with this same thing by Nicholas Amsdorf, he denied it.[57] Nonetheless, it seems certain that Hofmann was setting dates for the end. Not only does his statement in the commentary on Daniel suggest this, but remarks he made at the time of his imprisonment reveal the same thing. For instance, when he was taken prisoner in 1533, he said that the time had arrived for God's witnesses to be imprisoned,[58] and later he said that Christ would come in the third year of his confinement.[59]

Of special importance at the end time would be the two "witnesses," Elijah and Enoch, of which Hofmann claimed to be the former.[60] Evidently he believed the latter to be Leonard Jost, who, with his wife, was dreaming dreams and seeing visions as Joel had predicted; however, there is evidence that Cornelius Poldermann and perhaps Caspar Schwenckfeld were recognized as Enoch as well.[61]

In addition to the witnesses there would also be 144,000 followers, a number predicted by Revelation 7:4. Hofmann said that these would be the apostolic teachers, those who had received the full baptism of the Spirit in the wilderness, and who thus had power to lead their hearers into the wilderness for salvation. They would assemble at Strassburg, the site of the New Jerusalem, and venture forth under the leadership of the two witnesses to announce the imminence of the Last Day and urge their hearers to repent, be baptized, and enlist with the true followers of Christ.[62]

This final baptism, like all actions within the course of redemptive history according to Hofmann's view, would be composed of the inner reality or "spirit" and the outer figure. There would be nothing new about this baptism itself, for it would still be the inner baptism of trial and suffering which would be manifested in the outer covenantal baptism in water. However, the context would be changed, for baptism would now stand within the events of the Final Day and thus would serve to mark the elect of God in preparation for the advent of Christ. Like the baptisms of Israel and of Jesus, it would be given in the wilderness, this time the wilderness of a world ruled by the Beast, the new Pharaoh, the last manifestation of rebellion against God. Hofmann based his comments on Revelation 12:6 with its description of the woman fleeing into the wilderness for 1,260 days.[63] Although the usual Anabaptist interpretation understood this to refer to the period of the great "fallen" church founded by Constantine, Hofmann took it to speak of the second of the three-and-one-half-year periods of the end time. Thus, he said:

> And now in this final age the true apostolic emissaries of the Lord Jesus Christ will gather the elect flock and call it through the Gospel and lead the Bride of the Lord into the spiritual wilderness, betroth, and covenant her through baptism to the Lord.[64]

Supporting his views with a typological interpretation of Old Testament figures, Hofmann said that in this experience the believers would pass through the forecourt of the spiritual tabernacle, the antechamber of the spiritual temple and thereby move from the level of a literal birth in the Word to a spiritual birth to enter the spiritual holy of holies.[65] This would be the spiritual fulfillment of the Feast of Tabernacles, for now spiritual Israel, the woman of Revelation 12:1-6, would suffer the forty days in the wilderness. As with Christ, this would involve a betrothal and covenanting with God whereby the believer would yield his will fully to God to become absorbed in Him and enter into the power of eternal life.[66]

In this climactic way all of Hofmann's symbols were merged and both allegorical interpretations and typological interpretations were enlisted to show the significance of the baptism about to be poured out on the world. As these figures are drawn together, almost tumbling and cascading over each other, one can see Hofmann blending them, finding support on every hand for his belief that he stood at the redemptive center of his day and that he bore in himself the power of the mighty events of the end time. The baptism of which he spoke also contained this power, he said, for in both its internal action as redemptive suffering and its outer aspect as water baptism, it was the certain sign of the final events, and as such was a guarantee to the baptizand of his participation in the climax of the history of God's salvation.

Although Hofmann seems to have adopted no specifically "eschatological" mode of baptism as Hut did, he was, if anything, more convinced of the redemptive nature of the events coming to pass through him, and more powerfully expressive of his belief. In essence the two were very similar, for in their descriptions of the inner baptism in the Spirit both drew on the mystical tradition before them, both envisioned a climax to the baptismal experience in a full sanctifying, regeneration, and both understood baptism to serve as a sign gathering the elect for the coming of Christ at the Last Day.

The Administration of Baptism

One of the clearest indications of the strongly eschatological character of baptism in Hofmann's view is his order for a two-year *Stillstand* in the administration of the ordinance. On December 5, 1531, Jan Volkertz Trijpmaker, whom Hofmann left as his lieutenant in the Netherlands, was beheaded along with nine other Melchiorites by the imperial authorities. The grim event took Hofmann and his followers by great surprise, for in their understanding of the predicted course of the times it was still too early for the persecution of the elect to begin. Thus, Hofmann concluded that the time was not yet as advanced as he had thought, and he called for a two-year suspension of baptism.[67] The Biblical type for the decision was the comparable delay in the building of Zerubbabel's temple: the delay in building the physical temple was thus prophetically fulfilled in a delay in the spiritual temple.[68]

Whether Hofmann called for a renewal of the ordinance at the end of the two years is unclear. He was in the Strassburg jail by then and was of the opinion that the second half of the seven-year period had begun. This would mean that the task of evangelization would have then fallen to the 144,000 apostolic teachers. But no such number had rallied behind Hofmann by then, and due to his confinement his influence gradually began to wane in the face of the rise of other leaders. Whether this caused him to revise his eschatological calculations again, we do not know, but no evidence seems to survive to indicate that he called for a renewal of baptism on the scale once anticipated.

Hofmann said that the office of administering baptism would belong to the apostolic teachers. Kawerau observes that, as bearers of the divine message in their time, they would virtually have priestly authority: being possessed of the Spirit they would be able to interpret Scripture; they would mediate the grace of Christ and His revelation; and by virtue of participating in the heavenly Christ, the spiritual head, they would be the head of the church on earth.[69]

However, their primary function in the final days was to carry the message of Christ throughout the world and gather the elect in anticipation of the great marriage feast with Christ. They were to "gather the elect flock," lead the Bride into the spiritual wilderness, and there betroth and covenant her to the Lord in anticipation of His imminent return. As has been seen, this covenanting involved baptism, both the inner baptism of trial and purification, and outer baptism in water.

As compared with Hubmaier and Hut, Hofmann said little about baptism's power to form a congregation, but at the same time he was not without such concern. This will be seen in the story of his baptisms in Emden to be recounted in a moment. But beyond that, it is seen in the emergence of the Münsterite kingdom. Although the debacle there may be correctly judged as an illegitimate expression of Hofmann's own views, it nevertheless suggests the force his views had for creating a formally constituted community once these views were put fully into effect. The influence of Bernard Rothmann added to this, of course, but behind it lay the concern of Hofmann to gather the elect together and mark them with the sign of their participation in redemptive history. This was, of course, taken literally at Münster, so literally, in fact, that the baptisms were occasionally performed with no water at all—just the outer form.[70] Thus, Hofmann's eschatological sign became just that—a figure and sign to mark the gathering of the elect in the kingdom of the Last Day. At Münster this was constitutive indeed. One can assume therefore, that had Hofmann been free to carry out his own program of evangelization and baptizing, he too would have brought about the formation of formally constituted church groups, though hopefully less extreme than the experiment in Westphalia.

Hofmann recorded nothing about the mode of water baptism and only one instance of his own baptizing is preserved. Obbe Philips and the Lutheran preachers of Emden tell us of it. According to their account Hofmann baptized some three hundred persons there in 1530. Obbe said that this was done "publicly in the church."[71] The Lutherans report that it took place in the *Geerkammer,* a room which served as a vestry for the priests and an entrance to the altar and pulpit. They said further that the baptisms were performed "out of a barrel," suggesting that the mode was affusion.[72] They also reported that Hofmann baptized an infirm old man in the street, a report accepted by the Dutch chronicler, Eggerick Beningha, and a later historian (late sixteenth and early seventeenth centuries), Ubbo Emmius.[73] The Reformed preachers, who were in charge of the church at the time and were doubtless sensitive to the Lutheran claim that Hofmann and the Anabaptists had achieved so great an influence as to be able to conduct a public mass baptism, denied the report and asserted that the whole matter had been greatly exaggerated. They said that no one still alive from the time recalled any street baptisms.[74] Unfortunately all of these reports were composed some years after the event. Philips' *Bekentenisse* was written shortly before 1560, Beningha's *Volledige Chronijk van Oostfrieslant* dates from about the same time, and the account by the Reformed preachers is even later. However, even if the number of baptisms is exaggerated, the substance of the report would seem to be reliable.

That Hofmann should have chosen a church building as the location for the baptisms is notable, for the Anabaptists seemed generally to prefer houses or private places, doubtless often feeling that the ecclesiastical buildings were to be avoided since they housed the fallen church. Hubmaier had used his own church building of course, and Hofmann himself had once petitioned the authorities of Strassburg to provide a church for the Anabaptists;[75] so there was certainly precedent for the action. It was nonetheless unusual among the Anabaptists.

Hofmann on Infant Baptism: A Recantation

According to a document in the Strassburg archives, Hofmann forsook his position on adult baptism and in 1539 avowed acceptance of infant baptism.[76] The little document observes that Christians are enjoined to hear the counsel of the ancients, and thus the testimonies of Dionysius, Irenaeus, and Origen on infant baptism are recalled, all three of which are cited as having testified to it as an early practice. That infants were baptized should be no surprise, Hofmann says, for the Apostle Paul spoke of baptisms for the dead, and, if that was practiced, how much more acceptable infant baptism should be. He concludes: "I am, therefore, perfectly content for them to be baptized . . . , and if I myself had children, I would allow them to receive baptism in such fashion." By the phrase, "in such fashion," Hofmann means that such baptism would signify that the children were "received into the Christian church" and were to be "trained in holiness." "As such," Hofmann was evidently willing to accept infant baptism.

Kawerau comments that this is not a radical change in Hofmann: "This amounts to a very limited recantation which does not affect the significance of Hofmann's own teaching."[77] In a sense this is true, for the true baptism, if we may use Hut's phrase, is the inner baptism in the Spirit, and that baptism would remain. At least, Hofmann's recantation does not disavow the spiritual baptism, and his acceptance of infant baptism would not necessarily preclude his continued advocacy of it. Nonetheless, the change is considerable, for Hofmann, like other Anabaptists, had believed that infant baptism was not only contrary to the will of God but was of the devil since it was established on authority other than God's. It was therefore destructive of the true church, for it denied the voluntarism necessary to a fully disciplined congregation of believers. Hofmann had said: "All human notions are strongly forbidden; infant baptism is absolutely not from God but is practiced by the 'anti-Christians' and the Satanic crowd."[78] And further:

> Baptism is the sign of the covenant of God, instituted solely for the old, the mature, and the rational who can receive, accept, and understand the teaching and preaching of the Lord. It is not for the immature, the uncomprehending, and the unreasonable who are unable to receive, learn, and understand the teaching of the apostolic emissaries. Such are immature children. . . . Nowhere in the Old or the New Testament is there even one letter regarding children. The apostles of Christ Jesus gave no command concerning infant baptism, nor did they teach or write a syllable about it. There is no evidence that they baptized any child and no such will be found in all eternity.[79]

Thousands have been "slaughtered" by infant baptism,[80] and those who advocate it are only liars and blasphemers, Hofmann says.[81]

More important than signifying a simple withdrawal of Hofmann's opposition to infant baptism—aided certainly by the authority which he would have believed Dionysius and the others to have—is the matter of the separation of the "figure" and the "spirit" of the ordinance. The two had gone together, he said, and accordingly the apostolic heralds were charged with administering water baptism as well as encouraging the inner baptism of the Spirit. Together both served as a sign of belonging to the faithful of God, a sign of standing in the line of redemption. But with his recantation that was changed. This change found support in the fact that inner, spiritual baptism was always more important than outer baptism, and this further separation of the two only makes more clear the spiritualist center of Hofmann's thought. Nonetheless, the acceptance of infant baptism and the concomitant acceptance of the state church system was considerably more than a very limited recantation. It was a disavowal of the Anabaptist position and was accomplished in even stronger terms than Hans Denck had used at Basel in 1527.[82]

Scriptural Texts

The discussion of Hofmann's hermeneutics has already revealed that his use of Scripture differs from Hubmaier and Hut considerably, and thus it would be expected that his choice and interpretation of Biblical passages would vary as well. Two principal Scriptural bases underlay his theology of baptism: one is the great commission; the other is the exodus theme in Israel's Exodus, the Song of Songs, and Jesus' baptism, with the related texts in both Testaments.

The Great Commission is the "ordinance" itself, the express baptismal command of Christ which is binding upon all apostolic emissaries.[83] Like Hubmaier and Hut, Hofmann saw a threefold order in the command: preach, believe, and baptize, and in this sense his view is much like the two earlier subjects.[84]

However, the second group of texts—those relating to the exodus theme—embraced and undergirded more of his view than the great commission did. This was for the reason that they were susceptible to the typological hermeneutic which found greater value in Hofmann's eyes than the more literal (in the good sense of the term), grammatical, and contextual hermeneutic that much of Anabaptism took over from the magisterial reformers. Thus, Hofmann's collection and treatment of Biblical texts was entirely different from Hubmaier's. The latter combed the New Testament, collecting every text on baptism he could find, including those describing actual baptisms, but Hofmann did none of this. He sought rather to unfold the line of redemption which he saw linking the great events of salvation history. Hence he made no mention of the baptisms in Acts, nor is there any substantial use of many other Anabaptist *loci classici* such as I Peter 3:21 and Colossians 2:11, 12.[85] Instead, it was the passages explicating the exodus theme which provided the heart of the Biblical basis for his view: the accounts of the Exodus itself, the withdrawal of the bride in the Song of Songs, and the accounts of Jesus' baptism together with supporting passages like I Corinthians 10:1, 2 and Romans 6:3, 4. As has been seen, Hofmann's point was that the baptism he announced was the typological fulfillment of the earlier baptisms and was thus a critical part of the essential fabric of the divine and human history.

Mystical, nuptial, eschatological, and covenantal—these terms in this order describe Hofmann's theology of baptism. At bottom, Hofmann held to the mystical, regenerative baptism in the Spirit in the tradition of Müntzer, Denck, and Hut, but modified by the addition of the marital imagery of the medieval mystics. As with Müntzer and Hut, this baptism was the means of gathering the elect of the latter days in preparation for Christ's return. Also like Hut, this inner baptism was manifested and, in a sense, entered through the covenant in water baptism.

Further, Hofmann said that the outer action, when it was supplemented and empowered by the inner experience of the Spirit, served as a sign to the baptizand to confirm his participation in redemptive history. Though perhaps less bold than Hut's avowedly eschatological seal on the forehead, Hofmann's baptism nonetheless spoke to the believer to assure him that he stood in the center of the final and great "exodus." As such, baptism had objective power for Hofmann, just as it had for Hut, and, in a non-eschatological fashion, also had for Hubmaier.

Whether Hofmann went on to theorize about the significance of the baptismal covenant for the ordering of a congregation is unclear. Since his concern was principally on eschatological matters and upon the gathering together of the elect for the Last Day, the question may have been foreign to his mind. However, one can observe the power which his views possessed to form a solid, if aberrant, group at Münster. Fortunately, in the hands of his more moderate-minded successors, his view of the covenant with Christ finally came to a more balanced fruition.

CHAPTER V

Pilgram Marpeck

Pilgram Marpeck, the last subject of this study, has long been recognized as one of the most attractive of the Anabaptist leaders, for he exemplified an admirable balance of character and mind, even though often in the company of less balanced men. Further, he articulated perhaps the most thoughtful interpretation of baptism among the Anabaptists.

From the beginning of his Anabaptist career, Marpeck steered a course that brought him into conflict with two groups of opponents: on the one hand the Lutheran and Reformed churchmen who defended the traditional infant baptism, and on the other the Spiritualists who repudiated both the traditional infant baptism and the new adult baptism. Against the first group Marpeck contended that infant baptism lacked spiritual content and hence was an empty form; against the Spiritualists he said that the denial of all form was against both the explicit commands of Scripture and the underlying doctrines of creation and salvation.

The development of Marpeck's interpretation of baptism proceeded along two lines. He believed that his opponents were both guilty of the fundamental error of separating inner Spirit baptism from outer water baptism. He thus attempted to reunite these two aspects of this sacrament, and at this point he made perhaps his most interesting contribution to Anabaptist baptismal theology.

The second line of approach concerned the idea of the covenant. It was already an important element in the Anabaptist view of baptism, but Marpeck now expanded it to make it a key for reading redemptive history as well as understanding the baptismal ordinance. Since the covenant theme was basic to his framework of thought, our discussion begins with this topic.

Baptism and the Old and the New Covenants

In the discussion of Hubmaier it was observed that the Waldshut reformer found it difficult to counter Zwingli's argument for the unity of circumcision and baptism. In fact, it was at this precise point that Hubmaier yielded to Zwingli in his Zurich recantation.[1] The Anabaptist answer to Zwingli's argument was to be found in the distinction between the old and the new covenants—in this, together with Paul's statement in Colossians 2:11, 12 to the effect that inner circumcision of the heart is the fulfillment of the circumcision of the flesh. Hubmaier was well aware of the text in Colossians and employed it against Zwingli in his *Ein Gespräch auf Zwinglis Taufbüchlein*,[2] but he did not develop a satisfactory theological argument to support his view.

Denck came much nearer to solving the problem, for he recognized the relatedness of the inner covenant of the Spirit and the outer covenant in baptism and said that these stood in fulfillment of the ceremonies of the old covenant.[3] But still there was no attempt to read redemptive history in terms of covenant theology.

One of Marpeck's contributions was to provide such a reading. His confession to the Strassburg authorities in late 1531 or early 1532 (his first public statement) expressed a clear conception of the two Biblical covenants, and from that time on this was one of the basic building stones of his thought.[4]

Marpeck explained that God has always used a covenant to provide a framework for His work among men.[5] This may have begun even before the Fall,[6] but the more important aspect of it began immediately afterward when God covenanted to bring salvation to man. This promise or covenant of God (and Marpeck says that the terms "promise" and "covenant" are interchangeable[7]) was renewed with Noah, Abraham, and Moses. This was the only spiritual help the Old Testament believers had and without it they would have been lost, unable to know true goodness.

But the old covenant lacked the power of salvation brought with the new. It was only a promise of that power and brought only "figures" or symbols of salvation, not the true "reality" *(Wesen)*. "The ancients had a figured righteousness."[8] Not possessing a true spiritual rebirth within, it was only natural that they should have conceived of their salvation in material ways, thinking of it as a physical promised land to be inherited by natural progeny. Similarly, their ordinances were external "signs" which lack inner spiritual power. Their function was to point to a salvation yet to be given, not to speak of one already present. And, Marpeck says, even though one might speak with some accuracy of an inner circumcision under the old covenant, it was not the saving circumcision of the Spirit but only a token of that larger reality to come.[9]

In addition to the promise and the accompanying signs, Marpeck said that God gave the ancient believers the help of the law. This was a "first grace," which, as in Luther's view, revealed man's sin and need but brought no power to remedy that sin. But by convicting one of his sin and revealing how one is in bondage to it, it did prepare the way for the salvation given in Christ.[10]

Saving grace came through Christ's incarnation, crucifixion, and resurrection. The promise was fulfilled, so that what had been future promise now became present fact and "figure" gave way to "reality."[11] Following Catholic tradition, Marpeck said that this took place first in Hades to which Christ descended to bring salvation to the pious of the Old Testament who had awaited His coming since their death.[12] He descended to them and preached to them, urging them to believe on Him and receive the salvation previously unavailable to them.[13] All who responded in faith were led forth to share in Christ's kingdom. Upon His resurrection from the dead, this power of salvation was made available to persons on earth through the gift of the Holy Spirit who brought the promised salvation of forgiveness and regeneration. Marpeck says that the Spirit could not have come to man until Christ was raised and had ascended, for Christ Himself had said, "If I do not go away, the Counselor will not come to you."[14] Thus, the second grace of regeneration was given in addition to the first grace of the law, and the second covenant had arrived, the covenant of salvation.

Unlike the older, shadowlike covenant of promise with its external nature, the new covenant, according to Marpeck, brings the "covenant of a good conscience," i.e., the covenant of a heart cleansed of sin and made pure by Christ. And instead of signs which spoke only of the future, there are new ordinances or "witnesses" which testify to the presence of salvation in the regenerate heart. We shall see that this terminology carried an important interpretation of the nature of the sacraments, but for now we need simply observe that the principal difference in the ordinances, in Marpeck's view, was that under the old covenant they marked external things—the corporate and racial people of God, and the promise of salvation—whereas under the new covenant they represent a salvation already present within the believer.[15]

Following the argument from Colossians 2:11, 12 used earlier by Hubmaier,[16] Marpeck's *Vermanung* (here independent of Rothmann) argued that the true succession was from outer circumcision to inner circumcision and not from infant (outer) circumcision to infant (outer) baptism.[17] Just as the law is now written within the heart in fulfillment of Jeremiah's prophecy, so is circumcision performed within the heart through the work of the Holy Spirit.

> Just as he is not a Jew who is one externally, so is circumcision no circumcision which takes place only externally. Circumcision now is of the heart; it takes place in the Spirit and not in the letter.[18]

Marpeck distinguished three stages in this process of regeneration.

A summary statement of the matter in the *Glaubensbekenntnis* names only two of these, but the third is implied:

> First, one must be born through the Word as he dedicates himself to it in full faith. Second, he is born through water. At that time power is present to become a child of God [which begetting will take place later as the third birth] both here and in the life to come. "He who endures to the end will be saved,"[19] if he accepts Christ and desires to become a child of God and do His will.[20]

Doubtless recalling his earlier Lutheran instruction, Marpeck, like Hubmaier, believed that regeneration began by experiencing guilt before the law. He called this the birth from the "corporeal" *(leiblich)* Word, corporeal as distinguished from the spiritual Word that makes one alive through the Holy Spirit. This, of course, was known to the believers of the old covenant, and it now continues under the new. One can come to Christ in no other way, Marpeck said, for it is the experience which prepares one to receive Christ. In a figure reminiscent of Hubmaier, Marpeck spoke of the law as "battering man, slashing and breaking him," thereby making him ready for the healing care of the Great Physician.[21] This was the first stage of regeneration.

Following the birth in the corporeal Word came the birth in water and the Spirit. Building on John 3:5, Marpeck said: "No one enters the kingdom of God unless he is born again of water and the Spirit, that is, of affliction and consolation according to the manner of water and the Spirit."[22]

Like Müntzer and Hut, Marpeck emphasized the suffering involved in redemption. Water served as its symbol. This birth, he said,

> brings the mystery of the cross as water, for wherever water is spoken of in Scripture, it means affliction, anguish, woe, and suffering, and the watery deep means bodily death. This is the sign of Jonah unto which the whole world is condemned and through whose gates of hell we all must go with our flesh and bodily life.[23]

One should not fear this anguish, Marpeck said, for the Christian can be sure of victory. Christ warned that the gate was small and the way narrow that leads to life; and, since Christ suffered and was crucified, His disciples should expect nothing less. Indeed, Christ came, Marpeck observed, multiplying his metaphor, not with water alone, but according to I John 5:6 with water and blood.[24] Like his Master, the Christian must know both baptisms: the dedicatory baptism in physical water, and the redemptive baptism in blood, or metaphorical "water."

Part of this baptismal suffering is the inner anguish of redemption as one is thrust into the "deep" with Christ.

It is a hidden, penetrating water, this baptism, and it reaches beyond all reason. This baptism is to die in the deep with Christ and to be buried in His death.[25]

Aided by the idea of the Gospel of all creatures, Marpeck said that this is the way of *Gelassenheit* in which man submits to the dominion of God over his life, much as the creature submits to man,[26] and in this humiliation one participates in the sufferings of Christ.

Although he spoke of this inner suffering often,[27] he placed more emphasis on the outer suffering brought on by the world. One of the notable additions to Rothmann's text in the *Vermanung* concerns this. Marpeck criticizes those who have taken the sword to defend the faith of Christ or to impose it upon others and says that the Christian must suffer with Christ, not inflict suffering on His behalf.

> Those truly and genuinely baptized in Christ are baptized through patience under affliction (as companions in the suffering of Christ[28]) to suffer up to their bodily death, which affliction every Christian covenants in his baptism with Christ to withstand with the Word of truth in faith through patience, hating and resisting all temptations and evil.[29]

The Christian must expect this, but he can take hope whenever persecution comes, for he can know that this is part of the world which Christ has overcome.[30] Marpeck says that this suffering begins in both its inner and outer aspects immediately after one is baptized, just as it happened with Christ.[31]

In addition to the symbolic "water" of suffering, there is also the physical water of baptism. This too is closely related to the baptisms of the Spirit and blood. Marpeck argued against Bucer:

> [Christ] did not separate or divide the two substances, the Spirit of God and earthly water. Otherwise He would have said that infants must be born of water, but instead He clearly said [that one must be born] of water and the Spirit.[32]

Here He means physical water, the water of baptism. As we shall see shortly, Marpeck's view of the unity of these two aspects of baptism is one of the most interesting of his ideas. For now we simply recognize that baptism in physical water is also part of Marpeck's second stage of regeneration.

These two steps in the process of the new birth—birth through the Word as law and Gospel, and birth through water and the Spirit—give the power to become a child of God. Actual regeneration takes place after one has worked through these. By keeping the commands of Christ and sharing His sufferings as necessary, one can attain this final goal. Marpeck's assurance of this is found in the words of Jesus: "whoever does the will of my Father in heaven is my brother and sister."[33]

It will be recalled that Hut and Hofmann had a similar conception of regeneration. Hut made a clear separation between *Gerechtigkeit* and *Gerechtfertigkeit,* and Hofmann, like Marpeck, distinguished between having the power to become a child of God and being a child of God.[34] Hubmaier, on the other hand, placed regeneration before baptism. Although Marpeck followed the pattern of Hut and Hofmann at this point, there was a sense in which he did not agree with any of the three, for he refrained from saying that the life of relative perfection was attainable by the Christian, as Hubmaier, Hut, and Hofmann had said. When Marpeck believed this regeneration would finally be accomplished is unclear. Perhaps his earlier Lutheranism survived here too, and if so, he would have postponed complete regeneration to the day of resurrection. This seems to be the implication of his writings. At the same time, however, he agreed with his Anabaptist colleagues that salvation did effect a change within man which gave him power to meet the demands of the Christian life.

The Baptismal Covenant

A further distinction between the old and new covenants, according to Marpeck, is the fact that only under the new covenant does one have power to make the covenant pledge himself. This was not true under the old covenant. Since all men were still bound by sin at that time, the old covenant was founded principally upon God, who of His own will brought men into it. Man at best could only accept the covenant; he could not himself make the full pledge.[35] But under the new covenant the situation is different. Now God creates the good conscience within the believer through the work of the Spirit.[36] He thus restores to man the power of choosing good over evil and thereby gives him the power to pledge himself to the life demanded by this covenant. For this reason, the new covenant belongs "only to the one who covenants himself to God and promises [himself to Him] in the power of the Holy Spirit in faith."[37] It does not belong to all the people, young and old, as did the old covenant.

Marpeck called this "the covenant of the good conscience," a phrase coined by Luther in his translation of I Peter 3:21.[38] The expression was first adopted by Hans Denck as a tool for describing believer's baptism,[39] and it became common among the Strassburg Anabaptists from whom Marpeck presumably learned it. As already noted, Jacob Gross used it at Strassburg in 1526, and Jacob Kautz and Wilhelm Reublin reported in 1529 that the Anabaptists of Strassburg practiced a covenantal baptism.[40]

In the same tradition Marpeck described baptism as a covenant or pledge by which one who already knows the forgiveness of God promises to lay aside the old life and take up the new in Christ.

And this is the covenant *(verpundt)* in baptism, that we, through the knowledge of the Lord and Savior Jesus Christ, put off and flee the filth of the world and bind *(verpinden)* ourselves with Christ unto a new life, so that, just as Christ was raised from the dead, we too, as newborn from the dead, may enter into a new way of life.[41]

In direct contrast to the old covenant, the emphasis of the new covenant is upon man's dedication to God. Man makes this covenant in baptism, Marpeck says, even though he makes it on God's terms and in God's power.

Against those Zwinglians and Lutherans who held that baptism was God's pledge, Marpeck said that God's pledge had already been given in the cross, "an undoubtable sign of grace."[42] The baptismal covenant, therefore, is the baptizand's pledge on the basis of that earlier promise of God in Christ. To consider it as being principally the pledge of God would be only to perpetuate the old covenant, Marpeck says, for this would overlook the fact that the validity of the ordinances under the new covenant depends on the faith of the recipient.

Even so, Marpeck did not adhere strictly to those qualifications on the divine covenant, for he spoke at least twice of baptism as a betrothal or marriage,[43] which would seem to indicate a double-sided covenant. Even more tellingly, his conception of baptism as a testimony to the baptizand (to be discussed shortly) would also speak against this. But whatever the inconsistencies of his view may have been at this point, his intention was clear, namely, to ground the outer covenant in water on the prior presence of the inner covenant of the Spirit.

Thus the new covenant is a covenant within the heart of the believer, a heart cleansed and renewed by the grace of Christ. Marpeck stressed how this brings comfort to the soul, for the Christian now participates in Christ's conquest of the powers of evil.[44] The Gospel comforts because it can perform within the soul what was once only promised.[45]

Once again, this is the Anabaptist doctrine of regeneration as inner transformation and renewal. A trace of Luther survives in Marpeck's recognition that the regenerative process is not completed in a moment but requires a whole lifetime, but he still thinks of it in great measure as a present transformation already accomplished through the Word and Spirit of God.

Like Hubmaier, Marpeck linked the idea of regeneration with the common Anabaptist emphasis on human free will. He said that to accept predestination would be to threaten the reality of the redemptive events, for the doctrine undermines the substantiality of the created order. It would deny God's creatures their own place in the order of things[46] and would reduce the realm of human action to little more than "monkey-business and mimicry" taking place only "in the presence of God"[47] like a play or stage performance. The belief in predestination would mean, he said, that the history of salvation with its times of promise and fulfillment would not be substantial and real, and the incarnation with its avowed purpose of effecting salvation within a theretofore lost generation of men would be reduced to a stage-play.

Although the argument is not wholly convincing, it does reveal Marpeck's concern for a point seen in each of the Anabaptists we have examined, namely, their belief that man possesses freedom and responsibility within the process of redemption. That being so, both the reception and manifestation of salvation require man's voluntary participation. Thus salvation is operative only in the adult. And when it operates there, it is a genuine thing effecting a true transformation. Here again, Marpeck stressed the continuing aspect of regeneration rather than the more nearly instantaneous aspect seen in Hubmaier, but the import was the same: conversion and regeneration were within the individual, not just in heaven, as Marpeck thought Luther's doctrine of forensic justification implied. Thus, in Marpeck's view, there was truly a "good conscience" within the believer, and it was on this basis that the covenant in baptism was to be made.

The Unity of Inner and Outer Baptism

Another of Marpeck's important accomplishments was his description of the unity between inner and outer baptism. We have seen how two earlier Anabaptists divided these two aspects of baptism. Hubmaier, following the negative argument, said that material elements were unable to cleanse the soul; Denck, emphasizing the positive side, said that baptism was essentially a spiritual action. Though differently expressed, the two positions were essentially the same, and in each case inner and outer baptism were separate. Hut and Hofmann continued in principle the same point of view.

But as Marpeck debated the Reformed preachers of Strassburg on the one hand and the Spiritualists on the other, the question was brought into sharper focus. He concluded that both the error of infant baptism and the just as erroneous rejection of any outer baptism were caused by the separation of the two facets of what he thought should ideally be one baptismal action. Marpeck set himself to the task of describing the unity he felt baptism to have. His attempt to do so was perhaps his most interesting contribution to Anabaptist baptismal theology. Most of his writings contain passages dealing with the problem, and, notably, all such texts in the *Vermanung* are additions to the earlier *Bekentnisse* by Rothmann.[48]

As already observed, Marpeck held that regeneration began prior to water baptism and that the latter was an outer sign of a new birth already begun within. This much was standard Anabaptist thought. But Marpeck went beyond this to say that the sign participated in the very reality of regeneration and that it could be called part of that "reality":

> As in all other matters, the reality *(wesen)* must precede its own witness, so that the sign can be rightly taken or given. When otherwise, the sign is false and a vain mockery. If the reality is there and is known, then the sign is truly and wholly useful, and everything signified by the sign is [then] to be given to the sign, *for it is no more a sign, but a reality* (italics mark Marpeck's addition to Rothmann).[49]

This being the case, he could and did say that, although forgiveness of sin *preceded* baptism in that the Holy Spirit was already at work creating the good conscience, forgiveness was also bestowed *in* water baptism.

> Whoever is minded [to die to sin and be raised with Christ] and makes the proper confessions should be baptized. In this way, he will be correctly baptized and will obtain the forgiveness of sins in baptism.[50]

Attempting to clear himself of the possible charge of sacramentalism, Marpeck (here he followed Rothmann) went ahead to say that the power at work in this baptism was not the power of water or the Triune formula, but the power of the baptizand's confession of faith through the Holy Spirit. Whoever receives water baptism without having faith and repentance in his heart receives only the sign, i.e., washing of the body, but whoever receives baptism with such faith in his heart receives salvation.[51]

> Therefore, as Peter says, "baptism saves, not the laying off of the filth of the flesh, but the covenant of a good conscience with God through the resurrection of the Lord Jesus Christ, who is at the right hand of God."[52]

There are at least three ways—and all three are independent of Rothmann—in which Marpeck described the unity of this action. The first is in terms of the witness of the Spirit, who adds the "co-witness" of the outer ordinances to the inner testimony within the heart. The second, closely related to the first, involves the action of the Trinity, each member of which, in Marpeck's view, shares in the baptismal action and thereby contributes to baptism's unity. Finally, he interpreted baptism in terms of the inner and outer aspects of man, saying that the baptismal action includes the whole man. We shall discuss the three in turn.

Marpeck accepted the principle that the believer can know of his own regeneration by the inner testimony of the Spirit. He named four ways one could know that the inner witness was of the Spirit and not of one's self: love for God and neighbor, yieldedness to God even to death, willingness to teach the Gospel when God opens doors for it to be taught, and commitment to nothing but the sound Gospel of Christ.[53] But the inner witness of the Spirit was matched by an outer witness, or as Marpeck termed it, a "co-witness" *(Mitzeugnis)*.[54] It was this term that supplied Marpeck with his primary tool for reuniting inner and outer baptism.

Marpeck used the term to defend his view against threats from both the Spiritualists and the pedobaptists. Against the Spiritualists he wanted to do more than just cite the literalistic argument from the dominical commands, and so he looked for a rationale for the external ordinances. His conclusion was that the outer action is an external witness—he usually said *Mitzeugnis*—complementary to the inner witness of the Spirit. For instance, in a passage in which he describes the external ordinances as analogous to the external actions of the incarnate Christ, Marpeck says:

> Whoever, like a thief, steals from Holy Scripture all external teaching, speaking, action, baptism, and Lord's Supper, and then out of hearsay asserts that the external actions are performed without true faith—whoever says this has no truth in him, for the external action is a correct and true co-witness *(mitzeügnus)* of the Father and the Holy Spirit.[55]

The fact that the external action is considered as related to the work of the Trinity will be discussed more fully in a moment; for now, we simply note that the outer ordinance is described as serving as a co-witness to the inner testimony of the Spirit, and as such, is by implication as necessary and valid as the inner action itself.

On the other hand, Marpeck argued against the pedobaptists that the inner reality must precede the outer ordinance, and even there the element of baptism's being a co-witness of the inner action is stressed. Citing Tertullian's statement (like Rothmann before him) that baptism is a seal of faith, Marpeck asserted that faith and inner washing of sin must precede water baptism. He says:

> Since we all are already washed of sin, baptism (which means the outer action of immersion or pouring) is a co-witness *(mitzeüge)* of the inner reality *(wesen)* which is the covenant of a good conscience with God.[56]

Further, Marpeck associated this outer action with the operation of the Holy Spirit. This is well seen in the parallel question of the church's use of the keys. Marpeck said that the outer action of the church in discipline, when properly performed, is filled with the power of the Spirit who works both inwardly within the individual concerned and outwardly through the action of the church. His letter to the Anabaptists at Austerlitz (dated *ca.* 1545) discusses this at length. The Christian who sins is subject to the punishment of the Holy Spirit, he says, and if the sin is confessed and repented of privately before God very soon after its commission, the punishment will be performed secretly by the Holy Spirit within the offender. But if the lapsed refuses to repent unto God, the Holy Spirit will reveal his sin to the church, which then must carry out an external punishment "through the co-witness of the Holy Spirit." Once the outer discipline has been administered publicly by the body of Christ, the offender has another opportunity to repent. If he refuses, he may finally be visited by the Holy Spirit with the judgment of unbelief. But if he does amend his ways, atoning his sin through prayer by the death of Christ, aided by the prayers of the pure, he will receive forgiveness and the comfort of the Holy Spirit within his heart. The penitent will recognize this gift within, as will the church, which will then be able to forgive him in Christ through the Holy Spirit. All of this "is only one forgiveness," Marpeck says. As with baptism, the redemptive work is wholly of the Spirit, but the Spirit acts in conjunction with the church so that there is only one action. The outer works of the church are accomplished "through the collaboration *(mitwurckhung)* of the Holy Spirit."[57] Marpeck's principle is that, wherever the inner and outer realities are united, "the signs are no longer signs" empty and bare, but are the true "reality in Christ," for the Spirit of God acts in them.[58]

This is a rather high conception of the outer ordinances and it suggests that their power is considerable. Marpeck believed this to be true.

> In summary we can say that baptism is immersion in or affusion with water, which the baptizand desires, receives, and accepts as a sign or co-witness that he has died to sin, been buried with Christ, and is thereby raised to a new life.... Whoever is thus-minded and gives the proper confession should be baptized. In this way, he will be correctly baptized and will obtain the forgiveness of sins in baptism and thus be introduced into the fellowship of Christ and put on Christ.[59]

Marpeck added, however, that this would be accomplished through the power of the baptizand's faith; nonetheless, the outer action is very important for the believer, for it complements and fulfills the inner operation of the Spirit.

Marpeck's second way of describing the wholeness of baptism was grounded on the nature and operation of the Trinity and on the related pattern of the incarnation. Continuing his distinction between the inner and outer aspects of redemption, Marpeck gathered the facets of baptism together under the three rubrics of the Father, the Son, and the Holy Spirit. The *Vermanung,* in a statement not found in Rothmann's *Bekentnisse,* summarizes the matter thus:

> Regarding baptism and the Lord's Supper, those who are children of God, [who are born] through the birth of the Spirit and reality in Christ, who are members of the body of Christ—these do in every-

thing according to the external man what the Father does in them through the Spirit according to the inner man. The Father loves the Son and has given all over into His hand, so that, just as the Father as Spirit works internally, the Son of Man may work externally. Thus in Christ there is no more sign, only reality *(wesen):* one baptism, one faith, one God the Father of us all. For this reason one is baptized in the name of the Father, of the Son, and of the Holy Spirit, for the Son of Man is not without the Father and the Spirit, nor the Spirit and the Father without the Son of Man. Therefore, the external reality of the Son is one reality and work in the Father and the Spirit. And if a spirit appears who denies the external [side] of man, such as Christ's doctrine, baptism, or the Lord's Supper (which He taught, wrought, and accomplished), that spirit is a denier of the Son of Man and is not the Spirit of the Father.[60]

Behind this statement lies Marpeck's reading of the Gospel of John, where he found the Father performing the inner drawing of the soul to salvation while the incarnate Son performed the outer calling through preaching and baptism.[61] In part, this was the work of the obedient Jesus who performed outwardly the works which He saw the Father doing within, thereby revealing the Father.[62] But Marpeck says that this is also the *Ordnung Gottes* which requires that the external be used as much as the internal, or, to put it into christological terms relevant to Marpeck's controversy with Schwenckfeld, requires that the Word join flesh to spirit. Thus, when Christ was on earth He possessed a human body. Upon His resurrection His body was glorified. In His glorified body Christ ascended to the Father leaving on earth the church, His yet unglorified social body (as we may term it). It is through this still unglorified body that Christ works today, Marpeck says, and through it He still performs the "external" works of redemption.[63]

This present external work of Christ is performed through preaching and the administration of the ordinances by which Christ's ministers announce the Gospel just as He did when on earth, though now aided by the Spirit who makes the Word alive within the believer. In reliance on Ephesians 5:26, Marpeck calls this encounter with the Gospel a "waterbath in the Word," and thus a baptism. However, this is not a separate baptism, for it is part of the integral baptismal action that consists of both external and internal aspects. In a lengthy but important passage in the *Verantwurtung,* Marpeck describes his view in some detail. Denying that Christian baptism is only a washing in water like the ancient Jewish ablutions, he says:

> The apostolic baptism commanded by Christ has another way [of operation from that of Jewish baptism]. In Christian baptism the Holy Spirit and the blood of Christ wash and purify the heart and the conscience through the co-witness *(mitzeugen)* of the external Word through the Word's being received in faith. Thus, Christian

baptism is a "waterbath" in or through the Word, as Ephesians 5[:26][64] and our testimony [in the *Vermanung*][65] have said. Through this waterbath the whole man is cleansed in spirit, body, and soul and is manifested unto obedience toward Christ, i.e., the obedience of faith in Him. The believer receives this faith at that time through the prior and concomitantly-preached Word (John 14:15-26[?]; Romans 10:14-17). This waterbath in the Word of Christ, the only Savior, operates unto one single waterbath or baptism of Christ both [outside the baptizand] through Christ's minister *(diener)* or external ministry *(dienst)* and within the baptizand through Christ's Holy Spirit. Thus, we in no way injure the honor of Christ, but testify that it all takes place and is done by and in Christ to the cleansing and saving of the whole man.[66]

Interestingly, the role of the Father is not mentioned here. Two facts suggest that this may be due to a strain of Sabellianism in Marpeck's thought: (1) at least once he identified the Father and the Spirit by speaking of "the Father as internal Spirit,"[67] and (2) he often attributed to the Spirit the revelatory work done by the Father before the Spirit was given at Pentecost.[68]

Nonetheless, the principle of Marpeck's view remained the same: the conjunction of the inner and outer actions of God (as Father and Son) seen in the ministry of Christ is continued in the life of the church, as the inner operation of the Spirit is complemented by the outer action of the church, the successor on earth to the Son.[69] Thus, the term "co-witness" suggests that the unity of inner and outer baptism rested ultimately in the nature of God whose spiritual workings within man were always complemented by the outward actions of Christ, or His earthly successor, the church.

Finally, Marpeck's view sought to understand baptism as an action which included both the inner and outer aspects of man. This idea was mentioned before, when, in examining Hubmaier's relation to Zwingli, we saw that the Zurich reformer once spoke of inner baptism and outer baptism as complementing inner and outer man.[70] Hubmaier did not adopt the view, nor did Hut or Hofmann, but it appears again in Marpeck. Whether Marpeck took it from Zwingli we cannot know, but it would seem that a direct borrowing would have been unlikely since Zwingli voiced the view in private correspondence and not in his public writings. Whatever the source, the idea became important in Marpeck's controversy with Schwenckfeld.[71]

Schwenckfeld himself maintained that spirit and flesh were two different levels of reality and were recognized as such by God in His dealings with man. He said, therefore, that God had provided two kinds of baptism, the one a spiritual baptism which God Himself gives to the inner spiritual man, the other a water baptism bestowed by man. He held that only the former affects the real man—spiritual man. The latter, since it is only a creaturely action, cannot affect man's soul and is, thus, not only of less importance than Spirit baptism, but is virtually a completely separate baptism.[72] However, it is separate only in respect to man, for to God there is only one baptism, the baptism of rebirth of the believing heart.[73]

Marpeck could not accept this differentiation and argued that, although soul and body can be distinguished, they cannot be treated separately, for they form the unity of the whole man. He claimed that they are not contrary realities but are the inner and outer sides of one reality—man himself. In agreement with this unity of man's nature, the ordinance of baptism has both an inner and outer side, Spirit baptism and water baptism; these cannot be separated into two different actions.[74] Water baptism, therefore, cannot be dismissed or regarded lightly, for it serves outer man; nor can Spirit baptism be ignored, for man's inner nature is spiritual. Marpeck argued that this view does not bind the Holy Spirit to material elements or say that matter can effect a spiritual work, for the spiritual nature of baptism begins before water baptism is received, and it is only on the basis of the presence of Spirit baptism that water baptism may be received. But when it is then received, the two aspects of inner and outer baptism merge into a unity which embraces the whole man.[75]

Such is the nature of the unity that Marpeck saw in baptism as the covenant and knowledge of the good conscience before God, a unity which he believed both the Reformed theologians and the Spiritualists denied Against the former he argued that infant baptism separated inner and outer baptism by placing outer baptism before the inner baptism it was to signify. It was wrong, Marpeck said, to reduce the baptism of the living Spirit to second place after baptism in the dead element of water; Spirit baptism should begin first.[76] And against Schwenckfeld, Marpeck argued that the Spiritualists had created two baptisms, since they would admit no close connection of the two parts of baptism.[77]

Thus, against both extremes, Marpeck insisted that there was only one baptism composed of inner and outer aspects. Spirit baptism, with its powers of regeneration, began first and had to be present within the believer before water baptism could be validly given; but it was incomplete without the latter. Further, God was active in water baptism as well, even if only in an "external" way, so that the ordinance was a sign or witness to the baptizand that God was present within him and that he had died to sin and been raised to a new life. In this way there was an outer "co-witness" or "co-testimony" to complement the internal witness of the Spirit.

In this limited sense, then, one may say that Marpeck understood baptism to carry grace to the baptizand, not grace as a redemptive substance channeled through a sacrament, but grace as a divine word to the baptizand, assuring him of forgiveness and regeneration through his faith. It was with confidence, therefore, that Marpeck quoted Paul in saying that there is "one Lord, one faith, one baptism, one God and Father of us all, who is above all and through all and in all."[78]

A Threefold Baptism: Spirit, Water, and Blood

In addition to the three personal witnesses—Father, Son, and Holy Spirit—Marpeck spoke of three types of baptismal "witness"—water, Spirit, and blood. The text in I John, as preserved in the *Textus Receptus,* provided support for the view:

> There are three that bear record in heaven, the Father, the Word, and the Holy Ghost: and these three are one. And there are three that bear witness in earth, the Spirit, and the water, and the blood: and these three agree in one.[79]

Instead of stressing the successive baptisms seen in Hubmaier and Hut, Marpeck ordinarily concentrated on the unity of the three baptisms. Further, he usually understood the baptism of blood to refer to the inner washing of the heart by the blood of Christ, thereby reading I John 5 in terms of Hebrews 10:22: "our hearts sprinkled clean from an evil conscience ['by the blood of Christ' (Heb. 9:13, 14)] and our bodies washed with pure water." Thus the three baptisms were dissolved into two baptisms—inner and outer baptism—which are essentially one.

He spoke of the unity of the three baptisms in the following passage, which through its emphasis on the "witnesses" evokes the idea of "cowitness" even without the express term:

> Therewith is the whole baptism named [simply] "baptism" in the New Testament. . . . It consists of these three witnesses *(zeugnus)*: the Spirit, the water, and the blood. The text in I John [5:6-8] has conceived of these three as witnessing *(zeugen)* on earth in one thing, i.e., serving unto one single baptism. Whoever suspends one of these witnesses, or separates it from the others, divides and destroys the single baptism. . . . Christ comes with water and blood, not with water alone, meaning that whoever does not believe in the blood of Christ, which was poured out unto the forgiveness of sins, does not deserve the water unto the forgiveness of sins.[80]

By the same token, whoever receives all three baptisms receives the full cleansing of his heart, for that is the power of true apostolic baptism.

> The Holy Spirit and the blood of Christ wash and purify the heart and conscience through the co-witness of the external Word as it is believed, and thus baptism is a waterbath in or through the Word [Ephesians 5:26]. . . . Through this waterbath the whole man is cleansed in spirit, body, and soul.[81]

Although Marpeck's principal interpretation of the threefold baptism emphasized the unity of the three in the inner action of regeneration, he also recognized what was in principle very near the three baptisms of Hubmaier and Hut. That his view included a progression from Spirit baptism to water baptism is clear enough; but he also conceived of a baptismal suffering which one may, in Marpeck's stead, call a baptism of blood. We have already observed his discussion in the *Glaubensbekenntnis* of the affliction and suffering the Christian must undergo in following after the way of Christ. To inherit the kingdom, he says, one must be a "comrade in the afflictions of Christ" (an expression often used by Marpeck and his followers), which sufferings begin at the moment of baptism.[82] The *Vermanung* continued the same theme and spoke expressly of the baptismal covenant unto suffering:

> Those truly and genuinely baptized in Christ are baptized under tribulation in great forbearance as comrades of the afflictions of Christ, suffering even unto their death in the body. Every Christian covenants with Christ in his baptism to withstand patiently, holding the word of truth in faith, hating and resisting every temptation and evil.[83]

This suffering would partly be the result of imitating the way of Christ, a way that all His disciples must follow.[84] But it would also include the present sufferings of Christ in His unglorified body, the church.[85] This latter point Marpeck stressed against Schwenckfeld, who, because of his conception of the celestial flesh of Christ, was unwilling to accept Marpeck's emphasis on Christ's suffering in the flesh.

> [Schwenckfeld] teaches only the inner, glorified, ruling, and unsuffering Christ on earth, yea only the word of His glory and dominion. He will not speak of His cross and afflictions, neither earlier ones He bore as head [of the body] before His glorification and ascension, nor of the present ones which [the members of] His unglorified body fittingly bear.[86]

Like Hut, Marpeck found the image of the body of Christ full of meaning for the Christian life and he insisted that unless the Christian yielded to the sufferings of the cross in full *Gelassenheit* as Christ had, he could never reign with Christ.[87] One learns of Christ, he said, only through following in discipleship.[88]

The echoes of Denck and Hut are clear: one knows Christ in discipleship, which in turn involves suffering. To this extent Marpeck may be said to have envisioned a baptism of blood. The suffering would be partly internal and partly external, as one underwent both temptation and persecution, and each would have to be accepted as part of the Christian way. In recognition of this aspect of their faith, Marpeck and his fellow believers affixed as their signature to the *Vermanung* the simple statement, "the Christ-believing comrades of the covenant and afflictions in Christ."[89]

Arguments Against Infant Baptism

Although Hubmaier devoted considerable attention to the question of infant baptism, dedicating one tract to that issue alone, his treatment of the problem was neither as detailed nor as well developed theologically as Marpeck's, who of course had the assistance of an older, more thoroughly conceived Anabaptist theology. Marpeck's principal defense against infant baptism is found in the *Vermanung*. Part of the material is from Rothmann's *Bekentnisse*, but Marpeck also introduced new material. The earlier *Glaubensbekenntnis* discussed the matter, since that was an important point of debate between Marpeck and Bucer, but the *Verantwurtung* left it largely unmentioned, for precisely the opposite reason. The discussion will follow the order of the *Vermanung* which presents and refutes six arguments for infant baptism.

Following Rothmann, Marpeck first dealt with the argument from Old Testament circumcision. Both cited the view that since the time of Adam and Eve there has been only "one covenant of the promise of God." Arguing against this, they contended that the old covenant was only an external covenant, whereas the new covenant is internal. Further, the former was only a promise and appearance, whereas the latter is a reality. But following the first three paragraphs,[90] Marpeck broke away from Rothmann to argue in considerable detail that it was only with the new covenant that the Holy Spirit was given in regenerative power.[91] By the same token, he contended that new covenant baptism involved the whole Trinity in a way never true for old covenant circumcision.[92] Marpeck then asserted on the basis of Colossians 2:11, 12 that circumcision of the heart by the power of the Spirit is the true fulfillment of external circumcision.[93] At the same time Marpeck conceded that there are two similarities between old covenant circumcision and new covenant baptism: first, no dead children were circumcised just as no spiritually dead children are baptized now, and second, circumcision promised a reality which is now present in new covenant baptism.[94]

A second argument for infant baptism held that Jesus' blessing of the infants was precedent for the baptismal blessing. Bucer's first public statement in defense of infant baptism subsequent to the radicals' challenge of the practice had used the argument.[95] In saying this, Bucer was countering the views of Clement Ziegler and others who said that the words "of such" could not be understood to refer literally to children.[96]

The counterargument in the *Vermanung* is little more than a republication of Rothmann's material from the *Bekentnisse*, in which it is said that there is a marked difference between bringing children to Christ for His blessing and bringing them into the church for baptism. All parents should do the former and should pray daily that Christ will keep their children from harm. But baptism may be given only after repentance and confession of faith of which infants are incapable.[97]

Marpeck's third argument against infant baptism centered around the doctrine of original sin, a point which Rothmann had mentioned but had not developed into a full argument in his *Bekentnisse*.[98] Like many Anabaptists, Marpeck faced the dilemma of wanting to preserve a doctrine of the Fall of man in Adam; yet, he was committed to a rejection of infant baptism which had functioned to remove the guilt of original sin in the infant.

In an attempt to solve the problem, Marpeck articulated at least two distinct views. The first is found in both the *Glaubensbekenntnis* and the *Vermanung*. Basing his discussion on the principle that "where man has no knowledge [of good and evil] there is no sin,"[99] Marpeck argued that infants are without guilt, for they lack the knowledge of good and evil requisite for the reckoning of guilt. When the children come of age, that knowledge comes to life in them, knowledge inherited from Adam and Eve; but until then they remain "in creaturely innocence."[100]

Schwenckfeld, however, felt that Marpeck's position was open to the charge of Pelagianism and said so in his *Juditium* of 1541.[101] To counter the charge, Marpeck said that the creaturely innocence of the infants is not inherent in their nature but is a gift of God, first through the promise given to Eve following the Fall, and second (and foremost) through the sufferings of Christ. Marpeck told Schwenckfeld that until the infant comes into the power of "fleshly reason," as Marpeck terms it, "he is excused through creaturely innocence *and* the Word and blood of Christ [italics ours]."[102] But once the creaturely innocence is lost and the fleshly reason takes over, the "defect" of sin comes to life and the person becomes subject to its penalties.[103]

In spite of his arguments as to the innocence of infants, whether inherent or forensic, Marpeck was still of the opinion that not all who die before attaining the age of reason will be saved, for some, even most, are Esauites, not Jacobites. And thus, like Hans Denck, his final argument against infant baptism was that one cannot distinguish the one from the other, and to attempt to do so by baptizing some is to presume upon the very judgment of God.[104] Like Hubmaier, he said that one could only commend the infants to "the hidden judgment of God" who knows best and will treat them with mercy.[105]

The fourth argument for infant baptism dealt with by Marpeck—this also independently of Rothmann—was Luther's view of the *fides infantium*.[106] Marpeck argued that infants are not yet characterized by "unfaith," but neither have they come to the true faith attainable only through the believed Word. Without the latter and the prior hearing of the external Word, there is no need, and more important, no command for the external baptism. Both he and Rothmann (in a brief mention of the matter) admitted that God could create faith in an infant were He so pleased, but they believed that Scripture would not support the view that He actually does so.[107]

It was in this context that Marpeck presented one of his few statements about the Gospel of all creatures.[108] He argued that infants belong to the order of the creatures, i.e., to the order of those lacking the power of reason and hence subject to the dominion and guidance of man. But he expanded the point to include an observation about man's relation to God. "The rational man is a creature of all creatures," he says, i.e., the head of the creatures, "for all creatures are for the sake of man, [just as] man is for the sake of Christ, and Christ is for the sake of God."[109] Although Marpeck's letter to the Swiss Brethren mentions the fact that one must lead the ignorant to Christ with parables, as Christ Himself did, neither it nor the *Vermanung* say anything about the principle of redemptive suffering which Hut considered to be the dominant element of the Gospel in nature. Marpeck simply concluded that the command to be baptized concerns no unwitting infants, for they have "no dominion over the creatures."[110]

The text of Marpeck's fifth argument is taken from Rothmann with a few changes and additions by Marpeck.[111] The four principal points are from Rothmann and consist of two non-Biblical sources and two Biblical texts dealing with the question of the early practice of infant baptism. The first of the non-Biblical texts is a general reference to the *Corpus juris canonici,* perhaps made on the basis of Hubmaier's more detailed statements in his *Der uralten und gar neuen Lehrer Urteil.*[112] Marpeck and Rothmann simply note that baptism in the early church was preceded by a public confession of faith and renunciation of the devil by the baptizand in the presence of the bishop, inferring that this means that only adult baptism was practiced in the early church.

The other non-Biblical reference is to a note by Beatus Rhenanus appended to his edition of Tertullian's *De corona militis.* Marpeck cites Rhenanus' statement that until the times of Charlemagne and Louis the Pious baptism was given to adults only.[113]

The Biblical texts are the accounts of house baptisms in Acts and the reference to baptism for the dead in I Corinthians 15:29. The former were held by Rothmann and Marpeck to be valid baptisms, but baptisms which included no children; the latter they believed were abuses of true baptism, comparable to masses for the dead in their own time.[114]

Marpeck added two references to those of Rothmann's text, both of which related to the papacy. First he cited Luther to the effect that it is

Christ, not the pope, who confirms truth.[115] With that as a basis for argument, he then said that infant baptism was first confirmed as an official practice of the church by Pope Eugenius, thereby concluding that its practice is invalid.[116]

The last argument for infant baptism presented for refutation by Marpeck and Rothmann was the general one to the effect that, even though the New Testament, as it happens, expressly records only adult baptisms, infant baptisms are nonetheless valid and serve the child until he is old enough to claim the faith for himself. Further, the argument contended, even though the texts about belief and confession before baptism are descriptive of adult baptism, they ought not to be used to proscribe the baptism of infants. Rothmann and Marpeck answered that the Scriptures know only one baptism, the baptism of those who have died to sin and have been raised to a new life, and infants are incapable of that.[117]

The Dedication of Infants

Even though Marpeck rejected infant baptism, like Hubmaier he envisioned a dedication of the infant by the church, a service in which the church would join the parents in praying God's blessings upon the child, blessings which Christ Himself gave to children during His earthly ministry. The *Glaubensbekenntnis* says that the child would be given his name at this time and that the action should take place "before the church."[118] The *Vermanung* is less explicit, but it does insist that Christians should pray for their children, and that the example of Christ's blessing the children enjoins this.[119] At the same time, Marpeck argued that this provided no support for infant baptism.

Baptism and Marpeck's Use of Scriptural Texts

Several of the Biblical texts important in Marpeck's view of baptism have already been isolated and discussed: I Peter 3:21;[120] Colossians 2:11, 12,[121] and the accounts of Christ's blessing the children.[122] But several others deserve particular attention, as does Marpeck's general approach to Scripture.

Our discussion began by considering Marpeck's conception of the old and new covenants. The distinction is basic to his view of Scripture and redemptive history and, therefore, to his view of baptism as well. Not only did he distinguish between circumcision and baptism, claiming on the authority of Colossians 2:11, 12 that inner circumcision of the heart and not outer baptism of the flesh fulfilled old covenant circumcision, but, like Hubmaier and most Anabaptists, Marpeck distinguished between the baptism of John and the new covenant baptism of Jesus. He said that John's baptism was a preparatory baptism, a baptism unto repentance, which did no more than anticipate the kingdom to come. Jesus' baptism, on the other hand, was preceded by the reality of the Gospel of Christ, and whoever receives it properly receives eternal life.

> In sum, John baptized the people unto repentance, that is, that they should confess their sin and reform. The apostles, however, baptized those who believed in God's name, or in Christ, that is, those who yielded themselves unto God and were united with Him in Christ.[123]

The former was repentance; the latter is regeneration.

By the same token, Marpeck held that Christian baptism was instituted only with the command of the resurrected Christ, and not before.[124] The text of the great commission with which Jesus instituted baptism served Marpeck as a guide for the order of the baptismal action, just as it did for the other men of our study.[125]

Other passages received attention in Marpeck's writings, particularly Romans 6:3, 4 and the theme of death to sin and resurrection to new life.[126] Curiously, however, except for saying that the Christian's baptism is like Jesus' own baptism in that suffering begins immediately after it,[127] Marpeck made no use of the accounts of Jesus' baptism at the Jordan. The moving theme of the baptismal *imitatio Christi* in Hut and Hofmann, with its vivid imagery of the baptismal covenant and the subsequent struggle in the wilderness, is absent from Marpeck. The identification of the believer with the sufferings of Christ in the deep of the *descensus* fills something of the same role, but the pattern is found only in the metaphorical baptism of the cross and Hades, not in the literal baptism in the Jordan.[128]

The Administration of Baptism

Marpeck left no formal description of baptism like Hubmaier's baptismal order, nor do his writings yield any description of how the ordinance should be administered. The *Vermanung*, which contains more references to the mode of baptism than the other writings, speaks of both immersion and pouring. Notably, the references to pouring are largely additions to Rothmann's text which spoke principally of immersion.[129] Although Marpeck's retention of "immerse" in the *Vermanung* indicates that this was an acceptable mode to him, the fact that the *Verantwurtung* uses only "pour" *(übergiessen)* plus the fact that Marpeck added "pour" to the *Vermanung* text indicates that he must have preferred the latter.[130]

As to the administrator, Marpeck said very little except that those "who administer and receive the sign" of baptism must possess the good conscience from God.[131] How this was to relate to the order of the church Marpeck did not say.

Apart from this single exception Pilgram Marpeck presents the most developed of the Anabaptist baptismal theologies in our study. Concerned from the very first to give a better solution to the problem of baptism's place within the economy of redemption and to the question of the relation of inner and outer baptism, Marpeck carried the Anabaptist covenant idea to its fulfillment in his interpretation of the old and new covenants, and he found a way of reuniting inner and outer baptism.

So far as baptism itself is concerned, the latter was probably the more important of the two contributions, for it provided a way that could prevent water baptism from becoming only an empty formality, or from being discarded altogether, as Schwenckfeld and others had already done. In Marpeck's conception of the *Mitzeugnis*, he articulated a view of baptism which gave theological objectivity to the ordinance of baptism, and did so without finding it in the extreme apocalypticism of Hut and Hofmann and without erring to the side of sacramentalism which the Anabaptists had firmly renounced.[132]

Hence, Marpeck may be said to have found a middle way between the extremes of sacramentalism and spiritualism, a way whereby the order of salvation-history was preserved; the active participation of God, the church, and the baptizand was recognized in the baptismal action; and infant baptism was rendered unnecessary and unfounded. This was, without question, the most perceptive and profound of the theologies of baptism in our study.

CHAPTER VI

Conclusion

As the study has progressed, several themes have repeatedly emerged. The most important of these may be drawn together under three headings: the significance of the doctrine of regeneration; the Anabaptist use of the covenant in baptism; and the recognition of an objective power in baptism. In addition, we have seen how the baptismal motif was often used by these writers as a symbol for the whole of the Christian life in a manner more metaphorical than theological, although theological implications were present. We turn now to the final task of pulling the strands of these themes together for the purpose of consolidating their meaning and drawing the conclusions from them.

The Doctrine of Regeneration: A Key to Anabaptism

Each of the four subjects of this study grounded his interpretation of baptism in the doctrine of regeneration. They differed somewhat in their view of the time and manner of this inner transformation of the soul: Hubmaier placed it before baptism; Hut and Hofmann, although understanding it to begin before water baptism, thought that full regeneration would be accomplished only after continued submission to the inner baptism of suffering; and Marpeck, while placing the creation of the good conscience before baptism, believed that full regeneration would be accomplished only in the next life. However, they were at one in saying that the only legitimate basis for receiving baptism and entering the baptismal covenant was the experience of regeneration within, a regeneration which gave the believer power to make a valid confession of faith and to keep the commands of Christ under the watchful eye of a disciplining church.

This is a crucial point for understanding the Anabaptists, and one which is becoming increasingly recognized.[1] On the one hand this distinguished them from the developing Protestantism of Luther, Zwingli, and the other classical reformers, for the latter form of Christianity included, either implicitly or explicitly, the principle Luther pinpointed in his dictum *simul justus ac peccator*. Such a principle was unacceptable to the Anabaptists, for they thought that it opened the door to a compromise of the dominical mandates. It allowed Christians to bear the sword when they believed the Lord had explicitly proscribed this, and it seemed to them that it generally encouraged the citizens of the heavenly kingdom to encumber themselves too heavily with the burdens of this world. Therefore, the Anabaptists charged that Luther, Zwingli, and the rest were in the position of prohibiting a full commitment to the Gospel.

On the other hand, the Anabaptist insistence upon a virtually literal obedience to Christ's commands prompted Luther and his fellow reformers to protest that the Anabaptists had produced a new "works-righteousness," and they branded it a new Catholicism. In part they were right, for they saw that the Anabaptists, like the Catholics, believed that the regenerate heart could produce good deeds virtually unmixed with evil; at least the Christian could be largely *justus* and very little *peccator*. The fact that the Anabaptists often used the language of Luther and Zwingli—"the authority of the Scriptures," "by faith alone," "justification by faith," etc.—but with another meaning only caused the reformers to react all the more violently, for they felt that the new Anabaptist point of view was twice as dangerous as Catholicism. It not only contained the same errors of works-righteousness but did so under the guise of the new Reformation faith.

But Anabaptism was not a new Catholicism. It rejected the Catholic way: the Scriptures were to judge tradition, sacramentalism was repudiated, and the split between clergy and laity was, perhaps as nowhere else, almost completely overcome. At these points, and others as well, the Anabaptists did speak the Protestant language, even if with an Anabaptist accent.

Neither "Catholic" nor "Protestant," in a sense their nearest neighbors were the Spiritualists, for they often stressed the leadership of the Spirit and sometimes veered toward a rejection of the sacraments: Hans Denck is a good case in point. For this reason much scholarly opinion has tended to class them in this camp. But their commitment to Scriptural authority was consistent, and they kept and used the sacraments with great respect and perhaps even with new power. The latter has not been as well recognized as the former, perhaps because the informality of their kitchen baptisms and communions would seem to belie this. In regard to baptism, the stress has tended to be on its function as a confession of faith upon entrance into the brotherhood. That baptism was this is obvious, but it is also clear that in addition to this "subjective," almost spiritualist, quality, the sacrament spoke to the baptizand as an objective sign assuring him that his fellow believers recognized in him the gifts of the

Spirit. Thus the outer testimonies of prophet and people were added to the inner testimony of the Spirit within the baptizand's heart. Here lay the special power of Anabaptist adult baptism. Marpeck is the principal example here, for his interpretation of the sacrament was precisely this. But the same thing was true with Hubmaier, Hut, and Hofmann, each in his own way. For each of them baptism was the sign given by God's representative, whether the baptized congregation or an elect prophet, signifying to the baptizand that God's representative recognized in him the true gifts of the Spirit. Thus, Anabaptism, at least as found in these writers, was not Spiritualism.

Our study of Anabaptist baptism therefore supports the view that the movement was a third way alongside Catholicism and Protestantism, or fourth, if Spiritualism is added.[2] With the Protestants, the Anabaptists rejected the sacramentalism of the Catholic tradition; with the Catholics, they denied the solafideism of the magisterial reformers; and, with both, they criticized the implicit Gnosticism of the Spiritualists. For their own part they attempted to form a church which kept the doctrine of creation they believed the Spiritualists to deny, and a church faithful to the doctrine of redemption they felt both Catholic and Protestant to misinterpret.

The fact that the theological relationships of Anabaptism to the other strands of Christendom are dialectical suggests that the historical origins of the movement may also be complex. This is true more in respect to South German and Austrian Anabaptism where most of our discussion of this problem lay, than in respect to the Swiss Brethren and Balthasar Hubmaier. However, the case of Hubmaier himself is significant. We noted, for instance, that he was not simply a Zwinglian who felt the Zurich leader had gone wrong. He felt that Zwingli had erred, of course, but because he did not fully convert to the Reformation doctrines (preferring regeneration to justification, e.g.,) he operated on a basis different from Zwingli. The two were bound to find conflicts, therefore, and in a way belonged to two different rationales of the Christian faith, as the historical developments soon enough revealed.[3]

In regard to Hans Hut the situation is much clearer. Instead of dropping Müntzer completely when converted to non-revolutionary Anabaptism by Hans Denck, he reinterpreted the teachings of his erstwhile mentor, thereby developing a point of view similar to Denck but still Müntzerian in language, in the stress on redemptive suffering, and, to a degree, in eschatology. This means that in a sense, though a decidedly limited one, the old thesis of Karl Holl[4] has some truth to it, namely, that at least one strand of Anabaptism was indebted to the Saxon Spiritualists, or *Schwärmer* as Holl termed them. To admit this is not to say that the Anabaptists were guilty of the *Schwärmer* errors and excesses, nor that all of Anabaptism came from Müntzer and the Saxon radicals. The fallacies of that argument are well known. But this would say that the involvements and relationships of the Anabaptist groups were complex and included ancestors of more than one stripe, some of them admirable, and some of them perhaps not as admirable. This should be neither surprising nor disturbing, for the ferment of ideas and movements in the sixteenth century might be expected to produce unusual and even seemingly contradictory results. Nor should this necessarily be to the detriment of the Anabaptist movement which is now well recognized as having been largely a peaceful movement rather than a militant and revolutionary one. Indeed for Hut to have suppressed the revolutionary strains of the earlier movement while drawing good from it, and for his successors to have finally eliminated those radical elements altogether, would seem to be to their great credit.[5]

The Covenant of the Regenerate

The doctrine of regeneration also affected the concrete matters of church life and practice. In regard to baptism it mean that the sacrament was to be given only to those in whom the gifts of rebirth were evident. And those who had these gifts had the spiritual wherewithal to covenant themselves to God and His church. Thus the community of the reborn would be brought into life.

Hubmaier was the first to describe this covenant in baptism, though he used the word "pledge" instead of "covenant." This pledge bound the believer to God and to the fellow believers within the church. It included the commitment to abide by the teaching of Christ and by the discipline of the church which applied those teachings to life.

Hut, Hofmann, and Marpeck continued the same view and added to it particularly by stressing the inner covenant of God in the heart. For Hofmann this was a marital covenant as the soul was wedded to her heavenly lover as the earlier mystics had said; for Hut it was an inner operation of the Spirit as well as an eschatological seal which marked the band of covenanters who awaited their heavenly captain to lead them in the final attack upon evil; for Marpeck it was the covenant of the good conscience as Denck had earlier said. But in each case, the covenant in baptism identified the elect to each other and bound them together in mutual service to their Lord.

Here again the Anabaptists, particularly those of Southern Germany, may have been indebted to Thomas Müntzer, for they continued his aim of using the covenant to create a society of faithful Christians. But they differed from Müntzer in an important way, for their society would be a free, gathered church, whereas his was to have been a renewed Christendom. The full story of the transition from one aim to the other is yet to be told, but in principle it seems that the Anabaptist approach arose partly out of the collapse of Müntzer's attempt to put his views into effect. This was certainly true in the case of Hut, for, when he realized that Müntzer's attempted reformation of society through the *Bund* of the peasants had failed, he turned to a different kind of *Bund*. This covenant would involve only the church, the gathered and disciplined body of the baptized elect, separate from the world. It is notable that what happened with Hut and Müntzer also happened at Zurich. Conrad Grebel and Felix Mantz began to consider the possibility of a free church only when they became convinced that the city church was incapable of meeting their ideals.[6] In both cases, an attempt to reform Christian society failed, and when it did, the momentum of the attempt carried on, but now as a new movement separate from the "world."

Thus, the religio-political *Bund* of Müntzer gave way to the baptismal-ecclesiological *Bund* of Hut, much as the Swiss confederate *Eid*, which Johann Eberlin von Günzburg saw symbolized in baptism and which Zwingli related to the baptismal *Pflicht*, gave way to the voluntary *Taufpflicht* or *Taufgelübde* which formed the free church of Grebel and Hubmaier. The covenant thereby became the Anabaptists' tool for gathering the redeemed society, a society separate from the unregenerate world. Hubmaier's dictum that where there is no proper baptism there is no church is therefore revealed as no idle statement;[7] rather, it was the heart of the problem, for the church the Anabaptists had in mind could exist only as a brotherhood of regenerate believers covenanted together in mutual responsibility for living the life of the Spirit. Perhaps this also uncovers the reason for their consistent refusal to take the town oath, also called a *Bund:* through baptism they had now entered the covenant of the City of God (if we may employ Augustine's symbol), and they could therefore no longer be entrammeled with the covenant of the City of Man.

Since it was the baptismal *Bund* that bound the church together, baptism could then be interpreted as the dominical key of binding rather than the key of loosing, and the latter would then become the ban. This reversal of the traditional vocabulary was not universal among the Anabaptists—for example, neither Hubmaier nor Marpeck adopted it[8]—but it was so clear with Hans Hut as to suggest that he may not have been alone in altering the meaning of the terms.

The Objective Power of Baptism

Traditionally, interpreters of Anabaptist baptism have stressed the voluntarism that lay behind the action, and therefore their baptism has been understood principally as a confession of faith. This is correct, for the Anabaptists themselves repeatedly described their baptism as the confession and pledge of the baptizand. However, we have observed that there were objective elements in Anabaptist baptism as well as subjective elements. This was probably least true of Hubmaier, though it was not entirely lacking in him, for he understood water baptism to mark the entrance of the believer into the place of salvation, and this certainly attributed to the ordinance an objective value. However, the principle was expanded with the other three, first through the view of Hut and Hofmann that baptism was an eschatological sign assuring the baptizand of his membership in the elect, and second through Marpeck's conception of baptism as a co-witness complementary to the inner testimony of the Spirit.

In none of the four cases did the objective character of baptism rest simply in the ordinance itself, for behind the baptismal action stood the church of the regenerate, which administered the ordinance. The action, therefore, was more than a form—it was the testimony of the very people of God, which people would give the signs of Christ only to those in whom they recognized His Spirit. Leonhard Schiemer's analogy described this clearly: one seals an envelope only when one knows the contents.[9] Thus, the baptizand not only *gave* a testimony as he witnessed to his faith through the sign of baptism, but he *received* a testimony—specifically, he received from the church the sign of their belief that they recognized the gift of the Spirit within him. The formulation of the principle varied from one Anabaptist to another: for Hubmaier, it was the church's use of the keys to loose from sin; for Hut and Hofmann, this was the eschatological seal given by the prophet of God; for Marpeck, this was a sign from the body of Christ which, as Christ's earthly successor, stood in His place as it dispensed the ordinance. But the principle was the same in each case: baptism witnessed to the baptizand, assuring him of his inclusion within the covenanted people of God. Thus, Anabaptist baptism did possess objective value.

The Baptized Life

In summary, we can say that Anabaptist baptism symbolized all the basic elements of their view of the Christian life. Whether one looks to their experience of regeneration through the Holy Spirit, to their conception of the nature of the church and the foundation upon which it would stand, or to their understanding of the life the Christian would lead, their answer was the same—it was a "baptism."

The textual source for this broad application of baptism's significance was I John 5:6-8 which speaks of three baptisms: Spirit, water, and blood. Anabaptists, from the beginning, used this text to describe their whole life as a baptism.

The process began, of course, with the baptism of the Spirit which renewed man within, either instantaneously as Hubmaier said, or through a lengthy process as Hut, Hofmann, and Marpeck believed. In either event, this baptism was the gift of salvation itself, for it cleansed the person of sin and gave him the power to live the Christian life. The Spirit Himself witnessed within man that this was true.

But the birth of the Spirit was to be expressed in the baptism of water. Through this action the believer announced to the fellowship of the church that he was a brother in the Spirit; and through bestowing baptism on the candidate, the church announced to him their recognition of his membership with them in Christ.

From these two baptisms issued the third, the baptism of blood. The Anabaptists consistently claimed that the disciples of Christ, like their great Exemplar, would know suffering and affliction. This would sometimes be the inner suffering of guilt and despair. And, if the consciences of some may not have been sensitive enough to have created the expected trials within, the officials of the civic order were certain to create trials without. The Anabaptists expected both. And thus, they experienced the baptism of blood on two sides: the baptism of the mystics on the one side, and the baptism of the martyrs on the other.

If the Anabaptists seem to have welcomed persecution and martyrdom, it was partly because they believed that these persecutions were really the sufferings of Christ. He had suffered from the foundation of the world and for its salvation, and it was now their privilege to help fill up what lacked of that suffering. The baptism of blood thus had its own objective power, for in it the testimony of the godless was added to the testimony of the godly, and both served to assure the believer that he was indeed a member of the body of Christ. Finally, if one shared now in Christ's afflictions, he would later participate in His resurrection, when one's dying to sin and rising to a new life would be brought to completion.

Thus from the initial reception of the Spirit to the final death and resurrection of the body, the whole Christian life was a series of "baptisms." One can well reverse Hut's oft-quoted dictum that baptism is a lifelong struggle with sin[10] and say that the Christian life for the Anabaptists was a lifelong baptism.

There is also a sense in which the Anabaptists were as concerned about baptism, in the large sense of the term, as they were about the church. This is seen best perhaps in the branches of Anabaptism that were the most eschatological, for there, as with John the Baptist of old, the church was identified as the baptized faithful who stood awaiting a fuller baptism yet to come. But this was also true for the less eschatological strands of Anabaptism, for in creating a free, gathered church they were creating a "baptized" church, baptized not only by having received the baptisms of Spirit and water, but baptized also in that its life was a constant baptism in Spirit and in blood. Therefore, of the two basic ordinances of the New Testament, it was baptism, not the Lord's Supper, that drew their greatest attention. And rightly so, for theirs was basically a pilgrim church concerned to cross the Red Sea (to use the metaphor of the Exodus), not an institutional church concentrating on the gift of heavenly manna.

We see, therefore, that the roots of the Anabaptist theology of baptism went deep and its branches broadened out to include several types of baptism. As a result, every facet of their life and faith from conversion to resurrection and from Christian life to eschatology was bound together into a unity that could be encompassed metaphorically under the rubric of "baptism." Perhaps most of all, by serving as the entranceway into the church, the ordinance of water baptism, supported by the inner testimony of the Spirit, and the outer baptism in blood, signified that the baptizand had left the old order of death and sin and had now entered the new order of life and salvation. The ordinance was a sign to all who received it that they were thereby prepared for the final baptism unto eternal life to be given at the Day of Resurrection. Thus, baptism placed the believer in the center of redemptive history and assured him that, if he adhered faithfully to the teachings of Christ and kept to His example, the victory which Christ won would be his also and he would share in the glory of his Lord. And thus Anabaptist baptism was essentially a sign of hope and redemption, for it not only witnessed to the baptizand's death to sin and resurrection to new life in Christ, but it testified to his present victory over the powers of evil in the world and, most of all, to his future participation in the salvation to be given at the Last Day through the final redemption in Christ.

Appendix

BALTHASAR HUBMAIER'S BAPTISMAL ORDER[1]
AS FOLLOWED AT NICOLSBURG[2]

Whoever desires to receive water baptism should first present himself to his bishop[3] so that he may be tested as to whether he is sufficiently instructed in the articles of the law, Gospel, and faith, and in the doctrines which pertain to a new Christian life. Also he must give evidence that he can pray,[4] and that he can intelligently explain the articles of the Christian faith. This must all be ascertained about the candidate before he can be permitted to be incorporated into the church of Christ through external baptism unto the forgiveness of his sins.

If he meets these requirements, the bishop then presents him to his church. He admonishes all the brethren and sisters to kneel and with hearty devotion to pray to God, that God may graciously grant to the candidate the grace and power of His Holy Spirit, and that He will bring to pass that which He has begun in him through His Holy Spirit and divine Word.

The administration of baptism is then to proceed thus:
The bishop shall say: Come, Holy Spirit; fill the hearts of Thy believers and enkindle in them the fire of Thy love: Thou who hast assembled the peoples of many tongues in the unity of faith. Hallelujah! Hallelujah! Praise be to God! Praise be to God!

Then the bishop proffers the baptismal vow[5] to the candidate thus:

The Bishop: Believest thou in God the Father Almighty, Maker of heaven and earth?

The Candidate (in words for all to hear): I believe.

The Bishop: Believest thou in Jesus Christ, His only-begotten Son, our Lord; who was conceived of the Holy Ghost; born of the Virgin Mary; suffered under Pontius Pilate; was crucified dead and buried; that He also descended in His spirit and preached the Gospel to the spirits who were in prison; on the third day He was reunited with His body in the grave and rose in power from the dead; after forty days He ascended unto heaven, where He sits at the right hand of His Father Almighty; thence He shall come to judge the living and the dead; believest thou this?

The Candidate: I believe.

The Bishop: Believest thou also in the Holy Spirit; and believest thou one Holy Universal Christian Church, one communion of the saints which has the keys to remit sin; believest thou also one resurrection of the flesh, and one eternal life?

The Candidate: I believe.

The Bishop: Wilt thou also in the power of Christ renounce the devil, all his works, legions, and pomps?

The Candidate: I will.

The Bishop: If thou hereafter sinnest and thy brother knoweth it, wilt thou accept from him the first and the second steps of fraternal discipline, and then, if necessary, willingly and obediently allow thyself to be disciplined before the church?

The Candidate: I will.

The Bishop: Dost thou now desire, upon this profession of faith and pledge, to be baptized in water according to the institution of Christ, and thus to be incorporated and enrolled into the external Christian church unto the forgiveness of thy sins?

The Candidate: I desire this in the power of God.

The bishop then baptizes:

The Bishop: I baptize thee in the name of the Father, and of the Son, and of the Holy Ghost, unto the forgiveness of thy sins. Amen. May it thus be true.

The bishop admonishes the church a second time to pray for the one newly baptized. They are to pray that God will increase his faith, and the faith of all Christian men, and will grant us all power and perseverance, so that we finally may be found and be preserved in one Christian faith.

When the church has finished praying, the bishop lays his hands upon the head of the one newly baptized and says:

I give thee witness and authority, that thou henceforth shalt be numbered among the fellowship of Christians; that as a member of this fellowship thou shalt participate in its keys, and thou shalt break bread and pray with the other Christian sisters and brethren. God be with thee and with thy spirit. Amen.

Abbreviations

ANF	*The Ante-Nicene Fathers*
ARG	*Archiv für Reformationsgeschichte*
BRN	Cramer, Samuel, and Pijper, Frederik (eds.), *Bibliotheca Reformatoria Neerlandica*
CH	*Church History*
CR	*Corpus Reformatorum*
CS	*Corpus Schwenckfeldianorum*
LCC: Mysticism	Petry, Ray C. (ed.), *Late Medieval Mysticism*
LCC: Reform	Battles, Ford Lewis (ed.), *Advocates of Reform*
LCC: SAW	Williams, George Huntston, and Mergal, Angel M. (eds.), *Spiritual and Anabaptist Writers*
LCC: Zw	Bromiley, G. W. (ed.), *Zwingli and Bullinger*
ME	*The Mennonite Encyclopedia*
ML	*Mennonitisches Lexikon*
MPG	Migne, J. P. (ed.), *Patrologiae Cursus Completus: Series Graeca*
MPL	Migne, J. P. (ed.), *Patrologiae Cursus Completus: Series Latina*
MQR	*The Mennonite Quarterly Review*
TA: Bayern	Schornbaum, Karl (ed.), *Markgraftum Brandenburg: Bayern, I. Abteilung*
TA: Denck	Baring, Georg, and Fellmann, Walter (eds.), *Hans Denck: Schriften*
TA: Elsass, I, II	Krebs, Manfred, and Rott, Georg, *Elsass, I. Teil: Stadt Strassburg, 1522-1532; Elsass, II. Teil: Stadt Strassburg, 1533-1535*

TA: Glaubenszeugnisse	Müller, Lydia (ed.), *Glaubenszeugnisse oberdeutscher Taufgesinnter*
TA: HS	Westin, Gunnar, and Bergsten, Torsten (eds.), *Balthasar Hubmaier: Schriften*
TA: Oesterreich	Mecenseffy, Grete (ed.), *Oesterreich, I. Teil*
TA: Thüringen	Wappler, Paul, *Die Täuferbewegung in Thüringen von 1526-1584*
TA: Zürich	Muralt, Leonhard von, and Schmid, Walter (eds.), *Quellen zur Geschichte der Täufer in der Schweiz*, Vol. I: *Zürich*
TSK	*Theologische Studien und Kritiken*
WA	Knaake, J. C. F., et al. (eds.), *D. Martin Luthers Werke: Kritische Gesamtausgabe*
ZHVSN: Hut	Meyer, Christian (ed.), "Zur Geschichte der Wiedertäufer in Oberschwaben": Part I: "Die Anfänge des Wiedertäuferthums in Augsburg." *Zeitschrift des historischen Vereins für Schwaben und Neuburg*, I
ZHVSN: Langenmantel	Roth, Friedrich (ed.), "Zur Geschichte der Wiedertäufer in Oberschwaben": Part II: "Zur Lebensgeschichte Eitelhans Langenmantels von Augsburg." *Zeitschrift des historischen Vereins für Schwaben und Neuburg*, XXVII
ZKG	*Zeitschrift für Kirchengeschichte*
ZW	Egli, Emil, et al. (eds.), *Huldreich Zwinglis sämtliche Werke*

Footnotes

INTRODUCTION

1 Hans Denck, the other notable contributor to Anabaptist baptismal thought, is included obliquely in the study of Hut. Since he devoted no tract to baptism itself, and since his tradition is represented by Hut, one of his converts, he is not treated as a major subject of the study.

Certain sources referred to in the footnotes are distributed in North America by Herald Press, Scottdale, Pennsylvania. This information is given in the Bibliography following the various entries.

Chapter I. BALTHASAR HUBMAIER

1 The incident is reported by Heinrich Küssenberg, **Chronik der Reformation in der Grafschaft Baden, im Klettgau und auf dem Schwarzwalde**, ed. Johann Huber, **Archiv für schweizerische Reformationsgeschichte**, III (1875), p. 13.

2 **TA: Zürich**, I, pp. 391-92. These events along with the other principal ones of Hubmaier's career from his conversion to Anabaptism to his martyrdom are described by George Huntston Williams, **The Radical Reformation** (Philadelphia: The Westminster Press, 1962), pp. 134-41, 218-29, **passim**.

3 The involvements of Waldshut in the Reformation, the Peasants' Uprising, and political and social concerns in general are admirably described by Torsten Bergsten, **Balthasar Hubmaier: Seine Stellung zu Reformation und Täufertum, 1521-1528** (Acta Universitatis Upsaliensis: Studia historico-ecclesiastica Upsaliensia, No. 3; Kassel: J. G. Oncken Verlag, 1961), pp. 120-248. A summary description of Hubmaier's role in the Peasants' Movement is found in Williams, op. cit., pp. 64-68.

4 Bergsten, op. cit., pp. 94-119, 127-32, 144-57, 166-216.

5 **Ein Gespräch auf Zwinglis Taufbüchlein** (hereafter, **Gespräch**), TA: HS, pp. 172-73.

6 Ibid., p. 186; Bergsten, op. cit., p. 110. Hubmaier also mentioned the conversation during his court testimony in Zurich. TA: Zürich, I, No. 179, p. 195.

7 **Antwort über Balthasar Hubmaiers Taufbüchlein**, ZW, IV, p. 602.

8 Luther, in his letter of Jan. 13, 1522, to Melanchthon, reported the Zwickau prophets' use of Mark 16:16 as an argument against infant baptism. WA, Briefwechsel, II, No. 450, p. 425, 11. 85-86.

9 Wilhelm Mau and Johannes Martin Usteri believe Hubmaier's report is exaggerated. Mau, **Balthasar Hubmaier** (Abhandlungen zur mittleren und neueren Geschichte, ed. Georg von Below, Heinrich Finke, and Friedrich Meinecke, Vol. XL; Berlin and Leipzig: Walter Rothschild, 1912), p. 80. Usteri, "Darstellung der Tauflehre Zwinglis," TSK, LV, No. 2 (1882), pp. 211-12.

10 **Von der Taufe, von der Wiedertaufe und von der Kindertaufe**, ZW, IV, p. 228; trans. G. W. Bromiley, LCC: Zwingli, p. 139.

11 Op. cit., p. 112.

12 The complex story of the emergence of the radical, later Anabaptist, party in Zurich has been retraced by Robert Walton in "Zwingli's Theocracy" (unpublished Ph.D. dissertation, Yale University, 1964). Walton, chap. vi, finds the rise of this party to have begun at least as early as March, 1522, when the Lenten fast laws were broken at Christoph Froschauer's house. He believes that Grebel was connected with

this group as early as mid-1522. His helpful discussion of the October Disputation and the ensuing events is found in chap. xi, where he presents a more detailed account than the present one. Walton's major thesis is that Zwingli followed a generally consistent course of action through the whole process of reforming Zurich, and that the radical party which formed the Anabaptist congregation was a group which had differed with Zwingli for at least three years before the 1525 break.

13 Harold Bender, **Conrad Grebel, c. 1498-1526: Founder of the Swiss Brethren, Sometimes Called Anabaptists** (Studies in Anabaptist and Mennonite History, ed. H. S. Bender, et al., No. 6; Goshen, Ind.: The Mennonite Historical Society, 1950), p. 101. Fritz Blanke, **Brüder in Christo: Die Geschichte der ältesten Täufergemeinde** (Zürich: Zwingli Verlag, 1955), pp. 8-9.

14 Williams, op. cit., pp. 90-91; ZW, II, pp. 786-88.

15 ZW, II, p. 762.

16 Ibid. The concluding phrases allude to Isa. 55:10. Compare Zwingli: "Dass wort gottes so lebendig, so krefftig und stark ist, das im müssend alle ding gehorsam sin und das so dick und zü welcher zyt er will." **ZW, I,** p. 356.

17 In reply to Simon Stumpf's criticism of the possibility that the Council might decide matters of Christian faith itself, he said: "Ich wil ouch darwider predgen und tün, so sy ein anders erkantind. Ich gib inen das urteyl nit in ir hend. Sy söllend ouch über das wort gottes gantz nit urteilen. . . . Dise züsamenberüffung ist ouch nit darumb geschehen, dass sy darinn wellind urteilen, sunder ein wüssen haben und uss der geschrifft erfaren, ob die mess ein opffer sye oder nit. Dannethyn so werdend sy radtschlagen, mit was fügen das zü dem aller komlichesten on uffrür geschehen mög etc." ZW, II, p. 784.

18 Bergsten, op. cit., pp. 113-18, believes that the open break between the Grebel group and Zwingli did not come until December, when Zwingli and the other two people's priests of Zurich were overruled by the Zurich Council in their decision to administer the sacrament in both kinds at the Christmas communion. However, by not recognizing the implications of the divergent approaches to Scripture, he has overstressed the unanimity that prevailed between the developing parties. The same criticism may be raised against John Howard Yoder, **Täufertum und Reformation in der Schweiz,** Vol. I: **Die Gespräche zwischen Täufern und Reformatoren, 1523-1538** (Schriftenreihe des Mennonitischen Geschichtsvereins, No. 6; Karlsruhe: herausgegeben vom Mennonitischen Geschichtsverein e. V. Weierhof, 1962), pp. 20-28; and "The Turning Point in the Zwinglian Reformation," **MQR,** XXXII (1958), pp. 128-40. Yoder must be read in the light of Bergsten's identification of the time of the schism. Walton's dissertation, op. cit., is a criticism of Yoder and an argument on the other side.

19 Matt. 15:13. **Achtzehn Schlussreden, art. 11, TA: HS,** p. 73. Hubmaier quoted the same text at the October Disputation. **ZW, II,** p. 761. The text was used also by Clement Ziegler, the Strassburg gardener, sacramentarian, and spiritualist, in his attack on infant baptism in mid-1524. **Von der waren nyessung beid leibs und bluts Christi . . . und von dem tauff,** extracted by Manfred Krebs and Hans Georg Rott, **TA: Elsass,** I, No. 8, p. 17. For Ziegler's unusual combination of sacramentarian, iconoclastic, and eschatological views, see Williams, op. cit., pp. 245-48, and passim.

20 Op. cit., p. 130.

21 **TA: HS,** p. 73.

22 Ibid.

23 **Op. cit.,** p. 81.

24 Bergsten, op. cit., pp. 136-37.

25 Letter to Zwingli, Nov. (?), 1524, ZW, VIII, p. 254; Bergsten, op. cit., p. 213.

26 "Er ist wider den Zwingli dess taufs halb und wirt wider in schriben," **TA: Zürich,** I, No. 23, pp. 33-34.

27 Letter to Oecolampadius, Jan. 16, 1525, ed. Ernst Staehelin, **Briefe und Akten**

zum Leben Oekolampads, Vol. I (Quellen und Forschungen zur Reformationsgeschichte, Vol. X; Leipzig: M. Heinsius Nachfolger, Eger & Sievers, 1927), No. 238, pp. 341-44.

28 Bergsten, op. cit., p. 263.

29 Zwingli, Wer Ursache gebe zu Aufruhr (Dec., 1524), ZW, III, pp. 408-12; Bucer, Grund und Ursache (late Dec., 1524), Martin Bucers Deutsche Schriften (Martini Buceri opera omnia, Series I; Gütersloh: Gütersloher Verlagshaus Gerd Mohn, 1960-) I, pp. 254-62.

30 Letter to Francis Lambert and Brethren in Strassburg, Dec. 16, 1524, ZW, VIII, No. 355, pp. 261-78. The letter was a reply to Bucer's letter of Oct. 31. Ibid., p. 243. Whether Zwingli's reply arrived in time for Bucer to incorporate his suggestions is a question, for Bucer's Grund und Ursache was published between Dec. 26 and 31, 1524, which would have allowed very little time for the necessary writing and printing. Bucer's work contains most of the Biblical texts suggested by Zwingli, whether from Zwingli or gathered independently by Bucer.

31 Bucer, Grund und Ursache, loc. cit., pp. 259-61; Zwingli, Wer Ursache gebe, ZW, III, pp. 410-11.

32 Zwingli had expressed the view in his letter of Oct. 20, 1524, to Fridolin Lindauer; see p. 26. On Zwingli's later use of the distinction, see pp. 30-31.

33 Letter to Zwingli, Aug. 20, 1527, ZW, IX, No. 644, pp. 195-96.

34 Briefe und Akten zum Leben Oekolampads, I, p. 342.

35 Hubmaier says that the interpretation of talium to mean illorum is in a writing by the Argentinenses. Ibid., p. 343. He is referring to the Grund und Ursache of Bucer. The work was in fact a joint composition and is so signed. Martin Bucers Deutsche Schriften, I, pp. 259-60. The Bucer group may have been directing their remarks against Clement Ziegler who had been using the passage to argue that since the children are already blessed by Christ they do not need baptism. TA: Elsass, I, No. 8, pp. 14, 16.

36 Letter to Hubmaier, ca. Jan. 18, 1525. Briefe und Akten zum Leben Oekolampads, I, pp. 344-45.

37 Letter to Hubmaier, end of Jan. (?), 1525, ibid., pp. 355-56. Oecolampadius' letter to Zwingli reporting to the latter the contents of Hubmaier's letter survives: Letter to Zwingli, Jan. 18, 1525, ZW, VIII, No. 359, pp. 291-93. Zwingli's reply is lost.

38 "Placet supra modum ritus, quem servas in ecclesia; utinam arrideret omnibus."

39 TA: HS, pp. 106-7.

40 Der uralten und gar neuen Lehrer Urteil I (hereafter Urteil), TA: HS, p. 233; Urteil II, ibid., p. 250. Luther, WA, VI, pp. 363-64.

41 It is also true, of course, that Hubmaier elsewhere said that his questioning of baptism began in 1520. See above, p. 19.

42 Johann Loserth, Doktor Balthasar Hubmaier und die Anfänge der Wiedertaufe in Mähren (Brünn: Verlag der historischstatistischen Section, Druck von Rudolf M. Rohrer, 1893), p. 73.

43 Carl Sachsse, Doktor Balthasar Hubmaier als Theologe (Neue Studien zur Geschichte der Theologie und der Kirche, ed. N. Bonwetsch and R. Seeberg, No. 20; Berlin: Trowitzsch und Sohn, 1914), pp. 153, 158-60.

44 Op. cit., p. 202.

45 Op. cit., pp. 46-47.

46 Henry C. Vedder, Balthasar Hubmaier: The Leader of the Anabaptists (Heroes of the Reformation, ed. Samuel Macauley Jackson, [n. no.]; New York: G. P. Putnam's Sons, The Knickerbocker Press, 1905), pp. 100-12.

47 According to Zwingli's report, ZW, IV, p. 602. For the Zwickau prophets, see above, n. 8.

48 In the body of the epistle they say: "Dess touffs halb gfalt unss din schriben wol, begerend ouch witer bericht werden von dir." But in the postscript they add:

"Diner büchlin und protestationen halb so find ich dich on schuld, du verwerfist dann den touff gar, kan ich nit daruss verstan." **TA: Zürich,** I, No. 14, pp. 17, 20.

49 Bergsten notes that Müntzer's arrival would have been too late for him to have participated in the Waldshut **Bildersturm** or the rupture in the negotiations with the Austrian authorities. **Op. cit.,** p. 201.

50 A reductio ad absurdum: if baptism saves, then use **Malvasier** (a precious wine) instead of water. **TA: HS,** p. 144, n. 126; **Protestation oder Entbietung,** ed. Otto Brandt, **Thomas Müntzer: Sein Leben und seine Schriften** (Jena: Eugen Diederichs Verlag, 1933), p. 135.

51 "Die rechte Taufe ist nicht verstanden. Darum ist der Eingang zur Christenheit zum viehischen Affenspiel worden." **Ibid.**

52 Hans J. Hillerbrand, "The Origin of Sixteenth Century Anabaptism: Another Look," ARG, LIII (1962), p. 160. Hillerbrand cities Gottfried G. Krodel, "Die Abendmahlslehre des Erasmus von Rotterdam und seine Stellung am Anfang des Abendmahlsstreites der Reformatoren" (unpublished doctoral dissertation, University of Erlangen, 1955), pp. 73-78.

53 Grebel's letter to Müntzer says: "Allein an dem wort halten und schalten, wie allen gesanten, und dir und Carolostadio foruss, wol anstat, und ir mer tünd, weder alle predicanten aller nationen." **TA: Zürich,** I, No. 14, p. 18.

Gordon Rupp has recently suggested that Felix Mantz in writing his **Protestation** used as a guide Karlstadt's tract on baptism which Oecolampadius prevented from being printed in Basel. "Andrew Karlstadt and Reformation Puritanism," **Journal of Theological Studies,** X (1959), p. 321, n. 3. Hillerbrand, loc. cit., p. 163, considers the suggestion "altogether plausible." Even if that is not true, the contents of the tract were common knowledge to the Grebel group from Karlstadt's visit among them before his trip to Basel to arrange publication of his tracts.

54 Letter to Oecolampadius, Jan. 16, 1525, **Briefe und Akten zum Leben Oekolampads,** I, No. 238, p. 341.

55 **Etliche Schlussreden vom Unterricht der Messe, TA: HS,** p. 102. The view was later discarded. See Bergsten, op. cit., pp. 259-60.

56 See Hillerbrand, loc. cit., pp. 161-68, especially 166-67.

57 Letter to Fridolin Lindauer, Oct. 20, 1524, ZW, VIII, p. 236.

58 **Gespräch, TA: HS,** p. 210, quoting **Von der Taufe, von der Wiedertaufe und von der Kindertaufe,** ZW, IV, p. 333. Translated on p. 30.

59 Letter to Thomas Wyttenbach, June 15, 1523, ZW, VIII, p. 85.

60 **Briefe und Akten zum Leben Oekolampads,** I, No. 238, p. 342.

61 ZW, III, p. 773.

62 For instance, Hubmaier claimed that Zwingli had advocated that the church return to its early practice of having a catechumenate before baptism. Hubmaier, **Gespräch, TA: HS,** p. 186; **Urteil I,** ibid., pp. 234-35; **Urteil II,** ibid., pp. 250-51. He was citing Zwingli's **Auslegung und Begründung der Schlussreden oder Artikel,** ZW, II, pp. 122-23. But Zwingli only counseled that children baptized as infants should be instructed before being confirmed. Hubmaier, loc. cit., also charged that Zwingli had said that the New Testament provided no basis for infant baptism. Zwingli simply said that the New Testament neither confirmed nor denied it explicitly. **Wer Ursache gebe,** ZW, III, pp. 409-10. For Hubmaier that amounted to a denial of New Testament support, but not for Zwingli.

63 On the question of communications with the Grebel party, a point that has generally been weak in documentation, see Bergsten, **op. cit.,** pp. 203-7, 212-13.

64 Quoted by Loserth, op. cit., p. 73.

65 Published, respectively, in ZW, III, pp. 374-469; IV, pp. 206-337.

66 See above, n. 26.

67 **TA: Zürich,** I, No. 82, p. 87.

Footnotes / 151

68 Yoder's statement that "occasional rebuttal of Zwinglian arguments occurs only on the margin of this entire exposition" is an understatement. "Balthasar Hubmaier and the Beginnings of Swiss Anabaptism," MQR, XXXIII (1959), p. 10. While much of the work is simply "exposition," the rebuttal is hardly marginal, except in the sense that it occupies a relatively small number of pages due to the fact that the quotations from Scripture are extensive. Of the material composed by Hubmaier, the major portion is directly against the work by Zwingli, and most of the remainder is indirectly so.

69 TA: HS, pp. 108-15.

70 ZW, IV, pp. 585-642; TA: HS, pp. 164-214.

71 Articles 8-12, 16, TA: HS, pp. 92-93.

72 TA: HS, pp. 261-62. See also Gespräch, ibid., pp. 210-11; and Eine ernstliche christliche Erbietung, ibid., pp. 81-82.

73 Von der Taufe der Gläubigen, ibid., p. 146.

74 ZW, IV, pp. 231-34. Johannes Bader, in his Brüderliche Warnung vor dem neuen abgöttischen Orden der Wiedertäufer of 1527, cited Zwingli's argument against Hans Denck. TA: Denck, Part III, p. 106.

75 Von der Taufe der Gläubigen, TA: HS, pp. 127-31.

76 Zwingli, Taufe und Wiedertaufe, ZW, IV, pp. 238-39; Hubmaier, Von der Taufe der Gläubigen, chap. iii, TA: HS, pp. 127-34. The exegesis is sometimes strained. For instance, Hubmaier takes the order of Matt. 3:6 literally: "They were baptized . . . , confessing their sins." He asserts that public confession followed baptism in this case, but that baptism had been preceded by an inner confession and that, thus, there was no violation of the required sequence. Ibid., p. 128.

77 Ibid., pp. 146-51.

78 Hubmaier, ibid., p. 137; Zwingli, Taufe und Wiedertaufe, ZW, IV, pp. 237-38. In the same passage Hubmaier says that baptizing infants is like advertising wine at Easter, wine which will not mature until fall and then be of an unpredictable quality.

79 Hubmaier, ibid.; Zwingli, ibid., pp. 237, 243-44. In both passages Zwingli distinguishes between baptism in den Namen and im Namen, the former lending support to the idea of initiation.

80 Zwingli, ibid., p. 238.

81 Von der Taufe der Gläubigen, TA: HS, pp. 139-40. Similar passages on pp. 122, 136.

82 TA: HS, pp. 140-46.

83 Ibid., p. 146.

84 Above, p. 26.

85 "Von dem touff des geists spricht Christus (Act. 1[:5]): 'Joannes hat mit wasser getoufft; ir werden aber mit dem heligen geist getouft nach unlangen denen tagen.' Hie strycht Christus die beden underscheid des touffs us. Joannes toufft nun mit dem wasser oder usserlichen leere. Also touffend ouch noch hüt bi tag alle menschen nit anderst denn usserlich, eintweders, das sy usserlich leerend, oder das wasser angiessend oder tunckend. . . . Denn den touff des geists mag nieman geben weder got." ZW, IV, p. 220.

86 "Darumb wissen wir nur zweierley tauff, einen mit wasser, mit solchem hat Joannes geteüfft, der anfenger des neüwen testaments, die Aposteln und alle Christen. Der ander ist mit dem Christus teüffet durch den heylgen geist und das fewer, welchs eben der heilig geist ist." Grund und Ursache, Martin Bucers Deutsche Schriften, I, p. 256.

87 ZW, IV, p. 333; Gespräch, TA: HS, p. 210. Same quotations and format in Bergsten, op. cit., p. 369.

88 Ibid., p. 371.

89 In catabaptistarum strophas elenchus, ZW, VI, Part I, p. 172, n. 2.

90 ZW, IV, p. 221.

91 Zwingli, Taufe und Wiedertaufe, ibid., p. 318; Hubmaier, Von der Taufe der Gläubigen, TA: HS, p. 156.

92 Antwort über Balthasar Hubmaiers Taufbüchlein, ZW, IV, p. 621. See Bergsten, op. cit., pp. 374-75.

93 Eine christliche Lehrtafel, TA: HS, p. 313.

94 Von der Taufe der Gläubigen, TA: HS, pp. 136, 150. Hubmaier followed the translation of the 1524 Zurich Bible, "eine gewüsse kundtschafft," rather than Luther's "der bund eyns guten gewissens," which was of particular significance for other Anabaptists. On Luther's translation, see below, p. 180, n. 38. Zwingli translated $\dot{\epsilon}\pi\epsilon\rho\omega\tau\eta\mu\alpha$ variously as responsio (ZW, VIII, p. 236), interrogatio, following the Vulgate (ibid., VIII, p. 275), and erforschen (Angelobung) (ibid., IV, p. 248, n. 5).

95 Taufe und Wiedertaufe, ZW, IV, p. 248, n. 5.

96 "Nit das [der tauff] der selb die seelen reynige, sonder das ja eins gutten gwissens mit Gott, das da ist vorgangen im glauben inwendig." Von der Taufe der Gläubigen, TA: HS, p. 137.

97 Ibid., p. 150.

98 Ibid., p. 136.

99 Ibid., p. 142.

100 Ibid., p. 143.

101 Taufe und Wiedertaufe, ZW, IV, p. 224; trans. G. W. Bromiley, LCC: Zwingli, p. 136.

102 Zwingli explained to Fridolin Lindauer that water baptism was given, not to cleanse of sin, but to confirm to man externally what takes place internally. "Ut ergo toti, hoc est tam interiori quam exteriori, homini deus satisfaceret (ut exempli causa decamus), eum, qui iam credidisset, aqua tingi iussit, non ut animum ablui hac ratione voluerit—nam qui fieri posset, ut incorporea substantia elemento corporeo ablueretur?—sed ut exterior homo visibili signo initiaretur, quo eius quoque rei, quae apud interiorem vel fidei lumine vel manifesto gratiae dei verbo geritur, certior fieret." ZW, VIII, p. 236. It is of note that the passage is followed by the quotation of I Pet. 3:21.

103 Von der Freiheit des Willens, TA: HS, pp. 383, 386, 389.

104 Ibid., pp. 386-87.

105 Eine christliche Lehrtafel, TA: HS, pp. 321-23.

106 Ibid., p. 324.

107 Von der Freiheit des Willens, TA: HS, p. 394. Translation based on that by Williams, LCC: SAW, p. 129.

108 Das andere Büchlein von der Freiwilligkeit, TA: HS, p. 418. Also based on Williams, LCC: SAW, p. 135.

109 Regenerate man, thus, enjoys what is tantamount to the freedom of Adam, for if he keeps the commandments, the gift of eternal life will be preserved in him; but if he surrenders himself to sin, he will die, this time an irrevocable death. Ezek. 18:20 ("the soul that sins shall die") is applied literally to the Christian man. Von der Freiheit des Willens, TA: HS, p. 392.

110 Ibid., pp. 391-92.

111 Aware that he might be charged with reopening the door to the merit system of salvation and works-righteousness, Hubmaier insisted that the good works which the regenerate man does are performed through the power of the divine Spirit that brings him new life and not through man's own power. Eine christliche Lehrtafel, TA: HS, p. 321.

112 According to Fritz Blanke, ZW, VI, Part I, p. 172, n. 2.

113 The term Erbpräst, evidently coined by Zwingli, is a compound of the German

Erb and the Swiss dialect präst, the latter with a wide range of meanings, including: "(a) Körperlicher oder sittlicher Mangel; (b) Fehler, Schaden, Nachteil, Not, Elend, Plage; (c) Mangelhaftigkeit, Unvollkommenheit einer Sache." The term served a double purpose in Zwingli, for it allowed him to describe **Erbsünde** as sickness or defect and to differentiate it from **Erbschuld**. Rudolf Pfister, **Das Problem der Erbsünde bei Zwingli** (Neuruppin: Druck von E. Buchbinder [H. Duske] G. m. b. h., 1938), pp. 24-25. Pfister cites the meanings of präst from **Das Schweizerische Idiotikon**, V (1905), p. 836 ff.

114 Taufe und Wiedertaufe, ZW, IV, pp. 307-9; Pfister, op. cit., pp. 23, 28-30, 76-80.

115 Ibid., ZW, IV, p. 308. Zwingli illustrated this with the analogy of a young wolf which has it in him to kill sheep but knows nothing of this while his eyes are closed. With growth this inner character reveals itself and is put into action.

116 Ibid., p. 313.

117 Ibid., p. 315.

118 Von der Taufe der Gläubigen, TA: HS, p. 155.

119 Melanchthons Werke in Auswahl, ed. Robert Stupperich, Vol. II, Part I (Gütersloh: C. Bertelsmann Verlag, 1952), pp. 140-44.

120 Werner Jetter, Die Taufe beim jungen Luther (Beiträge zur historischen Theologie, ed. Gerhard Ebeling, No. 18; Tübingen: J. C. B. Mohr [Paul Siebeck], 1954), pp. 86-87.

121 Cc. 5, 6, D. II, de cons.

122 A statement by Thomas Aquinas reveals the problem within Catholic theology of attributing New Testament power to Old Testament ceremonies: "Manifestum est, quod a passione Christi, quae est causa humanae iustificationis, convenienter derivatur virtus iustificativa ad sacramenta novae legis, non autem ad sacramenta veteris legis, et tamen per fidem passionis Christi iustificabantur antiqui Patres, sicut et nos. Sacramenta autem veteris legis erant quaedam illius fidei protestationes, inquantum significabant passionem Christi et effectus eius." Summa theologiae, III, quest. 62, art. 6.

123 ZW, III, pp. 409-10. It was also mentioned in his letter of Dec. 16, 1524, to Francis Lambert. Ibid., VIII, p. 271. Bucer used the same argument in **Grund und Ursache**, perhaps deriving it from Zwingli. Bucers Deutsche Schriften, I, pp. 259, 261.

124 Zwingli listed three rules to follow in disputes within the church: (1) follow the Word of God, not man; (2) if two men both have Scriptural support, follow the man who best reveres God with his view; (3) if the New Testament contains no pertinent text, look to the Old Testament. Wer Ursache, ZW, III, p. 409.

125 "In him also you were circumcised with a circumcision made without hands, by putting off the body of flesh in the circumcision of Christ; and you were buried with him in baptism, in which you were also raised with him through faith in the working of God" (RSV).

126 Loci communes, ed. Stupperich, op. cit., pp. 141-44.

127 ZW, IV, p. 294.

128 Ibid., pp. 313-15.

129 Von der Taufe der Gläubigen, TA: HS, p. 150; Gespräch, ibid., pp. 175-76, 210.

130 Ibid., p. 180.

131 John Howard Yoder may be right in his suggestion that Hubmaier's inability to cope with Zwingli's covenant theology was one of the principal reasons for Hubmaier's recantation in Zurich. "Balthasar Hubmaier and the Beginnings of Swiss Anabaptism," loc. cit., p. 13; TA: Zürich, I, No. 147. However, the placing of the covenantal interpretation of baptism at the head of the points of the recantation could be attributed to Zwingli's own ordering of the elements as well as to Hubmaier's theological vulnerability.

132 Gespräch, TA: HS, pp. 196-97.

133 ZW, IV, pp. 258-77. The **Protestation und Schutzschrifft**, formerly attributed to

Conrad Grebel and now ascribed to Felix Mantz, refers occasionally to the baptism of John, principally to show that John required repentance and conversion of life before baptism and that, therefore, his baptism was unfitting for infants. A hint of the distinction between John's baptism and Christian baptism is caught in the statement, "töufft [er] sy alsso, das inen ire sünd nachgelassen söltend sein in dem künfftigen leiden Jesu Christi." TA: Zürich, I, No. 16, p. 24.

134 ZW, IV, p. 265. Martin Bucer presented the same position a few months earlier in his **Grund und Ursache** of late December, 1524. He claimed that John preached the same message as Christ and baptized with the same baptism. The column heading for the paragraph reads: "Joannis, der Apostlen und unser tauff ist einer." **Martin Bucers Deutsche Schriften, I**, p. 255.

135 **Von der Taufe der Gläubigen, TA: HS**, p. 124.

136 Ibid., pp. 126-27.

137 Ibid., pp. 125-27. **Gespräch**, ibid., pp. 196-97.

138 **Von der Taufe der Gläubigen, TA: HS**, pp. 125-27; **Gespräch**, loc. cit.

139 The question of the institution of baptism is more complicated than that of the institution of the Lord's Supper, for the former can be based on several texts (John's baptism of Jesus, the commissioning of the seventy to preach to the Jews, and the great commission, principally), while the latter has only one set of texts. Medieval theologians ordinarily made use of all or most of the events connected with baptism, thereby understanding baptism to have been instituted in a series of events rather than on a single occasion. Thus, Gabriel Biel said: (1) baptism was instituted potentially and materially in John's baptism of Christ which dedicated water (but did not consecrate it) for use in the sacrament; (2) Jesus' words to Nicodemus in John 3:5 gave baptism its purpose, and His commission in Mark 16:16 gave it its efficacy; (3) baptism was instituted formally in Matt. 28:19, symbolically in the water from Christ's side at His death, and officially in the commissioning of the disciples to Israel. **Collectorium in quattuor libros sententiarum** (Basilae impressum: 1507), **Lib. IV, dist. iv, quest. I, art, 3, dub. ult.** Similarly, Hugh of St. Victor had said that baptism was instituted ad usum with John the Baptist, ad consuetudinem with the baptisms by the disciples of Christ, and universally with Matt. 28:19. Cf. Jetter, op. cit., pp. 45, 92-93.

140 Catholic theology had sometimes done the same thing in other ways, to wit, the view of Hugh of St. Victor and Gabriel Biel that Christian baptism had been instituted (partially at least) at the baptism of Jesus. Above, n. 139.

141 **Von der Taufe der Gläubigen, TA: HS**, pp. 132-33.

142 **Das andere Büchlein von Freiwilligkeit**, ibid., p. 403.

143 **Von der Taufe der Gläubigen**, ibid., p. 158; **Eine Summe eines ganzen christlichen Lebens**, ibid., p. 111.

144 It is known that Hubmaier was hoping to read the notes which Matthew Beyr had made in Melanchthon's lectures on Romans and I and II Corinthians in 1521-1522. If he read them in either original or published form, he would have encountered this distinction in the roles of law and Gospel. Hubmaier says of John's baptism (and hence of the law), e.g.: It "bedeüt ein inwendige erkaltung der gewissen von wegen der erkantnuss der Sünden. . . ." It "Erschreckt, Tödtet, fiert in die Hell. Da kennt vnnd sicht man nichts den Sünden." **Gespräch**, ibid., p. 197. Compare Melanchthon's words: "Alterum officium legis est ostendere peccatum, et terrere conscientias. . . . Docet [Paulus] legem ut plurimum efficiat, tantum terrere conscientias, et occidere." **Annotationes Phil. Melanchthonis in Epistolas Pauli ad Romanos et ad Corinthios, CR: Mel, XV**, p. 460. Hubmaier could also have read Luther's **In epistolam Pauli ad Galatas commentarius** of 1519, which contains similar statements about the preparatory role of the law. **WA, II**, pp. 500, 526-27.

Luther, in articles prepared for debate in 1520 and published in the 1521 **Disputatio de baptismate legis, Iohannis et Christi habita, WA, VI**, p. 473, distinguished **baptisma legis** (exteriorem operum sanctitatem), **baptisma Iohannis** (gratiae avidos facit), and **baptisma Christi** (novas creaturas facit), the latter two being described and distinguished very much as Hubmaier was to do.

145 Trans. Ford Lewis Battles, LCC: Reform, p. 298.

146 "Die Tauff ist eyn eusserlich zeychen odder lossung, . . . das wir dar bey erkennet werden eyn volck Christi unssers hertzogen." **WA, II,** p. 727.

147 **Ibid.,** p. 731.

148 "Das hilfft dir das hochwirdig sacrament der tauff, das sich gott daselbs mit dyr vorpindet und mit dyr eyns wird eyns gnedigen trostlichen bunds." **Ibid.,** p. 730. The Franciscan conception of the **pactio** in baptism was related to the spiritual action of the sacrament. In their view, the power of the sacraments resided in the divine **pactio** which was God's promise that the sacraments would always be accompanied by His redemptive action. For instance, Bonaventure said: "Causalitas sacramentorum non est aliud, quam quaedam efficax ordinatio ad recipiendam gratiam ex pactione divina." Quoted by Friedrich Loofs, **Leitfaden zum Studien der Dogmengeschichte** (6th rev. ed., edited by Kurt Aland; Tübingen: Max Niemeyer Verlag, 1955), p. 471.

149 **Taufe und Wiedertaufe, ZW, IV,** p. 231.

150 **Ibid.,** p. 218.

151 **Ibid.,** p. 231.

152 **Ibid.,** p. 218.

153 Hillerbrand, loc. cit., p. 73, n. 101, believes that Eberlin probably influenced Zwingli's view of the covenant. Eberlin, a sometime Franciscan friar and later popular pamphleteer of the early Reformation, published a series of writings in late 1522 or early 1523 under the suggestive title, **Bundesgenossen,** in which he charged the Christian patriots of Switzerland that the responsibilities involved in fulfilling their civic **Eid** and their baptismal **Bund** (Eberlin used the term **Eid**) were the same:

You are named Swiss (**schwitzer**) and your highest glory should be in the sweating (**schwitzen**) of blood in defense of the holy, evangelical law and in keeping its teachings. . . . You are ridiculed as **Eidgenossen,** but you should hold to the vow (aid) that you made to God in baptism and have often reaffirmed by receiving the second sacrament. Help us, that we may preserve the vow that we made with God upon His evangelical law, so that we will not be driven from Christian doctrine.

Bundsgenoss XIII, Johann Eberlin von Günzburg: Ausgewählte Schriften, Vol. I, ed. Ludwig Enders **(Flugschriften aus der Reformationszeit,** No. XI; Halle a. S.: Max Niemeyer, 1896), p. 150.

Similarly: "Was ist dann eerlicher, wann [sic] der ayd, den wir christen unserem göttlichen houptman christo im touff geschworen haben." **Ibid.,** p. 144.

Eberlin is cited by Hillerbrand, who in turn cites Carl Hinrichs, **Luther und Müntzer: Ihre Auseinandersetzung über Obrigkeit und Widerstandsrecht** (Arbeiten zur Kirchengeschichte, ed. Kurt Aland, et al., No. 29; Berlin: Walter de Gruyter & Co., 1952), pp. 21-22.

154 Above, p. 41.

155 **Gespräch, TA: HS,** p. 187.

156 **Ibid.,** pp. 187-188.

157 **Von der Taufe der Gläubigen,** ibid., p. 120.

158 **Ibid.,** p. 160. The metaphor, **Herzog,** is applied to Christ by Hubmaier in the context of the Lord's Supper, which, as a sign of one's pledge to aid his neighbor, derives from the principal vow to serve Christ. **Etliche Schlussreden vom Unterricht der Messe,** ibid., p. 102.

159 **Von der Taufe der Gläubigen,** ibid., p. 122.

160. **Ibid.**

161 Letter to Thomas Müntzer, Sept. 5, 1524, **TA: Zürich,** I, No. 14, p. 17; trans. Williams, **LCC: SAW,** p. 80.

162 **Eine kurze Entschuldigung, TA: HS,** p. 275. Luther says: "Also folget, das die tauff alle leyden und sonderlich den tod nutzlich und hulsslich macht, das sie

156 / Anabaptist Baptism

nur dienen mussen der tauffe werck, das ist, die sund zu todten." Sermon von der Taufe, WA, II, p. 734.

163 Ethelbert Stauffer, "Märtyrertheologie und Täuferbewegung," ZKG, 3rd Series, LII, No. 4 (1933), pp. 583-87.

164 Von der Taufe der Gläubingen, TA: HS, p. 145.

165 Ibid.

166 Ibid.

167 An den christlichen Adel deutscher Nation, WA, VI, p. 407.

168 "Dan was ausz der tauff krochen ist, das mag sich rumen, das es schon priester, Bischoff und Bapst geweyhet sey, ob wol nit einem yglichen zympt, solch ampt zu uben." Ibid., p. 408.

169 Alfred Farner, Die Lehre von Kirche und Staat bei Zwingli (Tübingen: Verlag von J. C. B. Mohr [Paul Siebeck], 1930), pp. 14-22.

170 Auslegung und Begründung der Schlussreden oder Artikel, Article XXXI, ZW, II, pp. 276-86.

171 Von der Taufe der Gläubigen, TA: HS, p. 145; Eine christliche Lehrtafel, ibid., p. 316; Von der brüderliche Strafe, ibid., p. 345.

172 Von der Freiheit des Willens, TA: HS, pp. 390-93.

173 Bergsten, op. cit., p. 380.

174 Farner, op. cit., pp. 4-5.

175 Taufe und Widertaufe, ZW, IV, p. 318.

176 Bergsten, op. cit., p. 381.

177 Eine christliche Lehrtafel, TA: HS, p. 316.

178 Von der Taufe der Gläubigen, ibid., p. 125.

179 Von dem christlichen Bann, ibid., p. 369.

180 Grund und Ursache, ibid., pp. 335-36.

181 "Darumb als vil dem mennschen an der verzeyhunng seyner sünden vnd gmainschafft der heiligen, ausserhalb wölher khayn hayl ist, gelegen, so vill solle im an dem Wassertauff gelegen sein, durch wölhen er eingeet vnd eingeleybet wird der allgmainen Christenlichen Kirchen." Eine christliche Lehrtafel, ibid., p. 315.

182 "Die selbigen waren nit mit Johannes tauff, sonder auff Johannis tauff geteüffet oder zü Johannis tauff. Dann im kriechischen stat es εἰς τὸ Ἰωάννου Βαπτίσμα dann sust hetten sye von Christo und seinem tauff, der durch den geist beschicht, mer wissens gehabt." Martin Bucers Deutsche Schriften, I, p. 255.

183 woryn (worein [in quid]), not worinn (in quo). Taufe und Wiedertaufe, ZW, IV, p. 271, n. 7.

184 Ibid., p. 267. Christ did not say " 'im namen des vatters und etc.,' als ob die wort die sünd abweschind; sunder das man die so man toufft, in den namen, das ist: gwalt, maiestet und ghorsame, des vatters und sons und heligen geists touffen sölle."

185 Von der Taufe der Gläubigen, TA: HS, p. 131.

186 Ibid., p. 132; Gespräch, ibid., p. 183. Zwingli, Taufe und Wiedertaufe, ZW, IV, p. 271, n. 11.

187 Von der Taufe der Glaübigen, TA: HS, pp. 132-33.

188 Trent stated: "Si quis dixerit, baptismum Ioannis habuisse eamdem vim cum baptismo Christi, aut Christianes non alio baptismo baptizari, quam illo Ioannis, quo et Christus baptizatus est: anathema sit." Council of Trent, Session VII, "Canones de sacramento baptismi," canon 1. Concilium Tridentium, Diariorum, Actorum, Epistularum, Tractatuum: Nova Collectio, ed. Societas Goerresiana (Freiburg i. B.: B. Herder Typographus, Editor Pontificius V, 1901-1938), V, p. 995. Also, see above, n. 139.

189 Von der Taufe der Gläubigen, TA: HS, p. 125.

190 Ibid., pp. 136, 150.

191 Ibid., p. 150; Gespräch, ibid., pp. 175-76; Grund und Ursache, ibid., p. 336.

192 Taufe und Wiedertaufe, ZW, IV, pp. 329-30. Gespräch, TA: HS, p. 180.

193 Matt. 19:14; Mark 10:14; Luke 18:16.

194 Staehelin, Briefe und Akten zum Leben Oekolampads, I, No. 238, p. 343.

195 Oecolampadius, Letter to Hubmaier, end of January (?), 1525, ibid., I, No. 243, p. 356. Zwingli, Letter to Francis Lambert, Dec. 16, 1524, ZW, VIII, No. 355, pp. 271-72. Bucer, Grund und Ursache, Martin Bucers Deutsche Schriften, I, pp. 259-60.

196 Von der Taufe der Gläubigen, TA: HS, p. 155.
On the interpretation by other Anabaptists, see Franklin Hamlin Littell, The Anabaptist View of the Church: A Study in the Origins of Sectarian Protestantism (2nd ed.; Boston: Starr King Press, 1958), p. 83, with notes.

197 Chapter iii of Von der Taufe der Gläubigen is devoted to John's baptism, chapter v to Christian baptism. TA: HS, pp. 127-34, 146-51.

198 Ibid., pp. 150-51.

199 Ibid., p. 151.

200 Gespräch, ibid., pp. 194-95.

201 Von der Taufe der Gläubigen, ibid., pp. 153-54; Gespräch, ibid., pp. 210-11.

202 Op. cit., pp. 33-38.

203 Op. cit., pp. 361-66.

204 Ibid., pp. 361-62. Hubmaier reproduced Oecolampadius' statement: Von der Kindertaufe, TA: HS, p. 261.

205 Ibid. The references are quoted in Urteil I, ibid., p. 230, and Urteil II, ibid., p. 244.

206 The references seem to be: (1) Commentaria in Epistolam ad Romanos (on Rom. 6:3, 4), Bk. V, chap. 8, MPG, Vol. XIV, col. 1037. (2) Homiliae in Lucam, XXII (on Luke 3:1-4), ibid., Vol. XIII, col. 1855. (3) Homiliae in Leviticum, VIII, chap. 3, ibid., Vol. XII, col. 496.

207 Joachim Jeremias has identified Origen's relevant statements on the problem. Infant Baptism in the First Four Centuries (trans. David Cairns; London: SCM Press Ltd., 1960), p. 65. The sentence Hubmaier takes from the Homiliae in Leviticum, loc. cit., is in the same paragraph with a text on infant baptism. Origen's statement that infant baptism was an apostolic practice is in the Commentaria in Epistolam ad Romanos, loc. cit., col. 1047.

208 Von der Taufe der Gläubigen, TA: HS, pp. 153-54; Urteil I, ibid., p. 232; Urteil II, ibid., p. 248.

209 Sachsse, op. cit., pp. 35-38, identified each of the canonical citations with one error which Bergsten corrects, op. cit., p. 364, n. 47. The citations include papal documents (Popes Siricius and Leo I, e.g.), conciliar decisions (Laodicea in 343 and 381, the Fifth Council of Carthage in 401, etc.), and extracts from the Fathers (Jerome and Augustine).

210 Von der Taufe der Gläubigen, TA: HS, p. 153.

211 Urteil I, ibid., p. 231; Urteil II, ibid., p. 244. De corona, chap. iii: MPL, Vol. II, cols. 78-80. Hubmaier also cites Tertullian's De poenitentia, chap. vi: Urteil I, p. 231.

212 Urteil I, TA: HS, p. 231; Urteil II, ibid., p. 246. Identified by Sachsse, op. cit., p. 36, n. 3, as Cyril of Jerusalem. Catechesis, XVII, "de Spiritu Sancto," II, xxxvi: MPG, Vol. XXXIII, cols. 1009/1010-1011/1012. Hubmaier's description of Cyril as "ein Bischof zu Basel" is obviously an error.

213 Urteil I, TA: HS, p. 232. Hubmaier mistakenly attributes the account to Eusebius; it is actually found in Rufinus, Historia ecclesiastica, Bk. 1, chap. xiv: MPL, Vol. XXI, cols. 487-88; and Sozomen, Historia ecclesiastica, Bk. II, chap. xvii: MPG, Vol. LXVII, cols. 977/978-979/980. Sachsse, op. cit., p. 36, n. 1.

214 Urteil I, TA: HS, pp. 230-31; Urteil II, ibid., p. 245. The reference to Athanasius is uncertain.

158 / Anabaptist Baptism

215 **Urteil I, TA: HS,** pp. 231-32; **Urteil II,** ibid., pp. 244, 246. Theophylact, **Enarratio in Evangelium Marci** (on Mark 16:16), chap. XVI, vss. 14-20: **MPG,** Vol. CXXIII, cols. 679/680. The reference to Ambrose (Ambrosiaster?) is uncertain.

216 **Urteil I, TA: HS,** pp. 230-31; **Urteil II,** ibid., p. 245. Jerome: "Primum docent omnes gentes, deinde doctas intingunt aqua. Non enim potest fieri ut corpus baptismi recipiat sacramentum, nisi ante anima fidei susceperit veritatem." **Commentarius in Evangelium secundum Matthaeum,** Bk. IV, chap. xxviii, vs. 19: MPL, Vol. XXVI, col. 226.

Basil, speaking of baptism as a **sigillum fidei,** said: "Nam credere prius oportet, deinde baptismate obsignari." **Adversus Eunomium,** Bk. III, chap. 5: **MPG,** Vol. XXIX, col. 665/666. Hubmaier erroneously spoke of Basil as the twenty-second pope. He also referred to Basil's **Homilia in sanctum baptisma,** chap. 6: **MPG,** Vol. XXXI, cols. 437/438.

217 **Urteil I, TA: HS,** p. 231; **Urteil II,** ibid., p. 246. The reference is uncertain, but Sachsse, op. cit., p. 36, n. 3, suggests **Catechesis,** III, "de baptismo," chap. VI: **MPG,** Vol. XXXIII, cols. 433-36.

218 **Urteil I, TA: HS,** p. 230; **Urteil II,** ibid., p. 247. **Homilia in Psalmum XXIX,** chap. 8 (on Psalm 29:10): **MPG,** Vol. XXIX, cols. 303-304.

219 **Gespräch, TA: HS,** p. 197. The references, not located by Sachsse or Bergsten, are as follows: Origen, **Commentaria in epistolam B. Pauli ad Romanis,** Bk. V, par. 8: **MPG,** Vol. XIV, col. 1039. Cyril of Alexandria, **Commentarius in Evangelium Joannis, MPG,** Vol. LXXIII, cols. 257/258-259/260. Jerome, **Commentarius in Evangelium S. Matthaei** (on Matt. 28:19), **MPL,** Vol. XXVI, cols. 226-27.

The references in Chrysostom are uncertain. He may be referring to the spurious, "so-called" **Opus imperfectum** which was highly valued in the late Middle Ages and published at Basel in 1530: **Homiliae in Matthaeum,** chap. III, vs. 11, **MPG,** Vol. LVI, col. 653. Or it may be the genuine **Homiliae in Matthaeum** (on Matt. 3:1, 2), **MPG,** Vol. LVII, col. 185.

Theophylact was taken by Hubmaier to be a second-century figure. Williams, **LCC: SAW,** p. 80, n. 25. The references are to **Enarratio in Evangelium Matthaei,** chap. III, vs. 11: **MPG,** Vol. CXXIII, cols. 28-30: ibid., cols. 1219/1220-1221/1222.

220 **Gespräch, TA: HS,** p. 202. **Commentaria in Evangelium secundum Matthaeum,** XV, 8 (on Matt. 19:14): **MPG,** Vol. XIII, cols. 1273/1274-1275/1276.

221 Article 11, **TA: HS,** p. 73.

222 Bergsten, op. cit., pp. 363-65.

223 **De baptismo,** chap. xvi. Translated in **ANF,** III, p. 677. Tertullian, recalling the statement of Jesus in Luke 12:50 about His baptism to come, understood the water and blood from Christ's wound to signify the baptisms of water and blood and interpreted Matt. 20:16 in those terms: "called by water and chosen by blood."

224 **Epistola ad Fortunatum de exhortatione martyrii,** MPL, Vol. IV, col. 654. Cyprian is thinking of it principally as a second baptism additional to water, not in lieu of water.

225 **In consolationem de obitu Valentiniani admonitio,** MPL, Vol. XVI, col. 1435.

226 The statement about "crying to God with Christ" actually refers to the baptism of the Spirit. The expression here is very similar to that in **Von der Freiheit des Willens** in which Hubmaier described the gift of the Spirit as following the believer's plea for it. "God gives power and capacity to all men insofar as they themselves desire it." Above, p. 33.

227 **Eine kurze Entschuldigung, TA: HS,** p. 275. Another statement on the three baptisms, stressing the role of the Trinity, reads: "Der Tauff ist ein offennliche zeügnuss des glaubens, die der getaufft selbs thüt vor der kirchen. Nit Gotten oder Gfatern. Darzü so het ein yeder glaubiger Mensch drey zeügen im himel, Vater, Son, vnnd heiligen geyst, in dero namen vnd krafft er sich inwendig an Gott ergeben vnd eüsserlich in ein new lebenn nach der Regel Christi zefieren verpflicht hat. Er hat auch drey

zeügen auff erden, Geist, wasser, vnd blüt. Der geyst fieret, das wasser macht den durchbruch, dz blüt ligt ob in der krafft Gottes vnd siget entlich." **Gespräch, ibid., p. 209.**

228 **Von der Taufe der Gläubigen,** ibid., p. 122.

229 **Eine christliche Lehrtafel,** ibid., p. 310.

230 **Eine kurze Entschuldigung,** ibid., p. 275.

231 **Eine christliche Lehrtafel,** ibid., p. 314. In speaking of baptism in terms of death and resurrection, Luther said: "Das sacrament nit allein bedeut den todt unnd auffersteeung am jungsten tag, . . . ssondern das es auch gewisslich dasselb anhebe und wirck und unss mit gott vorpyndet, das wir wollen biss ynn den tod die sund todten und widder sie streyten." **Ein Sermon von der Taufe,** WA, II, p. 732.

232 Kessler, **Sabbata** (St. Gallen: Herausgegeben von Emil Egli und Rudolf Shoch, 1902), p. 144.

233 Reported by Valerius Rüd (sometimes known as Anshelm), physician and city chronicler of Bern. Bergsten, op. cit., p. 309. Waldshut was accused by the Austrians in January, 1525, of having destroyed the baptismal font, but the Waldshutians denied it. Since infant baptisms were at that time still being performed by Hubmaier, it would seem that the accusation was unjustified. Cf. the document from Waldshut in Bergsten, ibid., pp. 511-12.

234 **Eine Form zu Taufen,** TA: HS, p. 348. The order, with introduction, occupies pp. 347-52 of TA: HS; an English translation is to be found as the appendix to the present work: cf. pp. 143-44.

235 Appendix, p. 143.

236 Ibid., pp. 143-44.

237 Ibid., p. 144.

238 **Eine Summe eines ganzen christlichen Lebens,** TA: HS, pp. 111-12; **Von der Taufe der Gläubigen,** ibid., p. 160.

239 **Gespräch,** ibid., p. 181.

240 **Eine Form zu Taufen,** ibid., p. 352.

241 **Ibid.**

242 On the question of Hubmaier's Zurich recantations, cf. Bergsten, op. cit., pp. 383-95.

243 Article 25, TA: HS, p. 487.

Chapter II. HANS HUT

1 ZHVSN: Hut, p. 223, Answer 5; p. 245, Answer 5. The radicals—a miller, a tailor, and a wool weaver—are unknown by name. Presumably they belonged to the growing circle of Karlstadt's disciples.

2 Not Bibra in electoral Saxony, northwest of Naumburg and near Allstedt, as Austin P. Evans said. **An Episode in the Struggle for Religious Freedom: The Sectaries of Nuremberg, 1524-1528** (New York: Columbia University Press, 1924), p. 35, n. 2. Bibra in Saxony would actually seem to fit the events of Hut's life better, since it is near Allstedt and Weissenfels, the former figuring in his associations with Müntzer, the latter in his hearing opinions against infant baptism. But in the Augsburg **Urteilsbrief** of Aug. 6, 1527, Hut's home is given explicitly as "Bibra im land zu Franken," which can only be the Bibra near the border of Franconia and Thuringia, and near the town of Meiningen in Thuringia. ZHVSN: Hut, p. 252. Wilhelm Neuser located it near Meiningen. **Hans Hut: Leben und Wirken** [sic] **bis zum Nikolsburger Religionsgespräch** (Berlin, 1913), p. 10, n. 21. He followed H. Hartmann, "Hut, Hans H.," **Allgemeine Deutsche Biographie,** XIII (1851), p. 459. Herbert Klassen, who followed Neuser, has Memmingen, perhaps by typographical error. "The Life and Teachings of Hans Hut," MQR, XXXIII (July and October, 1959), p. 178.

3 ZHVSN: Hut, p. 223.

4 Von dem geheimnus der tauf and Ein christlicher underricht, TA: Glaubenszeugnisse, I, pp. 10-37. Gordon Rupp, "Thomas Müntzer, Hans Huth and the 'Gospel of All Creatures,'" Bulletin of John Rylands Library, XLIII (March, 1961), pp. 492-519, has argued that the Geheimnus (as we shall hereafter call it) is either by Müntzer or is a revision by Hut of a tract by Müntzer. See below, pp. 64-75.

5 Rathsbüchlein, extracts from which are edited by Friedrich Roth, ZHVSN: Langenmantel, pp. 38-40.

6 Ein sendbrief Hans Huthen, ed. Müller, TA: Glaubenszeugnisse, I, p. 12 (a portion of the letter is omitted). Rupp, loc cit., p. 498, n. 6, believes that the second letter in Urbanus Rhegius, Zwen Wunderseltsamen Sendbrieff an die Boten gen Augsburg gesandt (Augsburg, 1528), may be by Hut.

7 ZHVSN: Hut, pp. 220-53; TA: Bayern, I, pp. 41-44. The Bonn University dissertation by Wilhelm Neuser—only a portion of the work he originally planned—contains an extensive catalog of the extant manuscript and archival material relevant to Hut and provides the most detailed account available of his life through the Nicolsburg Disputation. "Hans Hut: Leben und Wirken [sic] bis zum Nikolsburger Religionsgespräch" (unpublished dissertation for the Licentiate in Theology, University of Bonn, 1913). The printed form of the dissertation (above, n. 2) contains only two of the five chapters of the original manuscript and omits most of the history. We are indebted to the Mennonite Historical Library, Goshen College, for the use of their specially prepared copy of the manuscript. The manuscript edition will hereafter be identified as MS.

8 Loc. cit. Walter Klaassen has also examined the influence of Müntzer on Hut and concluded that Hut's views of the "creatures," the cross, and Scripture were all derived from Müntzer, who in turn had adapted them from medieval mysticism. "Hans Hut and Thomas Muntzer," The Baptist Quarterly, XIX, No. 5, (Jan., 1962), pp. 209-27.

9 Heinrich Böhmer and Paul Kirn, Thomas Müntzers Briefwechsel (Leipzig: Verlag und Druck von B. G. Teubner, 1931), Anhang 4, pp. 135-38.

10 Ibid., Anhang 6, pp. 149, 157.

11 Annemarie Lohmann, Zur geistigen Entwicklung Thomas Müntzers (Beiträge zur Kulturgeschichte des Mittelalters und der Renaissance, ed. Walter Goetz, Vol. XLVII; Leipzig: Verlag und Druck von B. G. Teubner, 1931), p. 17.

12 Edited in modern German by Otto Brandt, Thomas Müntzer: Sein Leben und seine Schriften (Jena: Eugen Diederichs Verlag, 1933), pp. 133-44.

13 Ibid., p. 135.

14 Ibid., pp. 134-35.

15 Both Denck and Hut followed Müntzer in the view that contrary texts would yield the truth when compared, and all three agreed that only persons with the Key of David could correctly make this necessary comparison. The collection of such texts in Hut's Ein christlicher underricht (TA: Glaubenszeugnisse, I, pp. 29-31) contains thirty-nine of the forty references found in Denck's Wer die Wahrheit warlich Lieb hat. TA: Denck, Part II, pp. 67-74. Cf. Claude R. Foster, Jr., "Hans Denck and Johannes Buenderlin: A Comparative Study," MQR, XXXIX (1965), p. 117.

16 Protestation, Brandt, op. cit., pp. 134-35.

17 Isa. 44:3.

18 John 1:32.

19 John 2:7-9.

20 John 3:23.

21 John 4:14.

22 John 5:7.

23 John 6:19.

24 Protestation, loc. cit. This dialectical quality of Müntzer's idea of "spirit" has been well described by Thomas Nipperdey, "Theologie und Revolution bei Thomas

Müntzer," **ARG, LIV** (1963), p. 154. Nipperdey says that **Geist** for Müntzer is not just a substance given to man, but the way in which God meets man existentially. The term thus refers to a quality of religious experience and as such is dialectical, human and divine.

25 **Ausgedrückte Entblössung**, Brandt, op. cit., p. 167; Carl Hinrichs, **Thomas Müntzer: Politische Schriften mit Kommentar (Hallische Monographien,** ed. Otto Eissfeldt, No. 17; Halle, [Saale]: Max Niemeyer Verlag, 1950), p. 34.

26 Ibid., Brandt, pp. 166, 181; Hinrichs, pp. 33, 50.

27 George Huntston Williams, **Wilderness and Paradise in Christian Thought: The Biblical Experience of the Desert in the History of Christianity and the Paradise Theme in the Theological Idea of the University** (New York: Harper and Brothers, 1962), p. 53. For Eckhardt's statements, see Meister Eckhart: A Modern Translation, trans. Raymond Bernard Blakney (New York: Harper and Brothers, 1941), pp. 64, 115, 120.

28 **Von dem gedichteten Glauben,** Brandt, op. cit., p. 129. **Ausgedrückte Entblössung,** ibid., pp. 178, 181; Hinrichs, op. cit., pp. 47, 50. The phrase "die Wasser göttlicher Weisheit" is from Ecclesiasticus of Ben Sirach 15:3, which speaks of the man who masters the law as being given "the water of wisdom to drink."

29 Psalm 93:3, 4; 69:2. **Ausgedrückte Entblössung,** Brandt, op. cit., p. 165; Hinrichs, op. cit., p. 32.

30 Again, the quality of regeneration as an inner renewal and transformation is stressed. Müntzer felt that Luther and his followers lost this in the discussion of imputed righteousness. Nipperdey, loc. cit., pp. 158-70, has an excellent discussion of Müntzer on this point.

31 **Ausgedrücke Entblössung,** Brandt, op. cit., p. 186; Hinrichs, op. cit., p. 55.

32 **Protestation,** Brandt, op. cit., p. 135.

33 Above, pp. 41, 155 n. 153.

34 Carl Hinrichs, **Luther und Müntzer: Ihre Auseinandersetzung über Obrigkeit und Widerstandsrecht** (Arbeiten zur Kirchengeschichte, XXIX; Berlin: Walter de Gruyter & Co., 1952), p. 19. Compare a statement by Eberlin: "Was ist eerlicher vnd nötiger dann die sach, vmb der wir geschworen haben, das ist trew willfarung vnserem got, zu beschützen vnd behalten sein ewangelisch gesatz, vnd abgesage find sein des teüfels vnd aller siner gespänsten." **Bundsgenoss** XIII, loc. cit., p. 144.

35 The **Bürger** would own the town oath on at least three occasions: (1) when he became of age, usually at fifteen or sixteen; (2) when he moved to a new town and would have to pledge to take up work and to abide by the laws of the town; and (3) at the election of a new **Bürgermeister,** or perhaps annually even without such an election. Hans Planitz, **Die deutsche Stadt im Mittelalter** (Graz-Köln: Böhlau-Verlag, 1954), pp. 253-54.

36 Hinrichs, **Luther und Müntzer,** p. 19. The leaders of John Ziska's Taborite army entered their covenant in the same way, inscribing their names in the **Military Ordinance,** listing them in this case by social rank. Frederick G. Heymann, **John Ziska and the Hussite Revolution** (Princeton: Princeton University Press, 1955), pp. 374-76, 380-81.

Whether Müntzer employed the more dramatic military oath of raising weapons into the air, as Heinrich Pfeiffer once did, is uncertain. The Mühlhausen chronicle describes how Pfeiffer's hearers did this in response to his plea to the peasants there on April 1, 1523. The account records his question and their response: " 'Wer bei dem Evangelium stehen will, der recke einen Finger aufl' Da reckten alle zugleiche, Mann und Weib, jung und alt, den Finger auf und holten ihre Wehr." Alfred Meusel, **Thomas Müntzer und seine Zeit** (Berlin: Aufbau-Verlag, 1952), pp. 244-45. Bernard Rothmann and Pilgram Marpeck (reproducing Rothmann's text) spoke of the same military oath of the upraised finger or hand as an example of one meaning (that of "oath") which the word "sacrament" has. Rothmann, **Bekenntnisse van beyden Sacramenten,** ed.

162 / Anabaptist Baptism

Heinrich Detmer and Robert Krumbholtz, Zwei Schriften des Münsterschen Wiedertäufers Bernhard Rothmann (Dortmund: Druck und Verlag von Fr. Wilh. Ruhfus, 1904), p. 3. Marpeck, Vermanung, ed. Christian Hege in Gedenkschrift zum 400 Jährigen Jubliäum der Mennoniten oder Taufgesinnten: 1525-1925 (Ludwigshafen a. Rh.: Herausgegeben von der Konferenz der Süddeutschen Mennoniten E. V., 1925), p. 190.

Lowell Zuck has overstressed Müntzer's aversion to external ceremonies and thus overlooked the external owning of the covenant, but he is right in arguing that Müntzer did not adopt believer's baptism as the sign of the covenant. "Anabaptist Revolution through the Covenant in Sixteenth Century Continental Protestantism" (unpublished Ph.D. thesis, Yale University, 1954), pp. 93-96; "Fecund Problems of Eschatological Hope, Election Proof, and Social Revolt in Thomas Müntzer," Reformation Studies: Essays in Honor of Roland H. Bainton, ed. Franklin H. Littell (Richmond: John Knox Press, 1962), pp. 244-46.

37 Müntzer's Allstedt liturgy of 1523 contained a section on baptism which was essentially on continuation of Catholic infant baptism. It contains no elements peculiar to Müntzer. Ordnung und berechnunge des teutschen ampts zu Alstadt durch Tomam Müntzer, ed. Emil Sehling, Die Evangelischen Kirchenordnungen des XVI. Jahrhunderts (Leipzig: O. R. Reisland), I/1 (1902), p. 507. The theme of the covenant is mentioned several times in Müntzer's liturgies, usually in terms of the covenant created among the Lord's elect, often a covenant which places them in conflict with the godless. References to the covenant are found in the Sehling volume, pp. 472, 474, 479, 485, 487, 500, 501.

38 "Seht doch, allerliebsten, wehr es nit besser, das die tauf des jars zwier mit solcher andacht des volks gehalten wurde und den kindern also uberreicht, das sie ein frisch gedechtnuss alle yr lebenlank dran hetten, wie sie sie entpfangen hetten?" Appendix of letter to Allstedt, after Aug. 15, 1924, Müntzers Briefwechsel, No. 72, p. 106. The inner Word springs to life when one is six or seven: "Diese verwunderung ob es gotis wort sey oder nit hebet sich on wann eyner ein kint ist von 6. oder 7. iaren wie figurirt ist Num. am. 19." Die Fürstenpredigt, ed. Hinrichs, Müntzer: Politische Schriften, pp. 15-16. The chapter in Numbers describes how those rendered unclean by touching sacrifices or the dead are to cleanse themselves in water on the third and seventh day. Müntzer elsewhere speaks of this sprinkling on the third day as the beginning of the work of the Spirit of fear. Anschlag zu Prag, Müntzers Briefwechsel, Anhang 6, p. 146. This is when the Vernunft begins to emerge. Ibid., p. 140. It reaches fulfillment only at six or seven. Hinrichs, loc. cit., note to line 247, observes that Canon Law located the emergence of reason in the seventh year, as did the Schmalkald Articles. Hubmaier said that the human will arose in the seventh year and that baptism could be given then. Above, p. 55.

39 Müntzers Briefwechsel, No. 59, p. 76.

40 "Nu ist keyn kurtzer weyss oder weg, dann durch die tauff und tauffen werck, das ist leyden und sterben." Ein Sermon von dem heiligen hochwürdigen Sakrament der Taufe, WA, I, p. 734.

41 Described by Fritz Blanke, Brüder in Christo, pp. 10-11. Cf. Hans J. Hillerbrand, "The Origin of Sixteenth Century Anabaptism: Another Look," loc. cit., p. 174, n. 107.

42 Behind the earlier and later programs of radical reform lay two different views of the relation of the church to society. According to the first view, church and society were to be interrelated in a "Christian" society; in the second, they were to be separate and the church would be the "elect" called out of the world. According to the first view, reform would be needed whenever the leaders of society became corrupt and godless, and thus open revolution became a real possibility. The Müntzerite movement and the Hofmannite movement as led by Bernard Rothmann both tended in this direction. According to the second, there could be no revolution, only the restitution of the true church separate from the structures of civil power. Evangelical Anabaptism took this path. The difference in the two types is well seen in Müntzer's

socio-military covenant on the one hand and the Anabaptist baptismal covenant on the other. On the general problem of these two approaches to church and society, cf. Hans J. Hillerbrand, **Die politische Ethik des oberdeutschen Täufertums: Eine Untersuchung zur Religions- und Geistesgeschichte des Reformationszeitalters (Beihefte der Zeitschrift für Religions- und Geistesgeschichte, VII: Leiden-Köln: E. J. Brill, 1962)**, pp. 7-14, 60-69. Also, cf. Hillerbrand's article, loc. cit., pp. 173-75.

43 Walter Fellmann, "Das Leben Dencks," **TA: Denck**, Part II, p. 10.

44 Hut testified that he had stayed with Denck. **ZHVSN: Hut**, p. 224, Answers 4, 7; p. 229, Answers 3, 4. Fellmann has located twenty-two passages in Denck which indicate knowledge of Müntzer. Nine of these are references to the **Ausgedrückte Entblössung** which Hut seems to have had printed in Nürnberg at Müntzer's request. **TA: Denck**, Part II, pp. 21, 44, 59, 68, 92, 97, 106.

The possibility of Müntzer's influence is recognized by Robert Friedmann, who denies that Müntzer was a direct influence on the Anabaptist movement but admits the possibility of an indirect influence. "Thomas Muentzer's Relation to Anabaptism," MQR, XXXI (1957), p. 81.

45 **Bekenntnis für den Rat zu Nürnberg, TA: Denck**, Part II, pp. 23-24.

46 Psalm 69:2: "I sink in deep mire, where there is no foothold; I have come into deep waters, and the flood sweeps over me." Denck, ibid., p. 24. Müntzer, **Ausgedrückte Entblössung**, Brandt, op. cit., p. 165; Hinrichs, **Müntzer: Politische Schriften**, p. 32.

47 Denck, loc. cit. Müntzer, loc. cit.

48 See below, p. 118, with notes.

49 Denck, loc. cit. He quotes Mark 16:16: "He who believes and is baptized will be saved"; but he understood this saving baptism to be the inner baptism in the Spirit. Like Hubmaier, Denck understood man's response of faith to be prior to the regenerative action of the Spirit.

50 Ibid., pp. 80-81. Fellmann, ibid., p. 81, n. 2, and Williams, **The Radical Reformation**, p. 161, believe that this was probably the first such use of the term, **Bundzeichen.**

51 Hubmaier, using either the Vulgate rendering, docete, or a German translation, quoted the verb as leerent. **TA: HS**, p. 146. Denck, from his knowledge of Greek, translated $\mu\alpha\theta\eta\tau\epsilon\upsilon\sigma\alpha\tau\epsilon$ literally—macht zu jungern— and noted in his debate with Johannes Bader that this is the meaning of the Greek word. **TA: Denck**, Part III, p. 101. Zwingli did the same in his **Von der Taufe, von der Wiedertaufe und Von der Kindertaufe**, though with a different interpretation. Above, p. 28.

52 **Von der wahren Liebe, TA: Denck**, Part II, p. 83.

53 Ibid., p. 109.

54 **Hans Dencks Niederschrift über die Taufe für Johannes Bader**, ibid., Part III, p. 107.

55 Fellmann, "Das Leben Dencks," ibid., Part II, p. 12.

56 **ZHVSN: Hut**, p. 223.

57 Loc. cit. Walter Klaassen, in his recent article on Hut and Müntzer, has said that Rupp has now retracted his view that the **Geheimnus** was originally Müntzer's work. Loc. cit., p. 212. Whether Klaassen had this particular article of Rupp's in mind or not is unclear, for the statement is undocumented and his article contains no reference to Rupp's own article. However, in a letter to the present writer, Professor Rupp affirmed that Klaassen is in error; he still believes the tract originated with Müntzer.

58 Loc. cit., p. 503.

59 Müller, **Der Kommunismus der mährischen Wiedertäufer (Schriften des Vereins für Reformationsgeschichte**, Vol. CXLII; Leipzig: M. Heinsius Nachfolger, Eger und Sievers, 1927), pp. 74-75, after listing many of the terms common to both, observed that the tract seems almost to be one by Müntzer: "Sein Name ist nicht genannt. Er kann aber weder Latein noch Griechisch gekonnt haben, sonst könnte man fast meinen, eine unbekannte Schrift von Müntzer selbst vor sich zu haben." P. 74, n. 1.

Mecenseffy, "Die Herkunft des oberösterreichischen Täufertums," ARG, XLVII, No. 2 (1956), pp. 252-58. The article contends that Hut and his disciples lived in a thought world which derived principally from Thomas Müntzer and his type of spiritualism. It was a reply to Harold Bender, "Die Zwickauer Propheten, Thomas Müntzer und die Täufer," Theologische Zeitschrift, VIII (July-August, 1952), pp. 262-78, who claimed that the Anabaptists, including Hans Hut, were largely independent of Müntzer.

60 Loc. cit., pp. 504-5.

61 Ein anfang eines rechten warhaftigen christlichen lebens, TA: Glaubenszeugnisse, I, p. 12. Compare Müntzer's subtitle to the Protestation oder Entbietung: Zum Anfang von dem rechten Christenglauben und der Taufe, Brandt, op. cit., p. 133.

62 Rupp, loc. cit., pp. 505-6.

63 That is, both law and Gospel contain "Gospel." Hoch verursachte Schutzrede, ed. Brandt, op. cit., p. 189. Two other passages in Müntzer mention the idea. The first is found in the Anschlag zu Prag (all four versions) in the midst of a complaint against the religious leaders of the time. In the longer German version he charges that he has not heard the least word from the "donkey-pulling doctors" about the "ordnunge (in got und alle creaturen gesatzt)." Müntzers Briefwechsel, Anhang 6, p. 143. Ibid., pp. 140, 151, 155 for the shorter German, Czech, and Latin versions. The other passage is in Müntzer's undated letter to Jeori in which he says that the way of redemption through inner purgation is revealed by God "durch dye ordenung yn [Gott] und yn alle creaturn gesatzt." Ibid., No. 61, p. 79.

On Müntzer's view that the law contains grace, cf. Nipperdey, loc. cit., pp. 171-72.

64 TA: Glaubenszeugnisse, I, p. 17.

65 Geheimnus, ibid., pp. 17, 21-22, 26. Müntzer, Protestation, Brandt, op. cit., pp. 133-36.

66 Rupp, loc. cit., p. 506; Geheimnus, loc. cit., pp. 21, 24, 26, 28; Protestation, loc. cit., pp. 134-35.

67 Geheimnus, loc. cit., p. 25: "Die wasser, die in die seel dringen seind anfechtung, betrüebnus, angst, zitteren und komernus, also ist tauf leiden." Müntzer: "Die Wasser sind Bewegung unsres Geistes in dem Gottes. . . . Unsere Bewegungen werden lustig zu leiden." Protestation, loc. cit., p. 135.

68 Geheimnus, loc. cit., p. 23; Müntzer, loc. cit.

69 The Geheimnus summarizes its natural Christian theology in this way: "Im evangelion aller creatur wirt nichtz anderst anzaigt und gepredigt, dan allein Christus der gekreuzigete, aber nit allein Christus das haubt, sondern der ganz Christus mit allen glidmassen, disen Christum predigen und lernen alle creaturen." Loc. cit., p. 16.

70 Emile Male, The Gothic Image: Religious Art in France of the Thirteenth Century (New York: Harper Torchbooks, Harper & Brothers Publishers, 1958), pp. 27-63.

71 Walter Klaassen, loc. cit., pp. 213-14.

72 "Item primus liber sacer naturae non possit falsificari nec deleri, necque false interpretari, ideo heretici non possunt eum false intelligere, nec aliquis possit in eo fieri hereticus. Sed secundus possit falsificari et false interpretari et male intelligi." Theologia naturalis sive liber creaturarum ([Impressus Argentine per Martinum Flach, 1496]), Prologus, fol. A verso, col. 2. (Copy at Andover-Harvard Theological Library.)

73 Geheimnus, loc. cit., pp. 18-19.

74 Loc. cit., col. 1.

75 "Liber creaturarum debet primo sciri, antequam homo veniat at librum sacrae scripturae . . . et ideo liber creaturarum est porta, via, janua, introductorium et lumen quoddam ad librum sacrae scripturae." Op. cit., Tit. CCXI, fol. N 4, col. 2; Rupp, loc. cit., pp. 509-10.

76 Rupp, ibid., pp. 494-95.

Footnotes / 165

77 Raymond, op. cit., Tit. CCX, fol. N 2 verso, col. 2; Geheimnus, loc. cit., pp.16-19. Rupp, loc. cit., pp. 509-10.

78 Raymond, op. cit., Tit. XCIX, fol. E [6], col. 2: "Sic ergo creaturae ligantur cum homine, quia sunt propter hominem, et exinde homo ligatur cum Deo per talem obligationem." Also, Tit. CXVII, fol. G 2 verso, col. 2 through fol. G 3, col. 1. Geheimnus, loc. cit., pp. 17-18. Rupp, loc. cit., pp. 510-11. And both speak of the relation of the parts to the whole: the creatures are only parts of reality, always to be referred back to God, the Whole, in relation to whom alone they are understood. Ibid., pp. 496, 513, n. 2.

79 Brandt, op. cit., p. 126.

80 Not mentioned by Rupp. The statement reads: "Wye euch dye creaturn, also solt yr got untertanig seyn." Letter to Christoph Meinhard, Müntzers Briefwechsel, No. 47, pp. 53-54.

81 Rupp, loc. cit., pp. 503-4, 511.

82 Pp. 72-73.

83 Rupp, loc. cit., pp. 493-94.

84 Ibid., p. 508. The Geheimnus reads: "Da wirt der mensch in der langen weil seiner zeit, in der erduldung Gottes hand ein fertig und beraiter stuel und wonung Gottes." Loc. cit., p. 25. Müntzer's liturgy reads: "Darumb das du ein unwandelbar got bist/ Hast du den auserwelten gemacht zu deinem stule" (Psalm 93:2): and, "Do siht der mensch das er ein wonung gottis/ Sei in der lankweil seinen tage" (Psalm 93:5). Quoted in Rupp, loc. cit.

85 Georg Baring, "Hans Denck and Thomas Müntzer in Nürnberg, 1524," ARG, L (1959), p. 150.

86 Loc. cit., p. 508.

87 Again confirmed by F. W. Ratcliffe as unusual in late medieval Bibles. Ibid., p. 504.

88 Das Evangelion aller Kreatur may be read as either genitive or dative singular, of course. As a dative, it was the translation of Mark 16:15 adopted by Luther following the Greek, $τὸ$ $εὐαγγέλιον$ $πάσῃ$ $κτίσει$, and the Vulgate euangelium omni creaturae. Neither of the latter could be confused with the genitive singular, $τὸ$ $εὐαγγέλιον$ $πάσης$ $τῆς$ $κτίσεως$, and euangelium omnis creaturae.

89 "Das evangelion, das euch gepredigt ist, in allen creaturen." TA: Glaubenszeugnisse, I, p. 16. The RSV, following the Greek, $τοῦ$ $εὐαγγελίου$ $···$ $τοῦ$ $κηρυχθέντος$ $ἐν$ $πάσῃ$ $κτίσει$, reads, "the gospel ... which has been preached to every creature."

90 "Dz evangelion den Creaturen gepredigt werd als hunden und katzen. . . ." Loc. cit.

91 Ibid.

92 By modern scholarship: Neuser, op. cit. (MS), p. 9; Müller, TA: Glaubenszeugnisse, I, pp. 11-12, et al. The principal extant manuscript, Codex Ab 6 at the University Library, Budapest, names no author. The now well-known Kunstbuch in the Bern Bürgerbibliothek also has a copy of the tract, but it lacks the last section, "Nun volget das wesen des warhaftigen taufs." It also names no author. The Kunstbuch form of the tract bears the title, Ein Anfang eins rechten christlichen Lebens, which is also the subtitle of the Budapest version. Robert Friedmann, in his very helpful correspondence with the present writer on the problem, has said that his catalog of Hutterite codices lists no other copies of the tract.

Neuser, op. cit. (MS), p. 8, lists an Augsburg Stadtarchiv manuscript: Vom Geheimnus des Tauffs (das sogenannte Büchlein mit den siben sigeln). This was published by Roth in ZHVSN: Langenmantel, p. 40. It is not the baptismal tract but another piece evidently taken from Hut's concordance of Scriptural texts on the Last Day. See below, p. 89.

93 TA: Glaubenszeugnisse, I, p. 33.

166 / Anabaptist Baptism

94 **TA: Bayern,** I, p. 35. Spittelmaier said that Hut told him, "wie alle unvernünftige tier vil von des menschen wegen, ehe si dem menschen nutz werden, leiden müssen; dergleichen hab Cristus vil von des menschen wegen gelitten; und mit solchem und dergleichen fürhalten hab er inen zu der widertauf bewegt; und wie die creaturn von der menschen wegen leiden, also müssen die menschen von gotlichs worts wegen auch vil leiden." Also, **ibid.,** p. 48: "So es ainer begert, solchs zu wissen, den so zaigen wir im den willen gottes klärlich an durch alle creatur ainen jedlichem, darnach er ein hantwerk kan, durch seinem werkzeug . . . wie den Cristus geleret hat, das er durch sein hantwerk als durch ein puch, das im got geben hat seinen willen zu lernen, also auch ainem weib durch iren flags, den si spinnt, oder ander arbeit im haus, die si täglich im prauch hat."

See also statements in Wappler, **TA: Thüringen:** Martin Weischenfelder, pp. 237, 242; Veit Weischenfelder, p. 241; an account from the Bishop of Bamberg, p. 247.

Herbert Klassen considered Hut to be the creator of the theology of the creatures of the **Geheimnus** and said that neither Müntzer nor Denck used the term in the same way. From Hut it then spread to Spittelmaier, Schlaffer, Schiemer, and Marpeck. "Ambrosius Spittelmayr: His Life and Teachings," **MQR,** XXXII (Oct., 1958), p. 262, n. 70.

95 Rupp, **loc. cit.,** p. 506, n. 1. Our search through the Müntzer **corpus** (tracts and letters) has failed to uncover the term. The word occurs at least nine times in the Geheimnus, **TA: Glaubenszeugnisse,** I (once on p. 14, five times on p. 20 [in the section on the baptismal covenant], once on p. 25, and twice on p. 26); and at least twice in other known Hut material (once in reference to the inner covenant of Spirit baptism in his Augsburg testimony [**TA: Bayern,** I, p. 43] and once with the general meaning of the Anabaptist covenant [**Ein sendbrief Hans Huthen, TA: Glaubenszeugnisse,** I, p. 12]).

96 **Loc. cit.,** p. 20.

97 **TA: Bayern,** I, p. 43, Answer 13; also a similar statement in **ZHVSN: Hut,** p. 227, Answer 55.

98 **TA: Bayern,** I, p. 43, Answer 14; **ZHVSN: Hut,** p. 227, Answer 55. Other references to the covenant are in **TA: Bayern,** I, p. 42, Answer 9, and **ZHVSN: Hut,** p. 230, Answer 13.

99 Denck spoke of the **Bund** but without explicitly applying it to ecclesiology; Hubmaier had a covenantal ecclesiology in principle but without the term **Bund.**

100 **Geheimnus, loc. cit.,** p. 15.

101 "Sie sprechen mit blossen worten, wer do gleubet und ist getauft, der wird selig. Eyne solche gruntfeste rechenschaft geben sie den widdersachern und keine andere. . . . Man soll eine solche rechenschaft mit lumpen ausswerfen, und solte mit solchen ausredenern in abgrund der helle gestossen werden." **Müntzers Briefwechsel, Anhang** 6, p. 149.

102 **ZHVSN: Hut,** p. 223, Answer 6; also, p. 245, Answer 6, and **TA: Bayern,** I, p. 42, Answer 12.

103 **Loc. cit.,** p. 15.

104 **Loc. cit.,** pp. 19-20.

105 Denck had already begun this synthesis, of course. He understood baptism as the descent of the Spirit into the **abgrundt** of the soul, and as a personal dedication to the Christian life. **Bekenntnis, TA: Denck,** Part II, pp. 23-24. However, he lacked Müntzer's heavy emphasis on the suffering and anguish of the experience. Baring, **loc. cit.,** p. 174.

106 Rupp, above, p. 67; Müller, above, n. 59.

107 **ZHVSN: Hut,** p. 223, Answer 4; pp. 249-50.

108 **Ibid.,** p. 224, Answer 7.

109 **Anschlag zu Prag, Müntzers Briefwechsel, Anhang** 6, pp. 149, 157.

110 His litany for Easter in the Allstedt **Deutsch kirchen ampt** translated Psalm 2:3

to say that the kings of the earth have united and said: "Wir wöllen zurbrechen ire bund." (Boldface ours.) Ed. Sehling, op. cit., I/1, 487. A notable translation for more than one reason!

111 Loc. cit., p. 511, n. 2.

112 See the Latin form of the Anschlag zu Prag, Müntzers Briefwechsel, Anhang 6, pp. 154-59.

113 As noted above (n. 92), the extant manuscript copies of the Geheimnus name no author. A microfilm copy of the principal edition of the tract—the Budapest manuscript used by Müller in TA: Glaubenszeugnisse—reveals that no author's name is given. A later hand has added in the margin: "Hut? Schlaffer? 1527?" Nothing further is said. Robert Friedmann, who has seen the Budapest codex, informs the present writer that the Register in the front of the volume is also silent as to authorship. Müller did not report this in her published edition of the tract, but in her earlier Kommunismus der mährischen Wiedertäufer she did say of the author: "Sein Name ist nicht genannt." P. 74, n. 1. Contemporary treatments, following Neuser, op. cit. (MS), p. 8, and Müller, TA: Glaubenszeugnisse, I, pp. 11-12, have assumed Hut's authorship without question until Rupp introduced the question of Müntzer.

114 A comparison would have to include the following works, all of which contain the Geheimnus themes at one point or another, but in general assume the synthesis made in it rather than contribute to creating that synthesis. Leonhard Schiemer, Von dreyerley Tauf im Neuen Testament, TA: Glaubenszeugnisse, I, pp. 77-79; Hans Schlaffer, Ein kurzer Underricht, ibid., pp. 84-94, Ein kurzer bericht und leer eines recht christlichen lebens, ibid., pp. 94-96; Kurtze und ainfältige vermanung vom kindertauf, ibid., pp. 98-105; Die fünf artikel, ibid., p. 238.

115 Spittelmaier, above, n. 94; the Weischenfelders, TA: Thüringen, pp. 237, 241-42. Later influences of Hut's view are well seen in Mecenseffy's comparison of the Geheimnus, Schlaffer's Ein kurzer bericht und leer (loc. cit.), and the confession of the Freistadt Anabaptists (recently edited by Mecenseffy, TA: Oesterreich, I, pp. 21-24). "Die Herkunft des oberösterreichischen Täufertums," loc. cit., pp. 256-57.

116 TA: Thüringen, p. 237. One wonders whether the little book from which Hut read to Weischenfelder was the Geheimnus. He said that Hut "hab ime in einem puchlein etlich capitel gelesen." He then proceeded to describe the content of Hut's teaching, but he did not explicitly connect the teaching with the book. Ibid. Later, ibid., p. 242, he said that Hut read to him from the New Testament. This statement is also in the context of discussing Hut's ideas of the creatures and of baptism. Thus it may have been the New Testament to which Weischenfelder referred in the first instance.

117 Loc. cit., p. 511.

118 Lohmann, op. cit., pp. 48-49; Williams, The Radical Reformation, pp. 153-54, 304-6; Grete Mecenseffy, loc. cit., p. 285. Similarly, but without an explicit statement of this view, Grete Mecenseffy, "Das Verständnis der Taufe bei den Süddeutschen Täufern," Antwort: Karl Barth, zum siebzigsten Geburtstag (Zollikon-Zürich: Evangelischer Verlag Ag., 1956), pp. 642-46.

Chapter III. HANS HUT'S BAPTISMAL THEOLOGY

1 TA: Glaubenszeugnisse, I, p. 20.

2 Hubmaier spoke of the two keys which Christ gave to the church. The first is the power of the Holy Spirit, the power which looses from sin. The second is the power of the ban, which excludes the offender from the church, binding him within his unrepentant spirit. Von dem christlichen Bann, TA: HS, 369-70.

3 "Verbally": mit worten: i.e., not with the restraint of the civil sword. ZHVSN: Hut, p. 227, Answer 58. Similarly, TA: Bayern, I, p. 43, Answer 14.

4 TA: Bayern, I, p. 42, Answer 9; ZHVSN: Hut, p. 230, Answer 13.

5 Mark 10:38, 39.

6 TA: Bayern, I, p. 43, Answer 13; ZHVSN: Hut, p. 227, Answer 55.

7 Geheimnus, TA: Glaubenszeugnisse, I, pp. 21-22.

8 TA: Bayern, I, loc. cit.; ZHVSN: Hut, loc. cit.

9 Hut's term **Wesen** will ordinarily be translated "essence"; in Marpeck, where the term has a different signification, it will be translated "reality."

10 **TA: Glaubenszeugnisse**, I, p. 28. Denck speaks of God's gerechtigkeyt, barmhertzigkeyt, and almechtigkeyt but without identifying the qualities with the member of the Trinity. **Der Prophet Micha, Deutsch und Ausgelegt, TA: Denck, Part III,** p. 48. Although the work was not published until 1532, Denck composed it probably during his stay in Worms in 1527. Fellmann, ibid., p. 7. It would thus be an open question as to who depended upon whom. The idea plays a minor role in Denck's commentary and a major one in Hut's **Underricht.** Cf. further, Claude R. Foster, Jr., loc. cit., pp. 116-18.

11 **Ibid.**, pp. 32-33. Leonhard Schiemer developed a similar view in his **Das dreierlei gnad, ibid.,** pp. 60-65. Man receives a "first grace" from God, Schiemer says, which is "the light that enlighteneth every man." This reveals the Creator and His law. But not all use this grace wisely: some quench the light with works of the flesh; others follow as far as the cross and then fall away; yet others embrace it, accepting the cross and resisting evil wholeheartedly, thereby receiving "grace in addition to grace."

12 This differs from the **Geheimnus,** of course, which in good Müntzerian fashion locates the Gospel of all creatures in the first level. This difference between the **Geheimnus** and **Ein christlicher underricht** supports the arguments presented above regarding Müntzer's influence on the **Geheimnus.**

13 Mark 10:38; Luke 12:50.

14 "Wer di fuessstapfen und weeg nit wandlet und das creiz Christi nit tragen will, der hat und erkennt den sun nit." **Ein christlicher underricht, TA: Glaubenszeugnisse,** I, p. 34. Compare Denck: "Das mittel aber ist Christus, welchen nyemandt mag warlich erkennen, es sey dann, das er im nachvolge mit dem leben." **Was geredt sei, TA: Denck,** Part II, p. 45. Müntzer, to a different end, namely, the necessity of suffering, said: "Wir alle müssen den fussstapfen Christi nachfolgen." Letter to Hans Zeiss, Dec. 2, 1523, **Müntzers Briefwechsel,** No. 46, p. 51.

15 Müntzer, Hut, and Marpeck—all three—spoke of the experience of despair as the sign of Jonah. Müntzer, **Protestation oder Entbietung,** Brandt, op. cit., p. 135. Hut, **Geheimnus,** loc. cit., p. 23. Marpeck, **Bekenntnis, TA: Elsass,** I, p. 479.

16 **Geheimnus,** loc. cit., p. 21. Denck used the figure of the descensus in the same way: **TA: Denck,** Part II, pp. 23, 92-93, 95.

17 **Ein christlicher underricht, TA: Glaubenszeugnisse,** I, p. 34.

18 I Sam. 2:6; **Geheimnus,** loc. cit., p. 21.

19 **Op. cit.,** Prologus, fol. A verso, col. 2. Rupp, loc, cit., pp. 509-11.

20 "Sic ergo creaturae ligantur ium homine, quia sunt propter hominem, et exinde homo ligatur cum Deo per talem obligationem." Ibid., Tit. XCIX, fol. E [6], col. 2.

21 Above, pp. 66-67.

22 **Hoch verursachte Schutzrede,** Brandt, op. cit., p. 189.

23 **Geheimnus,** loc. cit., p. 17.

24 **Theologia naturalis,** XCIX, CXVII. **Geheimnus,** loc. cit. Müntzer also used the figure in **Von dem gedichteten Glauben,** Brandt, op. cit., p. 126, and **Protestation,** ibid., p. 139.

25 **Geheimnus,** loc. cit.; Hans Schlaffer, **Ein kurzer bericht,** ibid., p. 95.

26 **Geheimnus,** ibid., pp. 1819; Leonhard Schiemer, **Das dreierlei gnad,** ibid., p. 63; by inference, Schlaffer, **Ein kurzer Underricht,** ibid., p. 87.

27 **Geheimnus,** ibid., p. 16; Schlaffer, **Ein kurzer Underricht,** ibid., pp. 89-90; **Ein kurzer bericht,** ibid., pp. 95-96.

28 Geheimnus, ibid., pp. 21, 24-25.
29 Ibid., p. 23.
30 Ibid., p. 25.
31 Ibid., p. 21.
32 Ibid., pp. 20, 21, 24.
33 Ibid., pp. 25-26.
34 Brandt, op. cit., p. 135. Cf. Williams, The Radical Reformation, p. 52; and Lohmann, op. cit., pp. 46-47.
35 Geheminus, loc. cit., p. 23.
36 TA: Denck, Part II, pp. 23-24; also, Ordnung Gottes, ibid., pp. 93-94.
37 Deutsche Theologie, chap. ii, trans. Ray C. Petry, LCC: Mysticism, pp. 332-33. Herbert Klassen observes the double significance of the creatures in that they both tempt man to sin and reveal the truth of God. Loc. cit., pp. 291-92.
38 Vom Gesetz Gottes (1526), TA: Denck, Part II, p. 59.
39 Bekenntnis für den Rat zu Nürnberg, ibid., pp. 23-24.
40 Von der wahren Liebe (1527), ibid., pp. 80-81.
41 An unusual usage of rechtfertigen which could almost be translated "fulfill," since the teleological force of the term is dominant.
42 Marginal reference to I Cor. 10[:1, 2].
43 Marginal reference to I Sam. 2[:6].
44 Geheimnus, TA: Glaubenszeugnisse, I, pp. 20-21.
45 If we add the "baptism of blood" to the Geheimnus passage. See above, p. 78; below, pp. 92-93.
46 Geheimnus, TA: Glaubenszeugnisse, I, p. 25.
47 Ein Sermon von dem heiligen hochwürdigen Sakrament der Taufe (1519), WA, II, p. 730, ll. 30-31.
48 Bekenntnis für den Rat zu Nürnberg, TA: Denck, Part II, p. 24.
49 Geheimnus, loc. cit., p. 26. On this theme in Müntzer, see Rupp, loc. cit., p. 507, n. 1. Denck has the same theme of the unity of Christ in head and members, but with less emphasis upon suffering: Vom Gesetz Gottes, TA: Denck, Part II, pp. 52-53.
50 ZHVSN: Hut, p. 229, Answer 81; TA: Bayern, I, p. 43, Answer 16. The Anabaptists at Baiersdorf in 1528 answered similarly, ibid., p. 80. Ambrosius Spittelmaier revealed like views when he spoke of Christ as only a man and a prophet "according to the flesh"; however, after the Spirit of God came upon Him He was "truly God." Ibid., p. 64.
51 Ein christlicher underricht, TA: Glaubenzeugnisse, I, p. 35.
52 Ibid., pp. 35-36.
53 Geheimnus, ibid., p. 23.
54 Müntzer also distinguished these two forms of faith, not as different in time, but as different in kind, one invalid and the other valid. He claimed that justifying faith, as spoken of by Luther, was invalid. The only valid faith was that which was part of the inner transformation of the believer in regeneration. Nipperdey says: "An die Theologie der Rechtfertigung, für Luther die allein mögliche Theologie, schliesst sich bei Müntzer eine Theologie des Gerechtfertigtseins an." Loc. cit., p. 170. Müntzer evidently does not use the term gerechtfertigt but the idea is clearly central in his thought, so central in fact that Nipperdey (p. 158) speaks of Müntzer as having objectified the subjective experience of regeneration: he calls it a "massive objectivity." For a thorough discussion of Müntzer's treatment of justification and regeneration, see Nipperdey, ibid., pp. 160-70.
55 Walter Klaassen calls this faith by hearing "an interim faith." Loc. cit., p. 225.
56 Ibid. The point is a departure from Herbert Klassen, who recognizes the terms

170 / *Anabaptist Baptism*

but understands them to be identical in meaning: "Hut believed that when God declared a man righteous He also made him righteous." p. 292.

57 **Ein christlicher underricht, TA: Glaubenszeugnisse,** I, p. 36. Like Hubmaier, Hut held to a relative perfectionism. Above, pp. 33-34.

58 The baptism of blood was, as in Hubmaier, the third baptism alongside the covenantal water baptism and the mystical Spirit baptism. Cf. further, below, pp. 92-93.

59 Neuser mentions it. **Op. cit. (MS),** p. 51. Stayer, loc. cit., gives considerable attention to the eschatological and chiliastic elements in Hut. Herbert Klassen also recognizes that South German Anabaptists generally had an eschatological emphasis not found in Swiss Anabaptism. Loc. cit., p. 270.

60 **ZHVSN: Hut,** pp. 241, 249, 251.

61 In a letter to Herbert Klassen. Klassen, loc. cit., p. 179, n. 1.

62 This is ably defended by Stayer, **loc. cit.**

63 So Hut preached to his hearers at Königsberg. **ZHVSN: Hut,** pp. 241-42. It was still his view at the end. **Ibid.,** pp. 227-28, 231, 239. Whether he consistently supported a delayed revolution is uncertain. Hans Weischenfelder testified that Hut's followers had covenanted to overthrow the **Obrigkeit** at the Second Advent. **TA: Thüringen,** p. 281. Herbert Klassen cites opposing evidence and observes that this postponed radicalism is absent from many of the trial testimonies, although he recognizes their expectation of an imminent Advent with the enactment of divine judgment upon the godless. Loc. cit., pp. 202-5.

64 Martin Weischenfelder, **TA: Thüringen,** p. 243; Hans Nadler, **TA: Bayern,** I, p. 136. Cf. further, Stayer, **loc. cit.,** p. 184 ff.

65 **ZHVSN: Hut,** p. 228, Answers 67, 73; p. 239.

66 **TA: Thüringen,** p. 323.

67 **Ibid.,** p. 282.

68 Respectively, Nisius Schuster, **ibid.,** p. 258; Veit Weischenfelder, **ibid.,** p. 242; Hans Hübner, **ibid.,** p. 244. Hans Weischenfelder evidently expected it in 1528: **ibid.,** p. 281.

69 **TA: Bayern,** I, p. 44, Answer 23. Stayer, loc. cit., p. 186, believes the date was probably the midsummer of 1528.

70 **ZHVSN: Hut,** p. 228, Answer 69; p. 242.

71 Anwald and his master, Eitelhans Langenmantel, both disciples of Hut, were members of the Anabaptist congregation at Augsburg. The two men along with Anwald's wife and others were seized by officers of the Swabian League on April 24, 1528. Anwald and his wife were executed on May 11. Christian Hege, "Anwald, Hermann," **ME,** I, p. 135.

72 **ZHVSN: Langenmantel,** p. 29.

73 **Ibid.,** p. 23.

74 **Ibid.,** p. 30, art. 2.

75 **TA: Thüringen,** p. 244. The testimony was given shortly after the middle of March, 1527.

76 **TA: Bayern,** I, p. 83, Answer 11. Also Hans Zurl, p. 85, Answer 3; a young woman, p. 88, Answer 2; Katherine Schrenzin, p. 91, Answer 2; Gerhard Ottin, p. 92, Answer 2; Margaret Strieglin, pp. 92-93, Answer 2.

77 **Ibid.,** p. 124, Question 1.

78 **Ibid.,** p. 91, Answer 2.

79 Above, p. 88.

80 **ZHVSN: Langenmantel,** p. 20, Answer 1; p. 30, art. 2.

81 The original **wir** has been changed to **mir.** Repeated also in the trial testimony: ibid., p. 20, Answer 1.

82 Ibid., p. 40.

83 Testimony of Nov. 26, **ZHVSN: Hut,** p. 240. "Wol hab er Hut ain buechlin von dem buch und den syben sigeln, wie in Apokalipsi stande geschriben, das die brueder das buch mit den syben sigeln genant haben." Ursula Nehspitzin, an Anabaptist imprisoned at Salzburg in 1527, said that Hut had a book by that name "das der her dem Daniel propheten geschickt, aber solch puech werd nit geoffenbart biss an den jungsten tag." **Ibid.,** p. 248. Hut denied that his book on the seals was the one sent by the Lord to Daniel and the prophets. **Ibid.,** p. 240.

84 Testimony of Oct. 16, **TA: Bayern,** I, p. 44, Answers 26-29: "Er hab die articul in seinem buechlin umb deswillen zusamen verzaichnet, damit er denen, den er das evangelium verkonde, möge anzaigen, wie der her, so er das gericht halten, so schwerlichen strafen werde, damit er si dester mer von sunden möchte abwenden. Und hab solhs kainer arglistigen mainug getan, auch derohalben nichts args in seinem herzen gehabt und noch nit. Es seinen auch solh articul nit anderst gestelt, dann wie die in der heiligen geschrift begriffen sein; und die ort, so er anzaichnet hab, sagen alle vom gericht gottes etc."

85 **ZHVSN: Langenmantel,** p. 30, art. 1. Neuser reversed things and considered the **Geheimnus** (published after him by Müller, **TA: Glaubenszeugnisse,** I) as the **Buch mit den syben sigeln. Op. cit.** (MS), p. 9. It is an incorrect identification, however, for the **Geheimnus** contains none of the material from Revelation. Müller, p. 11, continued the error.

86 Torsten Bergsten's identification of the so-called **Ratsbüchlein** published in part by Roth, **ZHVSN: Langenmantel,** pp. 38-40, as the **Buch mit den syben sigeln** would seem to be incorrect, since the former covers so many topics beyond eschatology. **Op. cit.,** p. 458, n. 94. The perplexing **Sieben Urteile** have been identified with the **Buch mit den sieben Siegeln** by both E. Meissner, cited by Bergsten, p. 458, n. 95, and J. F. G. Goeters, **Ludwig Hätzer** (Quellen und Forschungen zur Reformationsgeschichte, Vol. XXV; Gütersloh: C. Bertelsmann Verlag, 1957), p. 115. Since the **Sieben Urteile** contained eschatological material there were probably similarities. Hut seems to have a separate work in mind, however. On the complex question of the **Sieben Urteile** and authorship by either Hut or Hubmaier, see Williams, **The Radical Reformation,** pp. 177-78, who surveys the problem citing the literature, and Bergsten, pp. 457-64, who has reinvestigated the problem. Carl Sachsse, **op. cit., Beilage** 8, has a useful chart comparing various versions of the articles.

87 **TA: Bayern,** I, p. 64.

88 **TA: Glaubenszeugnisse,** I, p. 27. The tract also speaks of suffering both fire and water, stating that the fire and Spirit of Matt. 3:11 and Luke 3:16 are the same as the water and Spirit of John 3:5. The same theme is developed by Hans Nadler, a disciple of Hut, who spoke of the Christians becoming one body through the suffering of the cross, just as grain becomes one loaf through water and the fire of the oven. **TA: Bayern,** I, p. 141.

89 **TA: Bayern,** I, p. 53. Also an account by Hans Weigel, an Anabaptist at Bussbach, ibid., pp. 57-58; and a summary by the authorities at Baiersdorf, ibid., p. 77. Spittelmaier adds: "Es sei hie oder dort, wir miessen purgiert wern in wasser oder feur." **Ibid.,** p. 54. This element is also found in the Gospel of all creatures: "Alle creatur, die uns nutz sein sollen, miessen gerainigt wern durch wasser und feur, also wern wir die kinder gottes hie in wasser und verzeruntem feur, das got selbs ist (Hebr. 4[:16?]) purgiert wern, und die gotlosen dort in dem ewigen feur." This statement, with its implicit universalism, was made in answer to a question on purgatory. Ibid., p. 55.

90 The designation occurs at many places in the trial testimony. The following is a representative sampling: Martin Weischenfelder, **TA: Thüringen,** p. 239; Veit Weischenfelder, ibid., pp. 241-42; Hans Hübner, ibid., p. 244; Hermann Anwald, **ZHVSN: Langenmantel,** pp. 23, 29.

91 Ambrosius Spittelmaier, **TA: Bayern,** I, p. 50, Answer 12. Hut claimed to have

been commissioned by an angel of God to gather and teach his brotherhood. ZHVSN: Hut, p. 225, Answer 14. Cf. further, Stayer, loc. cit., pp. 184-88.

92 Geheimnus, loc. cit., p. 20.

93 TA: Bayern, I, pp. 70-71. We can note once again that the "binding" of the dominical charge is interpreted as the Anabaptist baptismal Bund, not as the Catholic ban.

94 I John 5:8.

95 TA: Bayern I, p. 43; similarly, ZHVSN: Hut, p. 227.

96 We refer to Hut's statement that baptism is "a struggle with sin one's whole life." Above, p. 184.

97 We find no evidence in Denck's writings to suggest that Hut could have taken the idea from Denck. Herbert Klassen believes that Hut originated it himself. Loc. cit., p. 291.

98 TA: Glaubenszeugnisse, I, p. 77. Hut described the covenant in a similar fashion: ZHVSN: Hut, p. 230, Answer 13; TA: Bayern, I, p. 43, Answer 13.

99 TA: Glaubenszeugnisse, I, p. 78.

100 Bekandtnuss und verantwortung, ibid., I, p. 114.

101 Von dreyerley Tauf, ibid., I pp. 78-79.

102 Bekandtnuss und verantwortung, ibid., p. 114; also, Ein kurzer Underricht, ibid., p. 92.

103 Matt. 20:22, 23; Mark 10:38, 39; Luke 12:50. Ambrosius Spittelmaier also: "Dieser punt geschiecht im geist, tauf und trinkung des kölchs, das Christus haist die tauf des plüts." TA: Bayern, 1, p. 49.

104 Von dreyerley Tauf, TA: Glaubenszeugnisse, I, p. 78.

105 Bekandtnuss und verantwortung, ibid., p. 114; Ein kurzer Underricht, ibid., p. 93.

106 Ethelbert Stauffer's article, "Märtyrertheologie und Täuferbewegung," ZKG, 3rd series, LII, No. 4 (1933), pp. 545-98, has already shown the importance of the theme of suffering among the Anabaptists. His article includes a large amount of evidence from the Hutterite tradition which clearly perpetuated the views of Hut, Schiemer, Schlaffer, and the rest of Hut's group. The ideas of discipleship and imitation of Christ, the distinction of the three baptisms, and even the Gospel of all creatures— all of these survive in Hutterite hymnody. Stauffer, p. 208, quoted Anneken of Rotterdam in a hymn celebrating her martyrdom:

> Diesen Weg auch gegangen sind
> Alle die frommen Gottes Kind,
> Die den Tauf hond empfangen,
> **An ihren Stirnen versieglet** [bold ours],
> Folgen dem Lamm so es hingeht,
> Dienen ihm mit Verlangen.

> Solche mussen in diesen Thal,
> Und trinken den bittern Kelch all,
> Bis die Zahl ward erfüllet
> Zion der werthen Gottes Braut,
> Die ihm das Lamm selbst hat vertraut
> Und den Zorn Gottes stillet.

From the Ausbund: Das ist, etliche schöne Christliche Lieder (Lancaster, Pa.: Gedruckt bey Johann Bär, 1834) (pagination the same as in original), p. 112. Hans Betz makes express mention of the three baptisms (Stauffer, p. 207; Ausbund, p. 608):

> Wer den Tauf hat, der ist in Tod
> Christi gepflanzet worden,

All sein Begierd, gecreutzigt wird,
Dadurch ist neu gebohren.
Dess Geburt ist, in Jesu Christ,
Aus Wasser und Geist geschehen.
Also es hat göttlicher Rath
In Christo vorgesehen.

Also uns ist Herr Jesu Christ,
Drey Zeugniss he bescheiden.
Die zwey man heist, Wasser und Geist,
Die dritt, Blut das ist Leiden.
Gleichwie auch thun ins Himmelsthron
Drey in ein Zeugniss geben.
Der Vater, 's Wort, an allem Ort,
Der Heil'ge Geist merk eben.

107 ZHVSN: Hut, p. 223, Answer 6, repeated on p. 245; TA: Bayern, I, p. 42, Answer 12. For Hubmaier, see above, chap. i, pp. 39, 47.

108 TA: Glaubenszeugnisse, I, p. 25.

109 Müntzer spoke of Christ as saying, " 'Ich mus mit eyner andern taufe ubergossen werden denn mit der taufe Johannis, und ich werde seere gepeynyget, das ich solchs volfuere.' " Letter to Christoph Meinhard, Auslegung des 18. Psalms, May 30, 1524, Müntzers Briefwechsel, No. 49, p. 56. Denck says that John and the apostles as well baptized in water, since "Was dem wasser nit besteht, kan das feur noch wol weniger leyden." The true baptism, however, is in the Spirit within. Bekenntnis für den Rat zu Nürnberg, TA: Denck, Part II, p. 24.

110 ZHVSN: Langenmantel, p. 29; quoted in full above, p. 87.

111 TA: Thüringen, p. 256. Other accounts in ibid., pp. 259, 304; and TA: Bayern, I, p. 26.

112 TA: Thüringen, pp. 239-40, 249; TA: Bayern, I, pp. 58-59; ZHVSN: Langenmantel, pp. 26-28.

113 TA: Thüringen, pp. 239-40, 259; ZHVSN: Langenmantel, p. 26.

114 TA: Thüringen, op. cit., p. 240; TA: Bayern, I, pp. 26, 35, Answer 8.

115 Hut enjoined Martin Weischenfelder to say: "Gott gruss dich, bruder im Herrn." TA: Thüringen, ibid., p. 239. Others report the same: ibid., pp. 237, 244. Similarly, TA: Bayern, I, 51, Answer 15.

116 ZHVSN: Hut, p. 19.

117 TA: Bayern, I, p. 175.

118 TA: Bayern, I, p. 50. Spittelmaier seems also to have thought that the knowledge of good and evil arises within one at about the age of thirty. Cf. ibid., p. 36, Answer 18 and p. 37, Answer 31.

119 TA: Glaubenszeugnisse, I, pp. 92-93. Similarly, p. 114.

120 Ibid., p. 238. Hans Nadler also advocated baptism at thirty. TA: Bayern, I, p. 144.

121 Christianismi restitutio (Reprint; Nürnberg: 1790), p. 372.

122 Williams, The Radical Reformation, pp. 313, 317-18. On the practice of the Paulicians and the same custom among Polish Anabaptists, see ibid., pp. 414, 678. Theophylact and Servetus may have been following John Chrysostom. The latter commented that the age of thirty was appropriate for Jesus' baptism, for, in order to "fulfill all righteousness," Christ had to experience every stage of man's development; and sin, Chrysostom said, does not reach its full development until about the age of thirty when man's cupiditas erupts in its full power. Homiliae in Matthaeum, X (Matt. 3:1), par. 1, MPG, LVII, pp. 184-85.

123 Herbert Klassen's statement that Hut transformed "Müntzer's morbid view of

174 / Anabaptist Baptism

suffering into a positive concept for the imitation of Christ in a life of discipleship" would seem to be overdrawn. Loc. cit., pp. 303-4. But the other two results he sees from Hut's "free church" principle are better founded: "a change from Müntzer's individualistic view of the Spirit, new revelations, and dreams, to a view of the Spirit as a gift to the church"; and, "the modification of Müntzer's revolutionary eschatology into peaceful, though urgent, expectation of the return of Christ." Hut admitted to believing in dreams as possible divine revelations, however: **ZHVSN: Hut,** p. 232, Answer 6. He also claimed to have been commissioned by an angel of God: above, n. 91.

124 Herbert Klassen gives several instances of specific influences of Hut on Marpeck and the Hutterites. Loc. cit., pp. 289, 291, 294, 298, 304.

Chapter IV. MELCHIOR HOFMANN

1 **BRN**, V, pp. 125-70. English translation by Williams, **LCC: SAW**, pp. 182-203 (with **BRN** pagination inserted in the text).

2 "Die glaubigen sollen wissen den verstand der gschrifft, durch welchen sey glauben an den namen Jhesu, vnnd durch denselben glauben ist in der gwalt geben kinder gottes zu werden. Joan 1[:12]." **Von der vermehelung Marie vnd Josephs** (1524), **TA: Elsass,** I, p. 11.

3 "Nun, dise gepurd des wasserpads im wort gibt macht, aus ursach des leiblichen worts vnnd wassers, ain kind gottes zuwerden. Dan zum ersten mues man geperen durch wort, wann dem verwilligt vnd glaubt wirt; darnach durch das wasser; alsdann ist macht verhannden, ain kind gottes zewerden." **Pilgram Marpecks Glaubensbekenntnis** (Dec. 1532-Jan. 1531), ibid., pp. 474-75. See further, below, pp. 117-18.

4 "Dann so der mensch zu eyner neüwen creatur geborn ist, wirt jm dann macht geben eyn war kindt gottes zu werden, Johannis am ersten." **Eyn sendbrieff an alle gottsförchtigen liebhaber der ewigen warheyt** (hereafter **Ein sendbrieff** [1533]), June-July, 1533, **TA: Elsass,** II, No. 399, p. 105.

5 Through the Word of Christ God places man "in der hant zijns wils, daer gaetet dan an, dat die mensche een warachtich vry creatuer geworden is (Jn. 8[:32]), dat hi van die tijt aen met hem seluen mach beraden zijn eyghen koer ende verkies hebben, of hi na dat goet of nae dat quaet tasten wil." **Verclaringe van den geuangenen ende vrien wil** (hereafter Verclaringe), **BRN,** V, p. 194. Translated with context, below, pp. 98-99.

6 Fragments of the work are preserved in B. N. Krohn, **Geschichte der fanatischen und enthusiastischen Wiedertäufer vornehmlich in Niederdeutschland: Melchior Hofmann und die Secte der Hofmannianer** (Leipzig: bey Bernhard Christoph Breitkopf, 1758), pp. 86-89. The volume is rare; a copy is held by the Mennonite Historical Library, Goshen College.

7 Denck, **Was geredt sei dass die Schrift sagt** (1526), **TA: Denck,** Part II, pp. 27-47. Hofmann said: "Christus Jesus nit für eyn halbe welt gelitten hat, sonder für die gantzen wellt, das ist der gantz same Adams." **Eyn sendbrieff** [1533], **TA: Elsass,** II, pp. 104-5. Bucer credits him with the same. **Handlung inn dem . . . gesprech . . . gegen Melchior Hoffman,** ibid., p. 114.

8 See Alvin Beachy, "The Concept of Grace in the Radical Reformation" (unpublished Th.D. dissertation, Harvard University, July, 1960), pp. 100-2; and "The Grace of God in Christ as Understood by Five Major Anabaptist Writers," **MQR,** XXXII (1963), p. 15.

9 Verclaringe, **BRN,** V, p. 189; **Ordonnantie,** ibid., p. 149.

10 Ordonnantie, ibid., pp. 148-49; **TA: Elsass,** II, No. 444, p. 185. Hofmann recognized four principal occasions when God lifted the veil of history and allowed special knowledge of the kingdom. Each included the public proclamation of the new revelation. The first was the sending of the apostles to the Jews; the second was the turning to the Gentiles recorded in Acts 13; the third began with John Huss; the fourth was

taking place through Hofmann. Peter Kawerau, Melchior Hofman als religiöser Denker (Haarlem: de Erven F. Bohn N. V., 1954), p. 76.

11 The full Apocryphal quotation reads: "It was he who made man in the beginning, and left him in the hands of his own decision." The Wisdom of Sirach, 15:14. Edgar J. Goodspeed, **The Apocrypha: An American Translation** (New York: Random House, 1938). Hofmann elsewhere cites chapter 18:13: "The mercy of the Lord is for all mankind." **Verclaringe, BRN,** V, p. 188.

12 "You shall know the truth and the truth shall make you free."

13 **Verclaringe, BRN,** V, p. 194.

14 "Ende hier en wert geheelic niemant van Godt tot zijn rijck ghedwonghen, noch met ghewelt ghedronghen, maer ghelijc ghescreuen." Like Isaac's bride, Rebecca, the believer comes out of his own desire. As to the "compelling," Hofmann says that this is as one might constrain or urge a friend, but it is no more. **Ibid.,** pp. 193-94. See Beachy, **op. cit.,** pp. 102-4; and "The Grace of God in Christ," loc. cit.

15 **Verclaringe, BRN,** V, pp. 194-96.

16 **Ibid.,** pp. 194-95; **Ordonnantie, ibid.,** p. 163.

17 From the records of his trial, **TA: Elsass,** I, No. 67, p. 65. The text's reference to I Cor. 3 is an error for I Pet. 3:21.

18 **TA: Elsass,** I, No. 61, p. 59.

19 **Glaubensbekentniss** of Kautz and Reublin, Jan. 15, 1525. **Ibid.,** No. 168, p. 198.

20 **Ordonnantie, BRN,** V, p. 150.

21 **Ibid.,** p. 152. See the note by Williams, **LCC: SAW,** p. 185, n. 5.

22 **Ordonnantie, BRN,** V, p. 152.

23 Hofmann spoke of Christ as "een Coninck, Vorst ende Hertoch," and said that in baptism one leaves the kingdom of Satan and darkness and "weds and binds" himself to the Lord Jesus Christ. **Ibid.,** pp. 148, 150. Denck's reference to Christ as **Herzog** is not in a baptismal context but the implication is nonetheless clear, **Ordnung Gottes, TA: Denck,** Part II, p. 94.

24 **Ordonnantie, BRN,** V, pp. 150-51.

25 Similarly, Beachy said that water baptism was the "sign" of the betrothal, not the "means." **Op. cit.,** p. 201. The same transition of marital imagery from the inner mystical sacrament to the outer ordinance had already been made in respect to the Supper by Cornelius Hoen, whose view on the Eucharist Hofmann adopted. Hoen's letter spoke of the Eucharist as a token (**pignus**) from Christ symbolizing His love in a way analogous to the bridegroom's ring. He specifically spoke of the believer's loving response of faithful obedience as the true eating of the body of Christ, i.e., the true inner sacrament. **Epistola Christiana,** published in **ZW,** IV, p. 512. Hofmann used the same image in the **Ordonnantie, BRN,** V, p. 157.

26 Williams, **Wilderness and Paradise,** p. 50.

27 A stage in the soul's journey, i.e., as distinct from Meister Eckhardt's view that **desertum** is the divine **vastitas,** or abyss, and the contemplative side of man. **Ibid.,** pp. 50-52.

28 **Verclaringe, BRN,** V, p. 197.

29 Quoted by Williams, **Wilderness and Paradise,** p. 51, from **Selected Writings on Contemplation,** trans. Clare Kirchberger (London, [1957]), p. 224.

30 **Ordonnantie, BRN,** V, p. 150.

31 **Ibid.,** p. 151.

32 **Ibid.**

33 **Ibid.,** p. 165.

34 **Ibid.,** p. 151.

35 **Ibid.,** p. 164. Hofmann's Scriptural bases for this are Heb. 6:4-9 and 10:26, the texts customarily cited to deny a second repentance.

36 Verclaringe, BRN, V, p. 192.

37 Eyn sendbrieff (1533), TA: Elsass, II, No. 399, p. 105.

38 "You are those who have continued with me in my trials."

39 Eyn sendbrieff (1533), TA: Elsass, II, No. 399, p.108.

40 Ibid., pp. 107-8. That Hofmann believed men were condemned to hell only by their own choice is clear. "So er aber nun verdampt soll werden, muss er auss freiher wilkur den andern todt erwelen vnnd dessen sterben auss seinem eygenthumb vnnd freiem willen, dann gottes will wirt nit inn der hell brennen, nur eygen will; auch wirt gar nit eyner des ersten tods halb verdampt werden, sonder alle selig; alleyn die verdamnüs der ander todt wirt sein." Ibid., p. 105. This is a reversal of his position in Das 12. Capitel des propheten Danielis ausgelegt . . . , in which he said that one could fall as often as seven times a day (symbolically seven it would seem) and still have his wedding garment of redemption cleansed in the blood of the Lamb. Krohn, op. cit., p. 87.

41 Auszlegung der heimlichen Offenbarung Joannis . . . , 1:1; Kawerau, op. cit., p. 22.

42 Kawerau, ibid.

43 Dat erste Capitel des Evangelisten St. Mattheus . . . , Krohn, op. cit., p. 135.

44 Ordonnantie, BRN, V, pp. 150-53.

45 Kawerau, op. cit., pp. 21, 38; Krohn, op. cit., p. 105.

46 Adapting the images of Ezek. 1:10 and Rev. 4:7, Hofmann said that there are four levels of Scripture: lion, calf, man, and eagle. As lion, Scripture frightens man and kills him making him ready for salvation, a principle probably surviving from his Lutheran period. The calf symbolizes Scripture as a book of figures revealing to man his need of redemption. As man, it is full of parables by which one is born a child of the Spirit, and as eagle it is the Word of God available only to the Apostolic Teacher. Dat erste Capitel des Evangelisten St. Mattheus, Krohn, op. cit., p. 135. For a full discussion of the matter, cf. Kawerau, op. cit., pp. 33-36. The use of the symbols for the four senses of Scripture is first found in the 1526 An die gelöfigen vorsambling in Liflant ein korte formaninghe (reprint with dedication dated July 29, 1856: n.p.: n.n., n.d. [microfilm copy at Andover-Harvard Theological Library]), pp. A verso-Aij verso. Friedrich Otto zur Linden, Melchior Hofmann: Ein Prophet der Wiedertäufer (Haarlem: de Erven F. Bohn, 1885), pp. 82-83.

47 Dat erste Capitel des . . . St. Mattheus, Krohn, op. cit., p. 135.

48 Das freudenriche zeucknus . . . , reprinted in Linden, op. cit., p. 430.

49 Verclaringe, BRN, V, pp. 188-89.

50 Matt. 24:29-31. Das 12. Capitel des propheten Danielis ausgelegt, Krohn, op. cit., p. 99. Prophecey oder weissagung uss warer heiliger götlicher schrifft, Quart. A ij-B.

51 Verclaringe, BRN, V, pp. 189-90: Ordonnantie, ibid., pp. 150-51. The same principle is used in Hofmann's interpretation of the temple. Ordonnantie, p. 152; Das N. Amsdorf . . . nasengeist sey, Quart. [A iij]. See Kawerau, op. cit., pp. 23-26.

52 Weissagung uss heiliger götlicher geschrifft, Quart. [A] verso-A ij. See Linden, op. cit., p. 42, n. 10. Also, W. I. Leendertz, Melchior Hofmann (Haarlem: de Erven F. Bohn, 1883), pp. 15-16.

53 Das 12. Capitel des Danielis, Krohn, op. cit., pp. 97-98. Hofmann chided Nicholas Amsdorf for saying that one should constantly be alert for the Second Advent and claimed that "the figure shows clearly and brightly when one should watch for the Last Day." Das N. Amsdorf . . . nasengeist sey, Quart. [A iij] verso.

54 Our discussion is an expansion of Hofmann's brief comments. Das 12. Capitel Danielis, loc. cit., pp. 97-99. Also, Prophecey oder weissagung, Quart. A [iij]; B iiij verso; C ij.

55 Das 12. Capitel Danielis, loc. cit., p. 99; TA: Elsass, II, p. 114.

Footnotes / 177

56 Op. cit., p. 99. The work is now lost and only Krohn's excerpts and account of it survive.

57 Dat Nicolaus Amsdorff . . . nicht weth wat he setten, Quart. A ij.

58 Obbe Philips, **Bekentenisse**, BRN, VII, p. 124; trans. Williams, LCC: SAW, pp. 209-10.

59 TA: Elsass, II, No. 607, p. 386.

60 Ibid., No. 654, p. 444.

61 For Jost as Enoch, see Kawerau, op. cit., pp. 107-8. Obbe Philips provides the report about Poldermann and Schwenckfeld: **Bekentenisse**, BRN, VII, p. 126; trans. Williams, LCC: SAW, p. 212. On Hofmann's uncertainty about Enoch, see Leendertz, op. cit., p. 281, n. 1.

62 Bucer reports: "Auss disem Hierusalem, schreibt [Hofmann], sollen die junckfrawlichen apostolischen botten hundert tauset vnd vier vnd viertzig tauset aussgohn vnnd den bundt vnd tauff des wasserbadts über alle welt füren." TA: Elsass, II, No. 402, p. 114.

63 Above, p. 105.

64 **Ordonnantie**, BRN, V, p. 152; trans. Williams, LCC: SAW, p. 188.

65 **Ibid**.

66 Ibid.; Williams, LCC: SAW, pp. 188-89, with full notes on the details.

67 According to Obbe Philips, **Bekentenisse**, BRN, VII, pp. 124-25; trans. Williams, LCC: SAW, pp. 210-11.

68 The delay at Jerusalem is described in Ezra 4:24 and Hag. 1:1-15. Obbe's report that the **Stillstand** was ordered while Hofmann was in prison is in error. Linden, op. cit., p. 263, n. 1; ME, II, p. 782.

69 Kawerau, op. cit., pp. 71-73.

70 By the simple imposition of hands. G. Grosheide, "Verhooren en vonnissen der Wederdoopers, Betrokken bij de Aanslagen op Amsterdam in 1534 en 1535," **Bijdragen en Mededelingen van het Historisch Genootschap**, XLI (1920), pp. 172-73.

71 **Bekentenisse**, BRN, VII, pp. 122-23; trans. Williams, LCC: SAW, p. 208.

72 Linden, op. cit., p. 233.

73 Ibid.

74 Recounted in their **Gründtlicker Wahrhaftiger Bericht** of 1594. Ibid., p. 234.

75 TA: Elsass, I, No. 211, p. 261.

76 The original is lost but a copy survives. It bears the title, **Bekentnusz des MELCHIOR HOFMANNS vom kindertauff von der mutwilligen oder unvergebl. sünden und vom freyen willen.** . . . The document is reproduced by Abraham Hulshof, **Geschiedenis van de Doopsgezinden te Straatsburg van 1525 tot 1557** (Amsterdam: J. Clausen, 1905), pp. 180-81. Kawerau, op. cit., p. 120, presents most of the material on baptism in modern German.

77 Op. cit., p. 120.

78 **Ordonnantie**, BRN, V, p. 156.

79 Ibid., p. 155.

80 TA: Elsass, II, No. 444, pp. 184-85.

81 **Ordonnantie**, BRN, V, p. 156.

82 Denck actually continued to avow the correctness of believer's baptism, saying only that it does one no damage to have been baptized as an infant, and that it is a matter of **Menschengebott** and Christian freedom. **Widerruf**, TA: Denck, Part II, p. 109.

83 **Ordonnantie**, BRN, V, pp. 150-51.

84 Ibid., p. 155.

85 Inner circumcision of the heart, the theme of the latter passage, is found

178 / Anabaptist Baptism

developed at considerable length in the **Verclaringe**, but without reference to that Biblical passage or to baptism. **BRN**, V, pp. 195-96.

Chapter V. PILGRAM MARPECK

1 Above, pp. 37-38, 153 n. 131.

2 Above, pp. 47-48.

3 **Vom Gesetz Gottes, TA: Denck,** Part II, pp. 59-62; **Von der wahren Liebe,** ibid., pp. 82-83.

4 **Glaubensbekenntnis, TA: Elsass,** I, pp. 430-40. Jan Kiwiet presents a detailed discussion of Marpeck's conception of the covenants. **Pilgram Marbeck: Ein Führer in der Täuferbewegung der Reformationszeit** (2nd ed.; Kassel: J. G. Oncken Verlag, 1958), pp. 94-109. Cf. also, John C. Wenger, "The Theology of Pilgram Marpeck," **MQR**, XII (1938), pp. 208-12.

5 Marpeck's discussion of the two covenants in the **Vermanung** is an adaptation and expansion of Bernhard Rothmann's treatment of the topic in his **Bekentnisse**. References to the **Vermanung** and the **Bekentnisse** are to the respective editions by Christian Hege, and Detmer and Krumbholtz as cited on p. 161, n. 36. The discussions of the covenants are in pp. 225-28 of the **Vermanung** and pp. 41-46 of **Bekentnisse**. The important additions by Marpeck to the Rothmann material on the covenant concern the nature of regeneration (see below, pp. 119-21). On the interesting fact that Marpeck's **Vermanung** is an edited and expanded form of Rothmann's **Bekentnisse**, cf. Frank J. Wray, "The 'Vermanung' of 1542 and Rothmann's 'Bekentnisse,'" **ARG**, XLVII (1956), pp. 243-51. Wray gives a brief account of the modifications made by the Marpeck group.

6 Kiwiet, citing the **Testamentserleütterung** (n.p.: n.d. [1544-1550]), believes that Marpeck thought it did. **Op. cit.**, p. 88. Marpeck's statement is not explicit. In referring to various kinds of covenants, Marpeck says: "Das gesatz Ade vnd Moyse haisse ainen bundt." More important is the reference to Hos. 6:7 that follows: "But at Adam they transgressed the covenant." **Testamentserleütterung**, p. CXXXV recto. If it is true that Marpeck did conceive of a prelapsarian covenant, the fact is of note, for Marpeck would then have preceded the Reformed covenant theologians with the idea. According to Leonard J. Trinterud, Reformed theology did not speak of a prelapsarian covenant until the 1570's and 1580's when the theory of the double covenant was developed. "The Origins of Puritanism," **CH**, XX (1951), pp. 42, 48. Zwingli, Bullinger, and Calvin spoke of the divine covenant with fallen man. Gottlob Schrenk, **Gottesreich und Bund im älteren Protestantismus** (Gütersloh: Bertelsmann Verlag, 1923), pp. 37-39, 40-41, 45-47.

7 **Testamentserleütterung**, p. CXXXII recto.

8 **Vermanung, Gedenckschrift**, p. 232. The statement is Marpeck's, but the idea is paralleled in Rothmann's **Bekentnisse**, loc. cit., pp. 41-43.

9 **Glaubensbekenntnis, TA: Elsass,** I, p. 419, art. 11; **Testamentserleütterung**, pp. CLVII verso-CLVIII recto.

10 **Glaubensbekenntnis**, loc. cit., pp. 429-30, 434.

11 **Vermanung, Gedenkschrift**, pp. 225-27, in partial dependence on Rothmann's **Bekentnisse**, loc. cit., pp. 41-43.

12 **Glaubensbekenntnis, TA: Elsass,** I, pp. 430, 441, 447. Verantwurtung über Casparn Schwenckfelds Judicium, ed. Johann Loserth, **Pilgram Marbecks Antwort auf Kaspar Schwenckfelds Beurteilung des Buches der Bundesbezeugung von 1542** (Quellen und Forschungen zur Geschichte der oberdeutschen Taufgesinnten im 16. Jahrhundert; Wien und Leipzig: Kommissionsverlag der Verlagsbuchhandlung Carl Fromme Gesellschaft m. b. H., 1929), pp. 154-6. (Hereafter **Verantwurtung** I and II.) **Verantwurtung** II, p. 579.

The belief in the **descensus ad infernos**, a traditional article of faith preserved in the Apostles' Creed, was widely held within the Radical Reformation and was accepted by all four principal subjects of our study, as well as by Denck and Müntzer. Hut and Marpeck made the greatest use of it, the former interpreting it symbolically as the anguish of redemptive suffering (as Marpeck could do also; see below, p. 116), and the latter interpreting it as an event within the divine economy of salvation. For details in Marpeck and a brief sketch of the doctrine itself, see William Klassen, "The Hermeneutics of Pilgram Marpeck" (unpublished doctoral dissertation, Princeton Theological Seminary, 1960), pp. 123-26, 175-77.

On the descensus in general, as understood by medieval and Reformation theologians, see Erich Vogelsang, "Weltbild und Kreuzestheologie in den Höllenfahrtsstreitigkeiten der Reformationszeit," ARG, XXXVIII (1941), pp. 90-132. On its acceptance within the Radical Reformation, see Williams, The Radical Reformation, pp. 840-42.

13 Glaubensbekenntnis, TA: Elsass, I, pp. 440, 445-46. Marpeck fluctuates in his views on the nature and effect of the descent into Hades. According to the Glaubensbekenntnis, ibid., and the Verantwurtung II, pp. 202, 317, Christ descended to preach the Gospel to the Old Testament believers. But his Von der Tieffe Christi says that Christ suffered there as well. Kunstbuch, fol. 279-80.

Torsten Bergsten observes that Marpeck revealed an inconsistency in regard to the status of the Old Testament dead. On the one hand he said that they were in the hand of God, Abraham's bosom (Verantwurtung II, p. 202), and on the other that they were in hell (ibid., p. 317). "Pilgram Marbeck und seine Auseinandersetzung mit Caspar Schwenckfeld," Kyrkohistorisk Arsskrift, LVII (1957), p. 86.

14 John 16:7. Glaubensbekenntnis, TA: Elsass, I, p. 440.

15 "Die eüsserlich und figürlich zusag, ist allein Abraham und seinem geschlecht geschehen, und ist auch in denselben vollendet worden, und reychet gantz nit auff die christen." Christian baptism may not be compared "mit der leiblichen beschneidung . . . der alten, welch mit händen und bloss am fleisch geschehen ist, als an den abrahamskindern, so von seinem geschlecht und samen nach dem fleisch geboren wurden, welcher samen aller under das eüsserlich verbündtnus der eüsserlichen beschneidung genommen und gerechtnet ward." Vermanung, Gedenkschrift, p. 226. Rothmann, Bekentnisse, loc. cit., p. 42, but rather thoroughly rewritten by Marpeck.

16 Above, pp. 37, 48.

17 Rothmann held the same view, but Marpeck's text is independent of Rothmann. Marpeck's approach is also less typological. Vermanung, Gedenkschrift, p. 236; Bekentnisse, loc., cit., pp. 44-46.

18 Vermanung, loc. cit. Similarly, Glaubensbekenntnis, TA: Elsass, I, pp. 431-34. In the latter passage Marpeck interprets Gen. 17:10 ("Every male among you shall be circumcised") as a prophetic statement referring to the circumcision to come. "Redt hie nicht: Ir sollentz beschneiden, sonnder beschnitten werden. Hie redt got von der beschneidung on henndt, die erst verpracht muesst werden in Crissto, durch die predig des euangelion." Ibid., p. 433.

19 Matt. 24:13.

20 TA: Elsass, I, p. 475.

21 Ibid., pp. 449-50; also, Verantwurtung II, pp. 481-82.

22 Glaubensbekenntnis, loc. cit., p. 475.

23 Ibid., p. 479.

24 Ibid., pp. 480-82.

25 Von der Tieffe Christi, Kunstbuch, fol. 282.

26 Ibid., fol. 279. On Marpeck's use of the Gospel of all creatures, see below, p. 131.

27 Verantwurtung I, pp. 115-16, is perhaps the best statement of this inner suffering in Gelassenheit.

28 "Mitgenossen des trübsals Christi," a common phrase among Marpeck and his followers, used also in the signature to the Vermanung.

29 Vermanung, Gedenkschrift, p. 218.

30 Glaubensbekenntnis, TA: Elsass, I, p. 479. Kiwiet, op. cit., pp. 121-22, gives a large selection of references to the topic of redemptive suffering in Marpeck's writings.

31 Glaubensbekenntnis, loc. cit., p. 480.

32 Ibid., pp. 477-78.

33 Ibid., pp. 474-75. An important text for Marpeck's argument is Titus 3:5: "He saved us . . . by the washing of regeneration and renewal in the Holy Spirit." Marpeck read this as referring to two successive actions.

Bergsten rightly observes that Kiwiet erred in saying that the new birth is entirely prior to the reception of water baptism and that the latter is only an incorporation into the covenant. Bergsten, "Pilgram Marbeck" (1958), p. 59; Kiwiet, op. cit., p. 136. Kiwiet's error is in not recognizing that Marpeck, although he does speak of the new birth as beginning at a single point in time before baptism, also describes it as a process which continues throughout one's life. The reception of water baptism is a significant point in that process.

34 Above, 85-86, 97-98, 101-2.

35 Glaubensbekenntnis, TA: Elsass, I, pp. 486-87. Kiwiet, op. cit., p. 87, on the other hand, speaks of both covenants as involving a double-sided pledge.

36 Vermanung, Gedenkschrift, pp. 201-2; following Rothmann, Bekentnisse, loc. cit., p. 16.

37 Glaubensbekenntnis, loc. cit., p. 487. Compare Hans Denck: "Das bundzeychen, die beschneidung, gegeben ist, eer das man sein begeret hat, das alle die von Abrahams somen kamen, dem gsatz verpflicht worden sind, sie weren willig oder nit. Das new gsatz aber ist eyn kindtschafft, darumb das alle, die darunder seind, von keynem menchen darzu gebracht werden mügen, sonder alleyn von dem barmhertzigen Gott." Von der wahren Liebe, TA: Denck, Part II, p. 80.

38 The term "covenant" is virtually a mistranslation. The mistake was made by Luther in his September Testament of 1522 in which he used the translation "der bund eyns guten gewissens," perhaps thinking of stipulatio, once understood as the Latin equivalent of ἐπερώτημα. Die Deutsche Bibel, WA, VII, p. 308. Cf. H. G. Liddell and R. Scott, A Greek-English Lexicon (rev. ed.; Oxford: At the Clarendon Press, 1940), I, p. 618. The latter gives the first meaning of the Greek as "appeal," the translation used in the Revised Standard Version. The Zurich Bible of 1524 had used the word kundtschaft as had Hubmaier. See above, p. 152.

Schwenckfeld, even though he had once followed Luther's translation, later criticized Marpeck and the Anabaptists for using the term Bund, claiming that a better translation of ἐπερώτημα and interrogatio (as the Vulgate had it) would be zusagen, durchfrag, or vertädigung. CS, respectively, III, p. 795; VIII, p. 173.

Marpeck acknowledged Schwenckfeld's objection by quoting his statement in full but made no reply to the criticism, preferring to argue the matter on theological grounds. Verantwurtung I, pp. 85-86. It is notable that Marpeck based his defense on Old Testament passages, specifically Jer. 31:33, Isa. 59:21, and Ezek. 34:25.

39 Above, p. 63.

40 Above, p. 99.

41 Vermanung, Gedenkschrift, p. 203; following Rothmann, Bekentnisse, loc. cit., pp. 18-19. Although Marpeck is adopting Rothmann's material here, his own use of Luther's translation of I Pet. 3:21 antedates Rothmann's tract (1533), for it figured significantly in the Strassburg confession of late 1531 or early 1532. Glaubensbekenntnis, TA: Elsass, I, pp. 423 (art. 24), 433, 486.

42 Marpeck, Vermanung, Gedenkschrift, p. 204; Rothmann, Bekentnisse, loc. cit., p. 20.

43 Vermanung, Gedenkschrift, pp. 202, 204; Rothmann, loc. cit., p. 17. Verantwurtung I, p. 95.

44 Vermanung, Gedenkschrift, pp. 231, 235-36 (not in Rothmann).

45 Glaubensbekenntnis, TA: Elsass, I, pp. 444-46.

46 Vermanung, Gedenkschrift, p. 233 (not in Rothmann). Cf. also, Glaubensbekenntnis, loc. cit., pp. 490-92.

47 Vermanung, loc. cit. (not in Rothmann).

48 Although the discussion notes when the Vermanung follows Rothmann and when it is independent of him, a brief survey of the similarities and differences may be helpful. In general, Marpeck's distinctive theological interpretations and defense of believer's baptism are his own, namely, (1) his imaginative solution to the relation of inner and outer baptism, with the related concept of baptism's role as a Mitzeugnis joined to the inner witness of the Spirit, and (2) his view of the Trinitarian action in baptism. Marpeck's proposed solution to the problem of original sin is largely an addition to the material given by Rothmann, and his interpretation of the two covenants is more detailed and generally better integrated into his overall view of baptism than is Rothmann's. Thus, although the Vermanung is largely a literal reproduction of the Bekenntnisse, the weight of theological creativity in regard to baptism in the Vermanung lies on the side of Marpeck. In contrast, the section on the Lord's Supper is still largely Rothmann's, both in letter and in spirit.

49 Vermanung, Gedenkschrift, p. 209; Bekentnisse, loc. cit., p. 25.

50 Quoted more fully below on p. 123. Vermanung, Gedenkschrift, p. 209; Rothmann, Bekentnisse, loc. cit., p. 25. In this case Marpeck's text in the Vermanung follows Rothmann's Bekentnisse; but the theological solution to the problem, Marpeck's conception of the Mitzeugnis, is Marpeck's own contribution as is to be seen below.

51 Kiwiet's discussion of Marpeck's use of the term Zeichen is inaccurate. Op. cit., pp. 134-35. He rightly distinguishes between the Figur of the old covenant, as e.g., circumcision, and the Wesen of the new covenant, salvation itself, thereby noting Marpeck's distinction between promise and fulfillment. He is also correct in saying that Marpeck called the ceremonies of the old covenant "Zeichen." (See Glaubensbekenntnis, TA: Elsass, I, pp. 486-87.) He is wrong, however, in saying that Marpeck spoke of the ordinances of the new covenant as "signs" only when they are received improperly. It is true that the special term used by Marpeck for the ordinances when validly received is Zeugnis or Mitzeugnis, but it is also true that he used the term Zeichen, understanding it in his own way as a sign of something already present, and not a sign of something thereby given. See Vermanung, Gedenkschrift, pp. 208-9, for both his denial of the term and his positive use of it. (Marpeck's text follows Rothmann, Bekentnisse, loc. cit., p. 24, with a few phrases added, one of which includes the term Zeichen in reference to baptism.) However, Marpeck's vocabulary would have been more consistent, and perhaps more easily understood, had he actually done as Kiwiet reports.

52 I Pet. 3:21 (our translation of Marpeck). Vermanung, Gedenkschrift, p. 204; Rothmann, Bekentnisse, loc. cit., p. 20.

53 Von der Menschheit Christi, ed. Klassen and Bergsten, MQR, XXXII (1958), pp. 208-9.

54 Marpeck employs the term often in the Vermanung, always independent of Rothmann. For instance, p. 209 of the Gedenkschrift edition uses Mitzeugnis twice and Zeugnis once with this general meaning, all three of which are in place of or in addition to Rothmann's teken (Zeichen). Bekentnisse, loc. cit., pp. 24-25. In many instances Marpeck keeps Rothmann's term Zeichen; and in some instances both have Zeugnis, but never with the meaning of Marpeck's Mitzeugnis.

55 Vermanung, Gedenkschrift, p. 208 (not in Rothmann).

56 Ibid., p. 209; Rothmann, Bekentnisse, loc. cit., pp. 24-25. Rothmann's teken is replaced by mitzeüge in Marpeck.

57 Von der innerlichen Kirche, MQR, XXXII (1958), pp. 203-4. As in Hubmaier, the church plays an essential role in the forgiveness of sins. The same passage speaks of the body of Christ: "Das ist die gmeinschaft der heiligen, darjnn durch Christum

Jesum verzeichung der sundt ist." Although Marpeck makes no specific mention of the power of the keys in this passage, he does in the **Vermanung**, where he says that the church of the old covenant had no such power. Circumcision and the sacrifices were only **Wortzeichen** and hence possessed no real power. The church under the new covenant is different, however: its ordinances are **Bundzeichen**. The old church lacked the power of remitting and binding sins, but "die tauff in der kirchen Christi, befolhen und eingesetzt ist **zu eyner bundtzeügnus, die sünd zu verzeihen, und zu behalten.**" (Boldface ours.) Gedenkschrift, p. 231 (not in Rothmann). Interestingly, Marpeck, like Hubmaier, retained the traditional signification of the terms "loosing" and "binding."

58 **Vermanung, ibid.**, p. 207 (not in Rothmann).

59 Ibid., p. 209, following Rothmann, **Bekentnisse,** loc. cit., p. 25. The use of Mitzeugnis and the reference to affusion are additions by Marpeck.

60 **Vermanung, Gedenkschrift,** pp. 207-8. The **Vermanung** material cited in this discussion of the Trinity is all non-Rothmann material, as is true also of the ideas themselves.

61 **Ibid.,** pp. 207-8.

62 John 5:19. **Vermanung, Gedenkschrift,** pp. 229-30. This is an important text for Marpeck relating to the **imitatio Christi** theme: as the Son followed the Father, so are Christ's followers to follow Him. On the general problem of the importance of the "external" works of Christ in their relation to the incarnation and the Christian's **imitatio,** see Verantwurtung I, pp. 133-38, 142-45, 154-56.

63 **Ibid.,** pp. 134-35, 140, 160. It is worthy of note that this view gained clearest expression under the pressure of the debate with Schwenckfeld. The bases of it were laid earlier, however: **Vermanung, Gedenkschrift,** pp. 207-8.

64 "[Christ] gave himself up for her [the church], that he might sanctify her, having cleansed her by the washing of water with the word." Eph. 5:25, 26.

65 **Gedenkschrift,** p. 207.

66 Verantwurtung I, p. 109.

67 **Vermanung, Gedenkschrift,** p. 207.

68 For instance, citing Matt. 16:15-17, Marpeck observed that Jesus attributed Peter's recognition of His Messiahship to the revelation of the Father and not to the Spirit who has done this since Pentecost. **Vermanung, Gedenkschrift,** pp. 229-30.

69 The same principle of the cooperation of the members of the Trinity is seen in respect to the ban in Marpeck's 1545 letter to the Austerlitz Anabaptists. Interestingly, the roles of the Spirit and Christ are reversed here. Recalling the dominical statement that the Son repeats what He sees the Father doing (John 5:19), Marpeck says that the order is the same with the children of the Spirit. "What they see the Father do through Christ according to the inner man, they do in like manner through the co-witness in the Holy Spirit to the outer man. Thus, the body of Christ is built internally through the Holy Spirit and externally through [outer] actions." **Von der innerlichen Kirche,** MQR, XXXII (1958), p. 203.

70 Above, pp. 32, 152 n. 102.

71 The **Vermanung** makes only brief mention of the view: "Demnach, wa einer soll recht dz ausswendig zeychen empfahen, so muss er fürwar das innwendig und ausswendig wesen mit jm bringen, *wa und wann sollichs geschicht, so seind die zeychen nimmer zeychen sunder ein wesen in Christo, noch dem inwendigen und ausswendigen menschen [bold ours]." The portion beginning at the asterisk is Marpeck's addition to Rothmann's text. Gedenkschrift, p. 207; Rothmann, Bekentnisse, loc. cit., p. 24.

72 Bergsten, "Pilgram Marbeck," loc. cit. (1958), pp. 55-56.

73 Hans Urner, "Die Taufe bei Caspar Schwenckfeld," **Theologische Literaturzeitung,** LXXIII (June, 1948), col. 336.

74 "Es wirt nur das ampt und werk der apostel underschaiden und nit die tauff

noch das wasser als element von dem h. geist und feur, auch nit der mensch, weder fleisch, seel noch geist [here a tri-partite distinction], dann ye der ganz glaubig mensch wird getaufft zur verzeihung der sünd." **Verantwurtung I**, p. 113. See Bergsten, "Pilgram Marbeck," loc. cit. (1957), pp. 92-95; (1958), pp. 56-58.

75 **Verantwurtung I**, pp. 133, 149.

76 **Glaubensbekenntnis, TA: Elsass**, I, p. 478.

77 **Verantwurtung I**, pp. 113-14.

78 Eph. 4:5, 6. **Verantwurtung I**, p. 114.

79 I John 5:7, 8 (KJV).

80 **Verantwurtung I**, p. 110. Similiarly, p. 108.

81 **Ibid.**, p. 109.

82 **TA: Elsass**, I, p. 423, art. 26; pp. 432, 480-81.

83 **Gedenkschrift**, p. 218; similarly, p. 224 (neither passage in Rothmann).

84 **Verantwurtung I**, pp. 154-56.

85 **Ibid.**, p. 134.

86 **Ibid.**, p. 160. On the issue of the glorified-unglorified Christ, over which Marpeck and Schwenckfeld divided so sharply, see Bergsten, "Pilgram Marbeck," loc. cit. (1958), pp. 73-74.

87 **Von der Tieffe Christi, Kunstbuch**, fol. 281 verso.

88 **Verantwurtung I**, pp. 140-141, 154-56.

89 **Gedenkschrift**, p. 129.

90 Marpeck, ibid., pp. 225-26; Rothmann, **Bekentnisse**, loc. cit., pp. 41-43.

91 **Gedenkschrift**, pp. 227-28.

92 **Ibid.**, pp. 228-31.

93 **Ibid.**, pp. 231-33, 235-38.

94 **Ibid.**, p. 238. Included in the section is Marpeck's discussion of predestination (pp. 233-35) already alluded to. Believing that the doctrine of predestination denied the importance of human decision and action, Marpeck rejected it in favor of a characteristic Anabaptist voluntarism which required believers' baptism and precluded infant baptism.

95 **Grund und Ursache, Martin Bucers Deutsche Schriften**, I, p. 260. The Scriptural references are Matt. 19:13-15; Mark 10:14-16; Luke 18:15-17. Zwingli had suggested this to Bucer in a letter of Dec. 16, 1524, as one of several Biblical texts capable of being used to defend infant baptism. Bucer's work was published between Dec. 26 and 31, 1524. For details see above, pp. 22-23, with notes.

96 **TA: Elsass**, I, No. 8, pp. 14, 16.

97 **Vermanung, Gedenkschrift**, pp. 238-39; **Bekentnisse**, loc. cit., pp. 46-50. In his 1531 **Glaubensbekenntnis** Marpeck implicitly took the opposite view when he said that Jesus was recognizing the children's participation in the kingdom. Bucer replied with the question as to why they should not be baptized, and insisted that the children in the Gospel story were of believing parents, since no others would have wanted their children blessed. Marpeck denied that the parents were necessarily believers and rejected the inference concerning infant baptism. **TA: Elsass**, I, Nos. 302, 303, pp. 454-55, 459.

The **Verantwurtung II**, p. 199, discusses the passage in terms of foreknowledge, distinguishing between the Esauites and the Jacobites and arguing that God knows each by His foreknowledge.

98 **Vermanung, Gedenkschrift**, pp. 241-42, 250; **Bekentnisse**, loc. cit., p. 54, reproduced with changes and additions by Marpeck, p. 250. For a complete discussion of Marpeck's ideas on original sin, see Bergsten, "Pilgram Marbeck," loc. cit. (1957), pp. 74-82.

99 **TA: Elsass**, I, No. 312, p. 416, art. 1.

100 Vermanung, Gedenkschrift, pp. 215-16, 242, 246 (all of which are additions to Rothmann's text), and 250 (an adapted form of Rothmann's text, loc. cit., p. 54; the expression, in geschöpfflicher einfalt, is Marpeck's addition, however).

101 Juditium, CS, VIII, p. 190.

102 Verantwurtung II, p. 212. The Glaubensbekenntnis had approached this by saying that the children were made holy through the blessing of Christ. TA: Elsass, I, p. 454.

103 The winglian orientation is clear. Cf. above, p. 35. Schwenckfeld also may be reflecting Zwingli's influence in using the figure of a wolf to describe original sin. He said that, like the wolf's desire for sheep, original sin does not come to life in the very young. Juditium, CS, VIII, p. 193 (margin); above, p. 153, n. 115. Marpeck rejected Schwenckfeld's use of the image, saying that it is inappropriate, for a wolf (Marpeck says fox) cannot be reborn free of the desire, but man can. Verantwurtung II, p. 218.

104 Ibid., pp. 199-200. Denck, Widerruf, TA: Denck, Part II, p. 109, art. 8. Bergsten describes this fragmentary doctrine of election as a Tendenz in Marpeck's thought stemming from the Biblical sources, but he does not consider it part of the main line of Marpeck's thought. "Pilgram Marbeck," loc. cit. (1957), pp. 81-82.

105 Marpeck, Vermanung, Gedenkschrift, p. 250; Rothmann, Bekentnisse, loc. cit., p. 54. Hubmaier, above, p. 35.

106 Vermanung, loc. cit., pp. 242-46 (not in Rothmann). Marpeck's reference to Luther is vague: "Als Martinus Luther, der von der erbsünd wider den bapst in eynen büchlin schreibt, und die erbsünd der kinder mit vil argumenten widerficht." Ibid., p. 242. We have been unable to identify the work. Karl Brinkel's listing of the important texts for the idea of fides infantium in Luther includes no work identifiable as this. Die Lehre Luthers von der fides infantium bei der Kindertaufe (Theologische Arbeiten, ed. Hans Urner, et al., Vol. VII; Berlin: Evangelische Verlagsanstalt, 1958), pp. 20-23.

107 Marpeck, Vermanung, Gedenkschrift, pp. 248-49; Rothmann, Bekentnisse, loc. cit., pp. 52-53. This is a very brief statement; Marpeck's principal treatment of the matter is independent of Rothmann.

108 We have found only two passages dealing with it: the one presently under discussion, Vermanung, Gedenkschrift, p. 245 (independent of Rothmann), and his 1531 Gericht und Urteil, a letter to the Swiss Brethren, Kunstbuch, fol. 56-57, in a section which is headed, Evangelium der Creaturen.

109 Vermanung, loc. cit.

110 Ibid.

111 Marpeck, ibid., pp. 247-49; Rothmann, Bekentnisse, loc. cit., pp. 50-53.

112 Or perhaps from the briefer references in Von der christlichen Taufe der Gläubigen. See above, p. 50. Marpeck and Rothmann refer only to the section in which the relevant canons are found: de consecratione, distinctio 4; they name no specific canons.

113 Marpeck, Vermanung, Gedenkschrift, p. 247; Rothmann, Bekentnisse, loc. cit., p. 51. Tertulliani Opera, ed. Beatus Rhenanus (Basil: 1528), p. 451 (located by Detmer and Krumbholtz, op. cit., p. 51, n. 3). Elsewhere Marpeck, following Rothmann, refers to another passage from Tertullian in which the latter describes pre-baptismal penance, and to a passage from Origen which speaks of being buried with Christ in baptism. Tertullian, De poenitentia, chap. vi; Origen, Commentaria in Epistolam ad Romanos (on Rom. 6:3, 4). Both passages were cited by Hubmaier; for the references in Hubmaier and in the original texts see above, p. 157, nn. 206, 211. Marpeck, p. 209; Rothmann, p. 24.

114 Marpeck, Vermanung, Gedenkschrift, pp. 248-49; Rothmann, Bekentnisse, loc. cit., pp. 51-52.

115 Vermanung, Gedenkschrift, p. 247. A reference to Luther's Grund und Ursache

aller Artikel D. Martin Luthers, so durch römische Bulle unrechtlich verdammt sind? WA, VII, pp. 424/425.

116 Vermanung, loc. cit. The Eugenius with whom baptismal regulations are usually associated is Eugenius IV who approved the decision of the Council of Florence that infants should be baptized quamprimum after birth. Walter J. Conway, The Time and Place of Baptism (Canon Law Studies, No. 324; Washington: The Catholic University of America Press, 1954), p. 31.

117 Marpeck, Vermanung, Gedenkschrift, pp. 249-50; Rothmann, Bekentnisse, loc. cit., p. 54.

118 TA: Elsass, I, p. 501.

119 Gedenkschrift, pp. 239-40; following Rothmann, Bekentnisse, loc. cit., pp. 47-48.

120 Above, pp. 118-19.

121 Above, pp. 115-16, 129.

122 Above, pp. 129-30.

123 Vermanung, Gedenkschrift, p. 196; Rothmann, Bekentnisse, loc. cit., p. 10. A further distinction between John's baptism and Christian baptism is seen in the matter of a Bussezeit or catechumenate. Schwenckfeld criticized Marpeck for not insisting on an adequate catechumenate period before baptism. Marpeck replied that such a period has not been necessary since the resurrection, for the repentance brought through the Gospel is the work of God, not just of man. Hence, the period of preparation characteristic of John's baptism is not needed now. Verantwurtung I, pp. 73-74.

124 Vermanung, Gedenkschrift, pp. 196-98; following Rothmann, Bekentnisse, loc. cit., pp. 10-11.

125 Marpeck, Vermanung, loc. cit., p. 198; Rothmann, Bekentnisse, loc. cit., pp. 11-12.

126 Marpeck repeated Rothmann's interpretation of the passage in Romans 6. Vermanung, Gedenkschrift, p. 205; Bekentnisse, loc. cit., pp. 21-22.

127 Above, p. 117.

128 Von der Tieffe Christi, Kunstbuch, fol. 281, verso.

129 In three instances Marpeck simply reproduced Rothmann's term for immersion. The terms and references in the Vermanung, Gedenkschrift, and the Bekentnisse, loc. cit., are respectively: einduncken/intducken, pp. 196/10; gestossen/gestoten, pp. 200/14; gesteckt/gesteken, pp. 205/21. In one instance Marpeck reinforced the immersion idea by adding stossen to duncken (ducken), ibid., pp. 201/15. In several other instances Marpeck mentioned pouring in addition to Rothmann's immersion: ibid., pp. 201/16, 202/17, 202/18, 203/18, 207/24, 209/25, 211/27, 214/32, 241/49. Once, Marpeck softened Rothmann's int water gesteken to sey getaufft . . . mit wasser, ibid., pp. 203/18.

130 Verantwurtung I, pp. 133, 135, 169; Verantwurtung II, p. 456. The first of these is only an oblique reference to mode but is an interesting statement. Speaking of the fleshly reason which leads man into sin, Marpeck says that the reason "undergeen muess in dem kleinen tauffwässerlein."

131 Vermanung, Gedenkschrift, p. 208 (not in Rothmann).

132 However, Marpeck followed Rothmann in being willing to accept the term "sacrament" as technically appropriate for the Christian ordinance. Both interpreted the term narrowly as meaning a pledge or covenant, as it had meant in classical Latin, and both finally recommended against using it because of the misunderstanding it was liable to create. Vermanung, Gedenkschrift, pp. 190-93; Bekentnisse, loc. cit., pp. 3-5. One point which seems to suggest an important disagreement between Marpeck and Rothmann proves upon investigation to be a conflict only in words, if not simply an error. Marpeck says that "sacrament" properly means "ein wesslich ding," like body, bread, wine, or water; Rothmann says it means "eygentlicke geyn (the original reading is 'eygentlick egeyn') wesentlick dinck," which would seem to mean just the opposite.

186 / Anabaptist Baptism

Both draw the same conclusion, however, namely, that it is the "action" (werck), not the "thing," that makes the sacrament. Ibid., respectively, pp. 4, 191.

The term "sacrament" was accepted by several Anabaptists. On its use by Menno Simons and Dietrich Philips, e.g., see William Echard Keeney, "The Development of Dutch Anabaptist Thought and Practice from 1539-1564" (unpublished Ph.D. dissertation, The Hartford Theological Seminary, 1959), p. 109.

Chapter VI. CONCLUSION

1 It is one of the basic theses of Alvin Beachy's Harvard dissertation, op. cit., chap. iii of which is printed as "The Grace of God in Christ as Understood by Five Major Anabaptist Writers," loc. cit., pp. 5-33. Cf. also Hans J. Hillerbrand, "Anabaptism and the Reformation: Another Look," CH, XXIX (1960), pp. 415-18. Thomas Nipperdey, "Theologie und Revolution bei Thomas Müntzer," loc. cit., treats the same theme in Müntzer at considerable length.

2 Hans Hillerbrand, aware of Anabaptism's agreement at points with Catholicism, at points with Protestantism, and its disagreement with both in other matters, has suggested that the movement was sui generis. We judge this to be correct. "Anabaptism and the Reformation: Another Look," loc. cit., p. 418; and "The Origin of Sixteenth-Century Anabaptism: Another Look," loc. cit., pp. 177-80. This is, of course, in principle, what George Huntston Williams has said with his conception of a "Radical" Reformation alongside the Protestant and Catholic Reformations. It is also, in a way, what the Mennonite historians have long contended.

3 It would seem to this writer that something of the same must have been true for the Grebel group in Zurich. Followers and friends of Zwingli though they were, they were not thoroughgoing Zwinglians in their theology. It is notable, for instance, that they found some satisfaction in Müntzer (this fact should in no way color them with the shades of Müntzer's revolution of which they knew nothing since it had not yet begun), particularly in the ideas related to the new birth and the new life that was to issue therefrom. It is also notable that the Grebel group had theological difficulties with Zwingli as well as political ones. We are suggesting, therefore, that one of the factors operative in their split from Zwingli was a different conception of the Christian faith, and that this conception depended in part on non-Zwinglian sources. This is not to challenge the reconstructions of Dean Bender and Professor Blanke, but to suggest a refinement of them at the point of ideas and influences that are specifically theological. Cf. further, Hillerbrand, loc. cit.

4 "Luther und die Schwärmer," Gesammelte Aufsätze zur Kirchengeschichte, I (4th and 5th ed.; Tübingen: J. C. B. Mohr [Paul Siebeck], 1927), pp. 420-67.

5 The recent article by James M. Stayer shows well how Hut represents a midway point between the militancy of Müntzer and the pacificism of the Hutterites. "Hans Hut's Doctrine of the Sword," loc. cit., pp. 181-91.

6 Above, pp. 61-62, 76.

7 Above, pp. 43.

8 Above, pp. 77, 167 n. 2, 182 n. 57.

9 Above, p. 93.

10 Geheimnus, TA: Glaubenszeugnisse, I, p. 25.

APPENDIX

1 Translated from the critically edited text of Gunnar Westin and Torsten Bergsten, TA: HS, No. 19, pp. 347-52. The translation, from pp. 349-50, omits Hubmaier's introduction and his concluding comments about misinterpretations of baptism. The format is more formal than in Hubmaier's text, and the translation is free at points where the meaning or action deserves to be made explicit.

2 Hubmaier says in his introduction that this is "die Form des Wassertauffs, wie wir vns der selben zu Nickolspurg vnd andersswo gebrauchen." Ibid., p. 348.

3 Hubmaier here uses Bischof; this and Ältester were used interchangeably among sixteenth-century Anabaptists. See the introductory note by Westin and Bergsten, ibid., p. 348. Also ME, I, 347-49; II, 178-81.

4 Doubtless meaning to pray the Lord's Prayer, but perhaps also referring to the ability for free prayer.

5 Tauffglubd.

Bibliography

PUBLISHED SOURCES

Primary Sources: Works and Collections of Works

Die älteste Chronik der Hutterischen Brüder: Ein Sprachdenkmal aus frühneuhochdeutscher Zeit. Edited by A. J. F. Zieglschmid. Ithaca, N.Y.: The Cayuga Press, 1943.

Ausbund: Das ist, etliche schöne Christliche Lieder. Lancaster, Pa.: Gedruckt bey Johann Bär, 1834. Edition of 1962 available from Herald Press, Scottdale, Pa. 15683.

Battles, Ford Lewis. **Advocates of Reform: From Wyclif to Erasmus.** The Library of Christian Classics. Edited by John Baillie, et al., Vol. XIV. Philadelphia: The Westminster Press, 1953.

Bucer, Martin. **Martin Bucers Deutsche Schriften,** Vol. I. Edited by Robert Stupperich. Martini Buceri opera omnia, Series I. Gütersloh: Gütersloher Verlagshaus Gerd Mohn, 1960.

Concilium Tridentinum, Diariorum, Actorum, Epistularum, Tractatuum: Nova Collectio. Edited by the Societas Goerresiana. Freiburg i. B.: B. Herder Typographus, Editor Pontificius V, 1901-1938.

Cramer, Samuel, and Pijper, Frederik (eds.). **Bibliotheca Reformatoria Neerlandica.** 10 vols. 's Gravenhage: Martinus Nijhoff, 1903-1914.

Denck, Hans. **Hans Denck: Schriften.** Edited by Georg Baring and Walter Fellmann. Quellen zur Geschichte der Täufer, Vol. VI; Quellen und Forschungen zur Reformationsgeschichte, Vol. XXIV. Gütersloh: C. Bertelsmann Verlag, 1955-1960. Distributed in North America by Herald Press, Scottdale, Pa. 15683.

Eckhart, Meister. **Meister Eckhart: A Modern Translation.** Translated by Raymond Bernard Blakney. New York: Harper and Brothers, 1941.

Günzburg, Johann Eberlin von. **Johann Eberlin von Günzburg: Ausgewählte Schriften,** Vol. I. Edited by Ludwig Enders. Flugschriften aus der Reformationszeit, No. XI. Halle a. S.: Max Niemeyer, 1896.

Hoen, Cornelius. **Epistola christiana.** Huldreich Zwinglis sämtliche Werke, Vol. IV. Edited by Emil Egli, et al. Corpus Reformatorum, Vol. XCI. Leipzig: Verlag von M. Heinsius Nachfolger, 1927, pp. 505-18.

Hofmann, Melchior. **An de gelöfigen vorsambling in Liflant ein korte formaninghe.** Reprint with dedication dated July 29, 1856; n.p.: n.d. Microfilm copy at Andover-Harvard Theological Library.

———. **Bekentnusz des MELCHIOR HOFMANNS vom kindertauff von der mutwilligen oder unvergebl. sünden und vom freyen willen.** Reprinted by Abraham Hulshof. Geschiedenis van de Doopsgezinden te Straatsburg, van 1525 tot 1557. Amsterdam: J. Clausen, 1905, pp. 180-81.

———. **Dat erste Capitel des Evangelisten St. Mattheus geprediget unde uthgelecht.** Extracted by B. N. Krohn. Geschichte der fanatischen und enthusiastischen Wiedertäufer vornehmlich in Niederdeutschland: Melchior Hofmann und die Secte der Hofmannianer. Leipzig: bey Bernhard Christoph Breitkopf, 1758, pp. 134-36.

———. Das Freudenriche zeucknus. Partially reprinted by Friedrich Otto zur Linden. Melchior Hofmann: Ein Prophet der Wiedertäufer. Haarlem: de Erven F. Bohn, 1885, pp. 429-32.

———. Das N. Amsdorf ein lugenhafftiger falscher nasengeist sey. [Kiel]: 1528, Reprint by Gerhard Ficker. Schriften des Vereins für schleswig-holsteinische Kirchengeschichte, 4th Sonderheft. Preetz: 1926.

———. Dat Nicolaus Amsdorff . . . nicht weth wat he setten. [Kiel]: 1528. Reprint by Gerhard Ficker, Schriften des Vereins für schleswig-holsteinische Kirchengeschichte, 5th Sonderheft. Preetz: 1928.

———. Die Ordonnantie Godts. Edited by Samuel Cramer and Frederick Pijper. Bibliotheca Reformatoria Neerlandica, Vol. V. 's-Grevenhage: Martinus Nijhoff, 1909, pp. 125-70.

———. Prophecy oder Weissagung uss warer heiliger götlicher schrifft. [N.p.]: 1530. (Microfilm at Andover-Harvard Theological Library.)

———. Ein sendbrieff an alle gottsförchtigen liebhaber der ewigen warheyt. Edited by Manfred Krebs and Hans Georg Rott. Elsass, II. Teil: Stadt Strassburg, 1533-1535. Quellen zur Geschichte der Täufer, Vol. VIII; Quellen und Forschungen zur Reformationsgeschichte, Vol. XXVII. Gütersloh: Gütersloher Verlagshaus Gerd Mohn, 1960, No. 399, pp. 101-10. Distributed in North America by Herald Press, Scottdale, Pa. 15683.

———. Verclaringe van den geuangenen ende vrien wil. Edited by Samuel Cramer and Frederik Pijper. Bibliotheca Reformatoria Neerlandica, Vol. V. 's-Grevenhage: Martinus Nijhoff, 1909, pp. 171-98.

———. Weissagung uss heiliger götlicher geschrifft. [N.p.]: 1530. (Microfilm at Andover-Harvard Theological Library.)

———. Das 12. Capitel des propheten Danielis ausgelegt. Partially reprinted by B. N. Krohn, Geschichte der fanatischen und enthusiastischen Wiedertäufer vornehmlich in Niederdeutschland: Melchior Hofmann und die Secte der Hofmannianer. Leipzig: bey Bernhard Christoph Breitkopf, 1758.

Hubmaier, Balthasar. Balthasar Hubmaier: Schriften. Edited by Gunnar Westin and Torsten Bergsten. Quellen zur Geschichte der Täufer, Vol. IX; Quellen und Forschungen zur Reformationsgeschichte, Vol. XXIX. Gütersloh: Gütersloher Verlagshaus Gerd Mohn, 1962. Distributed in North America by Herald Press, Scottdale, Pa. 15683.

Hut, Hans. Ein christlicher underricht. Edited by Lydia Müller. Glaubenszeugnisse oberdeutscher Taufgesinnter, Vol. I. Quellen und Forschungen zur Reformationsgeschichte, Vol. XX. Leipzig: M. Heinsius Nachfolger, 1938, pp. 28-37.

———. Ein Sendbrief. Partially reprinted by Lydia Müller, Glaubenszeugnisse oberdeutscher Taufgesinnter, Vol. I. Quellen und Forschungen zur Reformationsgeschichte, Vol. XX. Leipzig: M. Heinsius Nachfolger, 1938, pp. 11-12.

———. Von dem geheimnus der tauf. Edited by Lydia Müller. Glaubenszeugnisse oberdeutscher Taufgesinnter, Vol. I. Quellen und Forschungen zur Reformationsgeschichte, Vol. XX. Leipzig: M. Heinsius Nachfolger, 1938, pp. 19-28.

Kessler, Johannes. Sabbata. Reprint; St. Gallen: Herausgegeben von Emil Egli und Rudolf Schoch, 1902.

Krebs, Manfred, and Rott, Hans Georg (eds.). Elsass, I. Teil: Stadt Strassburg, 1522-1532. Quellen zur Geschichte der Täufer, Vol. VII; Quellen und Forschungen zur Reformationsgeschichte, Vol. XXVI. Gütersloh: Gütersloher Verlagshaus Gerd Mohn, 1959. Distributed in North America by Herald Press, Scottdale, Pa. 15683.

———. Elsass, II. Teil: Stadt Strassburg, 1533-1535. Quellen zur Geschichte der Täufer, Vol. VIII; Quellen und Forschungen zur Reformationsgeschichte, Vol. XXVII.

Gütersloh: Gütersloher Verlagshaus Gerd Mohn, 1959. Distributed in North America by Herald Press, Scottdale, Pa. 15683.

Küssenberg, Heinrich. **Chronik der Reformation in der Grafschaft Baden, im Klettgau und auf dem Schwarzwalde**, ed. Johann Huber. Archiv für schweizerische Reformationsgeschichte, Vol. III. Solothurn: 1875.

Luther, Martin. **D. Martin Luthers Werke: Kritische Gesamtausgabe**. Edited by J. C. F. Knaake, et al. Weimar: Hermann Böhlaus Nachfolger, 1883 ff.

Marpeck, Pilgram. **Glaubensbekenntnis**. Edited by Manfred Krebs and Hans Georg Rott. Elsass, I. Teil: Stadt Strassburg, 1522-1532. Quellen zur Geschichte der Täufer, Vol. VII; Quellen und Forschungen zur Reformationsgeschichte, Vol. XXVI. Gütersloh: Gütersloher Verlagshaus Gerd Mohn, 1959, No. 302, pp. 416-528. Distributed in North America by Herald Press, Scottdale, Pa. 15683.

———. **Von der innerlichen Kirche**. Edited by Torsten Bergsten; translated by William Klassen. The Mennonite Quarterly Review, XXXII (1958), pp. 192-210.

———. **Von der Menschheit Christi**. Edited by Torsten Bergsten; translated by William Klassen. The Mennonite Quarterly Review, XXXII (1958), pp. 192-210.

———. **Pilgram Marbecks Antwort auf Kaspar Schwenckfelds Beurteilung des Buches der Bundesbezeugung von 1542**. Edited by Johann Loserth. Quellen und Forschungen zur Geschichte der oberdeutschen Taufgesinnten im 16. Jahrhundert. Wien und Leipzig: Kommissionsverlag der Verlagsbuchhandlung Carl Fromme Gesellschaft m. b. H., 1929.

———. Testamentserläuterung durch Auszug aus heiliger biblischer Schrift. [N.p.: n.d.] (Microfilm copy at Andover-Harvard Theological Library.)

———. Vermanung; auch gantz klarer/ gründtlicher vnd vnwidersprechlicher bericht. Reprinted by Christian Neff in **Gedenkschrift zum 400 jährigen Jubiläum der Mennoniten oder Taufgesinnten: 1525-1925**. Edited by Christian Hege. Ludwigshafen a. Rh.: Herausgegeben von der Konferenz der Süddeutschen Mennoniten E. V., 1925.

Mecenseffy, Grete (ed.). Oesterreich, I. Teil. Quellen zur Geschichte der Täufer, Vol. XI; Quellen und Forschungen zur Reformationsgeschichte, Vol. XXXI. Gütersloher Verlagshaus, Gerd Mohn, 1964. Distributed in North America by Herald Press, Scottdale, Pa. 15683.

Meyer, Christian. "Zur Geschichte der Wiedertäufer in Oberschwaben": Part I, "Die Anfänge des Wiedertäuferthums in Augsburg." Zeitschrift des historischen Vereins für Schwaben und Neuburg, I (1874), pp. 207-53.

Müller, Lydia (ed.). **Glaubenszeugnisse oberdeutscher Taufgesinnter**, Vol. I. Quellen und Forschungen zur Reformationsgeschichte, Vol. XX. Leipzig: M. Heinsius Nachfolger, 1938.

Müntzer, Thomas. **Thomas Müntzer: Politische Schriften mit Kommentar**. Edited by Carl Hinrichs. Hallische Monographien, ed. Otto Eissfeldt, No. 17. Halle [Saale]: Max Niemeyer Verlag, 1950.

———. **Thomas Müntzer: Sein Leben und seine Schriften**. Edited by Otto Brandt. Jena: Eugen Diederichs Verlag, 1933.

———. **Thomas Müntzers Briefwechsel**. Edited by Heinrich Boehmer and Paul Kirn. Leipzig: Verlag und Druck von B. G. Teubner, 1931.

Muralt, Leonhard von, and Schmid, Walter (eds.). **Quellen zur Geschichte der Täufer in der Schweiz**, Vol. I. Zürich: S. Hirzel Verlag, 1952. Distributed in North America by Herald Press, Scottdale, Pa. 15683.

Oecolampadius, Johannes. **Briefe und Akten zum Leben Oekolampads**, Vol. I. Edited by Ernst Staehelin. Quellen und Forschungen zur Reformationsgeschichte, Vol. X. Leipzig: M. Heinsius Nachfolger, Eger & Sievers, 1927.

Petry, Ray C. (ed. and trans.). **Late Medieval Mysticism**. The Library of Christian

Classics, edited by John Baillie, et al., Vol. XIII. Philadelphia: The Westminster Press, 1957.

Raymond of Sebonde. **Theologia naturalis sive liber creaturarum.** [Impressus Argentine per Martinum Flach, 1496.]

Roth, Friedrich. "Zur Geschichte der Wiedertäufer in Oberschwaben." Part II: "Zur Lebensgeschichte Eitelhans Langenmantels von Augsburg." **Zeitschrift des historischen Vereins für Schwaben und Neuburg,** XXVII (1900), pp. 1-45.

Rothmann, Bernhard. **Zwei Schriften des Münsterschen Wiedertäufers Bernhard Rothmann.** Edited by Heinrich Detmer and Robert Krumbholtz. Dortmund: Druck und Verlag von Fr. Wilh. Ruhfus, 1904.

Schiemer, Leopold. **Das dreierlei gnad.** Edited by Lydia Müller. Glaubenszeugnisse oberdeutscher Taufgesinnter, Vol. I. Quellen und Forschungen zur Reformationsgeschichte, Vol. XX. Leipzig: M. Heinsius Nachfolger, 1938, pp. 58-71.

———. **Die dritt epistel Leonhart Schiemers, darinnen wirt begriffen von dreyerley Tauf im Neuen Testament ganz clärlich enteckt.** Edited by Lydia Müller. Glaubenszeugnisse oberdeutscher Taufgesinnter, Vol. I. Quellen und Forschungen zur Reformationsgeschichte, Vol. XX. Leipzig: M. Heinsius Nachfolger, 1938, pp. 77-79.

———. **Vom Fläschlen.** Edited by Lydia Müller. Glaubenszeugnisse oberdeutscher Taufgesinnter, Vol. I. Quellen und Forschungen zur Reformationsgeschichte, Vol. XX. Leipzig: M. Heinsius Nachfolger, 1938, pp. 72-77.

Schlaffer, Hans. **Bekandtnuss und verantwortung.** Edited by Lydia Müller. Glaubenszeugnisse oberdeutscher Taufgesinnter, Vol. I. Quellen und Forschungen zur Reformationsgeschichte, Vol. XX. Leipzig: M. Heinsius Nachfolger, 1938, pp. 110-15.

———. **Ein kurzer bericht und leer eines recht christlichen lebens.** Edited by Lydia Müller. Glaubenszeugnisse oberdeutscher Taufgesinnter, Vol. I. Quellen und Forschungen zur Reformationsgeschichte, Vol. XX. Leipzig: M. Heinsius Nachfolger, 1938, pp. 94-96.

———. **Ein kurzer Underricht zum Anfang eines recht christlichen Lebens.** Edited by Lydia Müller. Glaubenszeugnisse oberdeutscher Taufgesinnter, Vol. I. Quellen und Forschungen zur Reformationsgeschichte, Vol. XX. Leipzig: M. Heinsius Nachfolger, 1938, pp. 84-94.

Schornbaum, Karl (ed.). **Markgraftum Brandenburg: Bayern, I. Abteilung.** Quellen zur Geschichte der Wiedertäufer, Vol. II; Quellen und Forschungen zur Reformationsgeschichte, Vol. XVI. Leipzig: M. Heinsius Nachfolger, 1934.

Schwenckfeld, Caspar. **Corpus Schwenckfeldianorum.** Edited by Chester David Hartranft, et al. 18 vols. Leipzig: 1907-1961.

Sehling, Emil (ed.). **Die evangelischen Kirchenordnungen des XVI. Jahrhunderts.** Vol. I: Sachsen und Thüringen nebst angrenzenden Gebieten; Part 1: Die Ordnungen Luthers: Die ernestinischen und albertinischen Gebiete. Leipzig: O. R. Reisland, 1902.

Servetus, Michael. **Christianismi restitutio.** Reprint; Nürnberg: 1790.

Wappler, Paul (ed.). **Die Täuferbewegung in Thüringen von 1526-1584.** Beiträge zur neueren Geschichte Thüringens, Vol. II. Jena: Verlag von Gustav Fischer, 1913.

Williams, George Huntston, and Mergal, Angel M. (trans. and eds.). **Spiritual and Anabaptist Writers.** The Library of Christian Classics, edited by John Baillie, et al., Vol. XXV. Philadelphia: The Westminster Press, 1957.

Zwingli, Ulrich. **Huldreich Zwinglis sämtliche Werke.** Edited by Emil Egli, et al. Vols. I-VI, VIII-XIV. Corpus Reformatorum, Vols. LXXXVIII-XCIII, XCV-CI. Leipzig: Verlag von M. Heinsius Nachfolger, 1905 ff.

———. **Zwingli and Bullinger.** Edited by G. W. Bromiley. The Library of Christian Classics, edited by John Baillie, et al., Vol. XXIV. Philadelphia: The Westminster Press, 1953.

SECONDARY SOURCES

Baring, Georg. "Hans Denck und Thomas Müntzer in Nürnberg, 1524," Archiv für Reformationsgeschichte, L, No. 2 (1959), pp. 145-81.

Baur, August. Zwinglis Theologie: Ihr Werden und ihr System. 2 vols. Halle: Max Niemeyer, 1889.

Beachy, Alvin J. "The Grace of God in Christ as Understood by Five Major Anabaptist Writers," The Mennonite Quarterly Review, XXXVII (1963), pp. 5-33.

Bender, Harold. Conrad Grabel, c. 1498-1526: Founder of the Swiss Brethren, Sometimes Called Anabaptists. Studies in Anabaptist and Mennonite History, edited by H. S. Bender, et al., No. 6. Goshen, Ind.: The Mennonite Historical Society, 1950.

———. "Die Zwickauer Propheten, Thomas Müntzer und die Täufer," Theologische Zeitschrift, VIII (1952), pp. 262-78.

Bergsten, Torsten. Balthasar Hubmaier: Seine Stellung zu Reformation und Täufertum. Acta Universitatis Upsaliensis: Studia historico-ecclesiastica Upsaliensia, No. 3. Kassel: J. G. Oncken Verlag, 1961.

———. "Pilgram Marbeck und seine Auseinandersetzung mit Caspar Schwenckfeld," Kyrkohistorisk Arsskrift, LVII (1957), pp. 39-100; LVIII (1958), pp. 53-87.

———, and William Klassen. "Two Letters by Pilgram Marpeck," The Mennonite Quarterly Review, XXXII (1958), pp. 192-210.

Blanke, Fritz. Brüder in Christo: Die Geschichte der ältesten Täufergemeinde. Zürich: Zwingli Verlag, 1955. Available in English translation as Brothers in Christ, Scottdale, Pa.: Herald Press, 1961.

Brinkel, Karl. Die Lehre Luthers von der fides infantium bei der Kindertaufe. Theologische Arbeiten, edited by Hans Urner, et al., Vol. VII. Berlin: Evangelische Verlagsanstalt, 1958.

Conway, Walter J. The Time and Place of Baptism. Canon Law Studies, No. 324. Washington: The Catholic University of America Press, 1954.

Evans, Austin P. An Episode in the Struggle for Religious Freedom: The Sectaries of Nuremberg, 1524-1528. New York: Columbia University Press, 1924.

Farner, Alfred. Die Lehre von Kirche und Staat bei Zwingli. Tübingen: Verlag von J. C. B. Mohr (Paul Siebeck), 1930.

Fast, Heinold. Heinrich Bullinger und die Täufer: Ein Beitrag zur Historiographie und Theologie im 16. Jahrhundert. (Schriftenreihe des Mennonitischen Geschichtsvereins, No. 7.) Weierhof: Mennonitischen Geschichtsverein e. V., 1959.

———. "Pilgram Marbeck und das oberdeutsche Täufertum: Ein neuer Handschriftenfund," Archiv für Reformationsgeschichte, XLVII, Part 2 (1956), pp. 212-42.

Fellmann, Walter. "Das Leben Dencks," Hans Denck: Schriften. Quellen zur Geschichte der Täufer, Vol. VI; Quellen und Forschungen zur Reformationsgeschichte, Vol. XXIV. Gütersloh: C. Bertelsmann Verlag, 1956-1960, Part II, pp. 8-19. Distributed in North America by Herald Press, Scottdale, Pa. 15683.

Foster, Claude R., Jr. "Hans Denck and Johannes Buenderlin: A Comparative Study," The Mennonite Quarterly Review, XXXIX (1965), pp. 115-24.

Friedmann, Robert. "Thomas Müntzer's Relation to Anabaptism," The Mennonite Quarterly Review, XXXI (1957), pp. 75-87.

Goeters, J. F. G. Ludwig Hätzer. Quellen und Forschungen zur Reformationsgeschichte, Vol. XXV. Gütersloh: C. Bertelsmann Verlag, 1957.

Grosheide, G. "Verhooren en vonnissen der Wederdoopers, Betrokken bij de Aanslagen op Amsterdam in 1524 en 1535." Bijdragen en Mededelingen van het Historisch Genootschap, XLI (1920), pp. 1-197.

Hall, Thor. "Possibilities of Erasmian Influence on Denck and Hubmaier in Their Views on the Freedom of the Will," The Mennonite Quarterly Review, XXXV (April, 1961), pp. 149-70.

Hershberger, Guy F. **The Recovery of the Anabaptist Vision: A Sixtieth Anniversary Tribute to Harold S. Bender.** Scottdale, Pa.: The Herald Press, 1957.

Heymann, Frederick G. **John Ziska and the Hussite Revolution.** Princeton: Princeton University Press, 1955.

Hillerbrand, Hans J. "Anabaptism and the Reformation: Another Look," **Church History,** XXIX (1960), pp. 404-23.

——. Bibliographie des Täufertums: 1520-1630. Quellen zur Geschichte der Täufer, Vol. X; Quellen und Forschungen zur Reformationsgeschichte, Vol. XXX. Gütersloher Verlagshaus Gerd Mohn, 1962. Distributed in North America by Herald Press, Scottdale, Pa. 15683.

——. "The Origin of Sixteenth-Century Anabaptism: Another Look," Archiv für Reformationsgeschichte, LII (1962), pp. 152-80.

——. Die Politische Ethik des oberdeutschen Täufertums: Eine Untersuchung zur Religions- und Geistesgeschichte des Reformationszeitalters. Beihefte der Zeitschrift für Religions- und Geistesgeschichte, VII. Leiden-Köln: E. J. Brill, 1962.

Hinrichs, Carl, **Luther und Müntzer: Ihre Auseinandersetzung über Obrigkeit und Widerstandsrecht.** Arbeiten zur Kirchengeschichte, edited by Kurt Aland, et al., No. 29. Berlin: Walter de Gruyter & Co., 1952.

Holl, Karl. "Luther und die Schwärmer." **Gesammelte Aufsätze zur Kirchengeschichte,** Vol. I. 4th and 5th ed. Tübingen: J. C. B. Mohr (Paul Siebeck), 1927, pp. 420-67.

Hosek, Frantisek Xaver. "Life of Balthasar Hubmeyer, the Founder of 'New Christianity' in Moravia." Translated by William W. Everts, Jr. **Texas Historical and Biographical Magazine,** I (1891), pp. 118-48, passim; II (1892), pp. 19-32, passim.

Hulshof, Abraham. **Geschiedenis van de Doopsgezinden te Straatsburg van 1525 tot 1557.** Amsterdam: J. Clausen, 1905.

Jeremias, Joachim. **Infant Baptism in the First Four Centuries.** Translated by David Cairns. London: SCM Press Ltd., 1960.

Jetter, Werner. **Die Taufe beim jungen Luther.** Beiträge zur historischen Theologie, edited by Gerhard Ebeling, No. 18. Tübingen: J. C. B. Mohr (Paul Siebeck), 1954.

Kawerau, Peter, **Melchior Hofmann als religiöser Denker.** Haarlem: de Erven F. Bohn N. V., 1954.

Kiwiet, Jan J. "The Life of Hans Denck (ca. 1500-1527)," **The Mennonite Quarterly Review,** XXXI (1957), pp. 227-59.

——. Pilgram Marbeck: Ein Führer in der Taüferbewegung der Reformationszeit. 2nd ed. Kassel: J. G. Oncken Verlag, 1958.

Klaassen, Walter. "Hans Hut and Thomas Muntzer," **The Baptist Quarterly,** XIX, No. 5 (Jan. 1962), pp. 209-27.

Klassen, Herbert. "Ambrosius Spittelmayr: His Life and Teachings," **The Mennonite Quarterly Review,** XXXII (1958), pp. 251-71.

——. "The Life and Teachings of Hans Hut," **The Mennonite Quarterly Review,** XXXIII (1959), pp. 171-205, 267-304.

Klassen, William. "Pilgram Marpeck in Recent Research," **The Mennonite Quarterly Review,** XXXII (1958), pp. 211-29, 248.

——, and Torsten Bergsten. "Pilgram Marbeck's Two Books of 1531," **The Mennonite Quarterly Review,** XXXII (1959), pp. 18-31.

Krohn, B. N. **Geschichte der fanatischen und enthusiastischen Wiedertäufer vornehmlich in Niederdeutschland: Melchior Hofmann und die Secte der Hofmannianer.** Leipzig: bey Bernhard Christoph Breitkopf, 1758.

Leendertz, W. I. **Melchior Hofmann.** Haarlem: de Erven F. Bohn, 1883.

Linden, Friedrich Otto zur. **Melchior Hofmann: Ein Prophet der Wiedertäufer.** Haarlem: de Erven F. Bohn, 1885.

Littell, Franklin Hamlin. **The Anabaptist View of the Church: A Study in the Origins of Sectarian Protestantism.** 2nd ed., revised. Boston: Starr King Press, 1958.

———. (ed.). **Reformation Studies: Essays in Honor of Roland H. Bainton.** Richmond: John Knox Press, 1962.

Lohmann, Annemarie. **Zur geistigen Entwicklung Thomas Müntzers. Beiträge zur Kulturgeschichte des Mittelalters und der Renaissance,** edited by Walter Goetz, Vol. XLVII. Leipzig: Verlag und Druck von B. G. Teubner, 1931.

Loofs, Friedrich. **Leitfaden zum Studium der Dogmengeschichte.** 6th rev. ed. Edited by Kurt Aland. Tübigen: Max Niemeyer Verlag, 1959.

Loserth, Johann. **Doktor Balthasar Hubmaier und die Anfänge der Wiedertaufe in Mähren.** Brunn: Verlag der historischstatistischen Section, Druck von Rudolf M. Rohrer, 1893.

Male, Emile. **The Gothic Image: Religious Art in France of the Thirteenth Century.** New York: Harper Torchbooks, Harper & Brothers Publishers, 1958.

Mau, Wilhelm. **Balthasar Hubmaier. Abhandlungen zur mittleren und neueren Geschichte,** edited by Georg von Below, Heinrich Finke, and Friedrich Meinecke, Vol. XL. Berlin and Leipzig: Walter Rothschild, 1912.

Mecenseffy, Grete. "Die Herkunft des oberösterreichischen Täufertums," **Archiv für Reformationsgeschichte,** XLVII, No. 2 (1956), pp. 252-59.

———."Das Verständnis der Taufe bei den Süddeutschen Täufern." Antwort: Karl Barth, zum siebzigsten Geburtstag. Zollikon-Zürich: Evangelischer Verlag Ag., 1956, pp. 642-46.

Meusel, Alfred. **Thomas Müntzer und seine Zeit.** Berlin: Aufbau-Verlag, 1952.

Müller, Lydia. **Der Kommunismus der mährischen Wiedertäufer. Schriften des Vereins für Reformationsgeschichte,** Vol. CXLII. Leipzig: M. Heinsius Nachfolger, Eger und Sievers, 1927.

Neumann, Gerhard J. "The Anabaptist Position on Baptism and the Lord's Supper," **The Mennonite Quarterly Review,** XXXV (1961), pp. 140-48.

Neuser, Wilhelm. **Hans Hut: Leben und Wirken bis zum Nikolsburger Religionsgespräch.** Berlin, 1913.

Nipperdey, Thomas. "Theologie und Revolution bei Thomas Müntzer," **Archiv für Reformationsgeschichte,** LIV (1963), pp. 145-81.

Pfister, Rudolf. **Das Problem der Erbsünde bei Zwingli.** Neuruppin: Druck von E. Buchbinder (H. Duske) G. m. b. h., 1938.

Planitz, Hans. **Die Deutsche Stadt im Mittelalter.** Graz-Köln: Böhlau-Verlag, 1954.

Quiring, Horst. "The Anthropology of Pilgram Marbeck," **The Mennonite Quarterly Review,** IX (1935), pp. 155-64.

Rupp, Gordon. "Andrew Karlstadt and Reformation Puritanism," **Journal of Theological Studies,** X (1959).

———. "Thomas Müntzer, Hans Huth and the 'Gospel of All Creatures,'" **Bulletin of John Rylands Library,** XLIII (1961), pp. 492-519.

———. "Word and Spirit in the First Years of the Reformation," **Archiv für Reformationsgeschichte,** XLIX, No. 1 (1958), pp. 13-26.

Sachsse, Carl. **Doktor Balthasar Hubmaier als Theologe. Neue Studien zur Geschichte der Theologie und der Kirche,** edited by N. Bonwetsch and R. Seeberg, No. 20. Berlin: Trowitzsch und Sohn, 1914.

Schrenk, Gottlob. **Gottesreich und Bund im älteren Protestantismus.** Gütersloh: C. Bertelsmann Verlag, Gütersloh: 1923.

Schulze, R. Wilhelm. "Neuere Forschungen über Balthasar Hubmaier von Waldshut." **Alemannisches Jahrbuch: 1957.** Lahr/ Schwarzwald: Moritz Schauenburg Verlag, 1957, pp. 224-72.

Stauffer, Ethelbert. "Märtyrertheologie und Täuferbewegung," Zeitschrift für Kirchengeschichte, 3rd series, LII, No. 4 (1933), pp. 545-98.
Stayer, James M. "Hans Hut's Doctrine of the Sword: An Attempted Solution," The Mennonite Quarterly Review, XXXIX (1965), pp. 181-91.
Theobald, Leonhard. "Balthasar Hubmaier," Zeitschrift für Bayrische Kirchengeschichte, XV (1941), pp. 153-65.
Trinterud, Leonard J. "The Origins of Puritanism," Church History, XX, No. 1 (1951), pp. 35-57.
Urner, Hans. "Die Taufe bei Caspar Schwenckfeld," Theologische Literaturzeitung, LXXIII (June, 1948), cols. 329-42.
Usteri, Johannes Martin. "Darstellung der Tauflehre Zwinglis," Theologische Studien und Kritiken, LV, No. 2 (1882), pp. 205-84.
Vedder, H. C. **Balthasar Hubmaier: The Leader of the Anabaptists. Heroes of the Reformation,** edited by Samuel Macauley Jackson, [n. no.]. New York: G. P. Putnam's Sons, The Knickerbocker Press, 1905.
Vogelsang, Erich. "Weltbild und Kreuzestheologie in den Höllenfahrtsstreitigkeiten der Reformationszeit," Archiv für Reformationsgeschichte, XXXVIII (1941), pp. 90-132.
Wappler, Paul. "Thomas Müntzer in Zwickau und die 'Zwickauer Propheten.' " Wissenschaftliche Beilage zu dem Jarhesberichte des Realgymnasiums mit Realschule zu Zwickau, Program No. 734. Zwickau: Druck der Firma Zwickauer Zeitung, Amtsblatt, R. Zückler, 1908.
Wenger, John C. "The Theology of Pilgram Marpeck," The Mennonite Quarterly Review, XII (1938), pp. 205-56.
Williams, George Huntston. **The Radical Reformation.** Philadelphia: The Westminster Press, 1962.
———. "Studies in the Radical Reformation (1517-1618): A Bibliographical Survey of Research Since 1939." Church History, XXVII (1958), No. 1, pp. 46-69; No. 2, pp. 124-60.
———. **Wilderness and Paradise in Christian Thought: The Biblical Experience of the Desert in the History of Christianity and the Paradise Theme in the Theological Idea of the University.** New York: Harper and Brothers, 1962.
Wiswedel, W. Hubmaier der Vorkämpfer für Glaubens- und Gewissensfreiheit. Kassel: Verlag von J. G. Oncken, 1939.
Wray, Frank J. "The 'Vermanung' of 1542 and Rothmann's 'Bekentnisse,' " Archiv für Reformationsgeschichte, XLVII, Part 2 (1956), pp. 243-51.
Yoder, John Howard. "Balthasar Hubmaier and the Beginnings of Swiss Anabaptism," The Mennonite Quarterly Review, XXXIII (1959), pp. 5-17.
———. **Täufertum und Reformation in der Schweiz.** Vol. I: Die Gespräche zwischen Täufern und Reformatoren: 1523-1538. Schriftenreihe des Mennonitischen Geschichtsvereins, No. 6. Karlsruhe: Herausgegeben vom Mennonitischen Geschichtsverein e. V. Weierhof, Buchdruckerei und Verlag H. Schneider, 1962. Distributed in North America by Herald Press, Scottdale, Pa. 15683.
———. "The Turning Point in the Zwinglian Reformation," The Mennonite Quarterly Review, XXXII (1958), pp. 128-40.
Zuck, Lowell. "Fecund Problems of Eschatological Hope, Election Proof, and Social Revolt in Thomas Müntzer." **Reformation Studies: Essays in Honor of Roland H. Bainton.** Edited by Franklin H. Littell. Richmond: John Knox Press, 1962.

UNPUBLISHED SOURCES

Primary Sources

Hubmaier, Balthasar. "The Writings of Balthasar Hubmaier." Translated by George D. Davidson. (Unpublished typescript at William Jewell College; microfilm at Andover-Harvard Theological Library.)

[Hut, Hans.] **Ein Anfang eins rechten christlichen Lebens.** Das Kunstbuch, fol. 15 recto-26 verso.

———. **Von dem geheimnus der tauf, baide des zaichens und des wesens: ein anfang eines rechten warhaftigen christlichen lebens.** In Codex Ab 6, pp. 59-107, University Library, Budapest. Microfilm possessed by author.

Das Kunstbuch. Edited by George Maler. Sixteenth-century manuscript collection of Anabaptist tracts and letters at the Bürgerbibliothek in Bern, Switzerland. (Typescript copy at the Mennonite Historical Library, Goshen College.)

Marpeck, Pilgram. **Epistel an die Schweizer Brueder von wegen der jähen Gricht und Urteil (1531).** Das Kunstbuch, fol. 27 recto-62 verso; pp. 56-93 of the Mennonite Historical Library typescript.

———. **Von der Tieffe Christi.** Das Kunstbuch, fol. 278 recto-301 recto; pp. 320-46 of the Mennonite Historical Library typescript.

Secondary Sources

Beachy, Alvin. "The Concept of Grace in the Radical Reformation." Unpublished Th.D. dissertation, Harvard University, July, 1960.

Keeney, William Echard. "The Development of Dutch Anabaptist Thought and Practice from 1539-1564." Unpublished Ph.D. dissertation, The Hartford Theological Seminary, 1959.

Klaassen, Walter. "Word, Spirit, and Scripture in Early Anabaptist Thought." Unpublished Ph.D. dissertation, University of Oxford, Regent's Park College, 1960.

Klassen, William. "The Hermeneutics of Pilgram Marpeck." Unpublished Th.D. dissertation, Princeton Theological Seminary, 1960.

Krodel, Gottfried G. "Die Abendmahlslehre des Erasmus von Rotterdam und seine Stellung am Anfang des Abendmahlsstreites der Reformatoren." Unpublished doctoral dissertation, University of Erlangen, 1955.

Neuser, Wilhelm. "Hans Hut: Leben und Wirken bis zum Nikolsburger Religionsgespräch." Unpublished dissertation for the Licentiate in Theology, University of Bonn, 1913. Typescript at the Mennonite Historical Library, Goshen College.

Walton, Robert. "Zwingli's Theocracy." Unpublished Ph.D. dissertation, Yale Univerversity, 1964.

Zuck, Lowell. "Anabaptist Revolution Through the Covenant in Sixteenth Century Continental Protestantism." Unpublished Ph.D. dissertation, Yale University, 1954.

Indexes

SUBJECT

Adiaphora, 23
Administration of baptism, 54-56, 84, 87-89, 93-95, 107-09, 124-24, 133, 143-44
  forehead, on the, 78-89, 94, 172 n. 106
  milk pail, from a, 19, 54
  See also Mode of baptism
Administrator of baptism, 94-95, 107-8, 125, 133, 143, 187 n. 3 unworthy, 55
Age for baptism
  old enough to remember, 61
  seven as minimum, 55
  shortly after birth, 185 n. 116
  six or seven, 61
  thirty, 93, 95
  three, 23
Anabaptism
  emergence of, 147 n. 12, 148 n. 18
  origins in Zwingli, 26
  sui generis, 34, 137, 186 n. 2
Anfechtung, 60-61, 65, 80
Anguish, in guilt, 54, 116-17, 141; spiritual, 80, 100, 116-17
Apostles' Creed, 54-55
Apostolic practice of baptism, 27, 59; "house" baptisms, 22
"Apostolic teachers" (Hofmann), 103, 105, 107-8, 110
Aristotelian teleology, 65, 83-84
Atonement: satisfaction theory, 84-85
  universal, 84-85, 98-99
Austrian authorities, 22

Ban, 43-46, 69, 77, 92, 122-23, 182 n. 69; See also Keys of binding and loosing
Baptism: confession or testimony, a, 31-32, 43, 47, 115, 119, 139-40 a "co-witness," 121-25, 127, 133, 140
  "essence" of, the, 83-84
  lifelong death and resurrection, a, 61-62, 92, 118-19, 140-142
  lifelong struggle with sin, a 54-55, 57, 84, 119, 140-42
  objective power of, the 46-47, 57, 90-91, 93, 96, 111-12, 133, 136-37, 139-41
  penalty for lack of, 30, 32, 52-53, 59, 89-90
  seal, a, 36, 88-89, 91, 93, 111, 122, 138, 140
  sign, a, 23, 26, 29, 37, 41-42, 48, 76 f., 83 f., 88-89, 102-07, 120-124, 140, 181 n. 51
  See also the many related topics
Baptism of blood, 42, 52-54, 78, 92-93, 116-17, 127-28, 141
Baptisms of Spirit, water, and blood, 42, 52-54, 78, 92-93, 116-17, 127-29, 140-42
  unity of, 127
Believers' baptism 21, 24-25, 27-35
  arguments for, 40, 70-71
  in the New Testament, 29-30
  practiced by the early church 49-52, 131
Bible translations
  late medieval, 24, 67, 165 n. 87
  Luther, 24, 63, 67-68, 152 n. 94, 180 n. 38
  Vulgate, 48, 68, 73, 163 n. 51, 180 n. 38
  Zürich, 24, 48, 67, 152 n. 94, 180 n. 38
Bishop, 54 f., 131, 143-44, 187 n. 3
Body of Christ, 45-46, 80, 84-85, 123-24, 128, 140, 182 n. 69
Bundezeichen, 63, 76, 78, 163 n. 50, 180 n. 37, 182 n. 57

Catechumenate, 59, 150 n. 62, 185 n. 123
  See also Preparation for baptism
Catholic elements in:
  Anabaptism 136-37
  Hofmann, 102
  Hubmaier, 33-34, 39, 45-46, 52-53
  Marpeck, 115
Catholic view of baptism, 51-53, 102
  circumcision, and, 36-37
  institution of baptism, 39, 48
  of John and Jesus, 39
  Keys, and the, 46
Children:
  age of discretion, 130, 162 n. 38, 173 n. 118
  blessed by Christ, 22, 48, 132, 184 n. 102
  dedication of, 23-24, 129-30, 132-33
Church, 28, 31, 33, 40, 77-78, 84, 94, 108, 124-25, 128, 132-33, 140-43
  ark of Noah, the, 45
  baptismal vow, and the, 43, 55, 69-70
  Bride of Christ, the, 45

197

fallen, 106
Keys, and the, 43-46, 69, 122-23
purity of, 44
society, and, 162 n. 42
Woman in the Wilderness, the, 106
universal-particular, 45-46, 144
visible-invisible, 45-46, 55, 57, 144
Church councils:
Cartnage V and Laodicea, 157 n. 209
Florence, 185 n. 116
Trent, 156 n. 188
Circumcision, 36-38,
inner, 37, 48, 177 n. 85
original sin, and 36
succeeded by inner baptism, 37, 48-49, 63-64, 114-15, 129, 132
unity with baptism, 22, 36-38, 113-14
Cloven hoof, principle of the, 103
Comfort, 42, 82, 119, 123
Confession of:
Christ, 23, 131
faith through baptism, 29-33, 43, 47, 115, 119, 139-40
sin, 29, 122-23
Congregation's role in baptism, 43, 45, 55
Conscience, the good, 48, 118,
knowledge of, 31
covenant of, 99, 115, 118, 122, 138; See I Pet. 3:21
Covenant, 23, 26, 31, 36-44, 55-56, 61-63, 76-79, 88, 90-92, 95-96, 129, 138-39
ban, and the, 43-44
in baptism, 71-72, 99-100, 106, 111-20, 133, 138-39, 143 f., 187 n. 5
church, and the, 69-70
conscience, of a good, 63, 83, 126
Franciscan view of, 41, 181 n. 57
inner and outer, 60-62-64, 70, 83-84, 129, 133
military oath, analogy to, 40-42, 161 n. 36
nuptial, 100, 119
Old and new covenants, 39, 51, 63, 113-20, 129, 132, 181 n. 57
peasants, of the, 61
tool for reforming society, a, 41, 61-62, 76, 138-39
theology of, 36
See Oath, civic
Creatures and creaturely 60, 65-68, 72, 78-83, 100-1, 119, 131
See Gospel of all creatures
Cross, 40, 85-86, 89-90, 141-42
for all creatures, 81
mystical, 80

suffering of, 42, 61, 65-67, 77-79, 128, 141

Death and resurrection, 54, 56, 80-81, 85, 99, 119, 132
in baptism 49, 85, 92, 116-17, 133, 140-42
Death, second, 101-2
Deathbed baptism, 53-54
Dedication service for infants, 23-24
descensus ad infernos—see Hell
Devil, 99
renunciation of, 23, 131
Discipleship, 25, 80, 85, 93, 95, 128, 172 n. 106
Discipline, 29, 43-46, 55, 69-70, 77-78, 122-23, 144
Disputations:
Waldshut (proposed), 21
Zürich, Second (Oct., 1523), 20-21, 26, 28, 148 n. 12
Third (First Baptismal, Jan. 17, 1525), 22

Early church,
baptismal practice, 19-20, 49-52, 131
Fathers of, 49-52
Effect of baptism,
on the baptizand, 32
on others, 32
See Baptism, the objective power of
Elect, 84-85, 87, 90-91, 96, 100-2, 106, 111-12, 138-139
church of the, 76
covenant of the, 76, 106, 138
"elect friend of God," the, 65, 85
Eschatology, 86-91, 95-96, 102-7, 111-12, 137-38, 140-42, 148 n. 19
Eucharist
See Lord's Supper
Examination for baptism, 54-55
See Catechumenate
Exodus experience, 82, 99-102, 104-6, 111-12, 142
Ex opere operato, 36

Faith, 85-86, 169 n. 54
baptizand, of the, 29, 31, 49, 119, 123
"believed" and "known" 80, 86
church, of the, 23
future, 28-29
infants, of, 130-31

objective and subjective, 31
parents, of the, 23, 31
sacraments, and the, 24, 26, 31-32, 49, 51-52, 72, 119
sola fide, 24, 34, 36, 137
Fall of man, 32, 34-35, 114, 130
Fire, baptism of, 89-90
Foreknowledge 183 n. 97
Forgiveness of sin, 31, 39, 122-23
and baptism, 38, 48, 144, 181 n. 57
baptism necessary for, 46
baptism a sign of, 48
given in water baptism, 121-23
power of, 45-46
Frankenhausen, battle of, 74

Gelassenheit, 56, 80, 117, 128
Good and evil, knowledge of, 32-33, 102, 118, 130
Gospel of all creatures, 64-68, 71-74, 80-83, 94, 117, 131, 171 n. 89, 172 n. 106
Grace, 168 n. 11
 alone, 34
 Catholic and Protestant conceptions of, 33-34, 102
 in baptism, 126-27
Great commission, 38-39, 70, 97, 111, 133
Greeting to the baptized, 94

Hell (Hades), 38, 82, 84-85, 90, 102
 descent into, 115, 133, 168 n. 16, 178 n. 12
 spiritual, 38, 60-61, 65, 80, 82-83, 133
Hermeneutic, 70, 103-4, 111
Holy Spirit, 26, 30-33, 59-60, 63, 78, 85-86, 91-93, 99, 11, 115-16 118, 129 143-44, 169 n. 50, 180 n. 33
 inner testimony of, 121-22, 137, 140
"House" baptisms (N.T.), 22
Hutterites, 75, 93, 172 n. 106, 174 n. 124, 186 n. 5

Icons, 20
Image of God, 32-33
Imitation of Christ, 54, 93, 95, 99, 102, 128, 133, 172 n. 106, 174 n. 123, 182 n. 62
Imposition of hands, 55, 144
Infant baptism, 19-24, 63
 arguments against, 20, 25, 28-29, 49, 129-32, 148 n. 19
 arguments for 22-23, 36-37, 129-32
 Hubmaier's first denial of, 22-23

Infants, status of, 31, 35, 130-31
Inner and outer baptism, 22-23, 25-26, 30-32, 37-38, 48-49, 59, 62-64, 76-77, 82, 86, 94, 101, 111, 113, 133
 unity of 120-27, 133
Institution of baptism, occasion of, 39, 48, 133
Jews, 82, 89, 115, 174 n. 10
Justification, 34, 36, 44, 79-86, 120, 135-36, 161 n. 30, 169 n. 54
Key of David, 103-4, 160 n. 15
Keys of binding and loosing, 43-46, 122-23, 139-40, 144, 167 n. 2
 in relation to baptism, 45-46, 55, 77
 See also Ban
Law and Gospel, 38-40, 48, 54, 114-17, 164 n. 63
Liturgies of baptism, ancient, 32
Lord's Prayer, 55, 187 n. 4
Lord's Supper (Eucharist, Mass), 20, 22, 25, 56, 123, 142, 144, 155 n. 158, 175 n. 25
Masses for the dead, 131

Man, nature of, 32-33
 inner and outer, 32, 125-26
 spirit and flesh, 125-26
 See also Free will
Marital imagery, 99-100, 106, 111, 119, 138
Martyrdom, 52-54, 83, 86, 141, 172 n. 106
Martyrs' Synod, 87
Mass
 See Lord's Supper
Miles Christi, 40-42
Military symbolism in baptism, 40-42, 99-100
Mode of baptism:
 affusion, 54-55, 94, 108, 133, 151 n. 85, 185 n. 129
 immersion, 123, 133, 151 n. 85, 185 n. 129
 without water, 108
 See also Administration of baptism
Mystical tradition, 60-61, 65, 82-83, 100-2, 107, 111

Naming and baptism, 23, 132
Natural theology, 64, 66-67, 79, 81-83
New Israel, 41
New Jerusalem, 105-6
New Testament and baptism 28-30, 47-49, 111, 132-33

Oath, civic, 61, 139
Original sin, 23-24, 35-36, 95, 130
Parables, 81
  Good Samaritan, 40, 53
  Great Physician 40, 116
  Great Supper, 33, 98-99
  Mustard Seed, 29
  Tares and wheat, 59
  used in preaching, 131

Paulicians, 95, 173 n. 122
Peasants' Revolt, 19, 87, 147 n. 3
Pelagianism, 34, 130
  See also Will, human
Perfectionism, 29, 34, 41-42, 101, 118, 136, 170 n. 57
Persecution, 42, 53-54, 78, 80, 83-84, 88-89, 92-93, 105, 107, 117, 128, 141, 172 n. 106
Pilgram church 142
Place of baptism:
  church, 55, 108-9
  homes, 55
  street, 108-9
Polish Anabaptists, 173 n. 122
Pope (Papacy), 44, 50, 131-32, 157 n. 209
  See also popes by name
Postponement of baptism, 58
  adopted by Hubmaier, 22-23
  accepted by Zwingli, 19-20
  considered by Oecolampadius, 22-23
Prayer for infants, 23, 132
Predestination, election, 31, 34-35, 119-20, 184 n. 104
  basis for baptism (Zwingli), 35
Preparation for baptism, 31, 54-55, 95
  See also Catechumenate
Priesthood of all believers, 21, 44
Promised land (spiritual), 100-1
Protestant influence on Anabaptism, 136-37
  See also Luther, Zwingli
Purgatory, 171 n. 89

Rebaptism, 39, 48, 93-94
Reformed tradition, 113, 120, 126, 178 n. 6
Regeneration, 60, 80, 106, 129, 133
  a key to Anabaptism, 44, 119, 135-38
  and baptism, 57, 111, 120-22
  distinguished from water baptism, 26, 31
  distinguished from justification, 85-86, 169 n. 54
  stages of, 97-102
  related to the will, 33, 98-99, 119-20

Repentance 20, 39-40, 51, 60, 132-33
  no second, 101
Resurrection, hope of, 26
Revolution, 61, 87, 90, 138, 162 n. 42, 166 n. 110, 174 n. 123
Righteousness:
  forensic, 34, 85-86, 120, 161 n. 30
  inherent, 34, 85-86, 102, 117-20, 161 n. 30

Sabellianism, 125
Sacrament, the term, 56, 185 n. 132
Sacramentalism, 34, 46, 121, 134
Sacramentarianism, 148 n. 19
Saints, invocation of, 21
Salvation, 59, 115
  and baptism, 45-46
  and the church, 45-46
  See also Justification, Regeneration
Sanctification, 79, 85-86, 99, 101-2
Scholastics, 34, 36-37, 48, 51
Schwärmer, 137-38
Scripture:
  allegorical interpretation of, 103, 111, 176 n. 46
  radical and moderate positions on, 20-21, 24, 28, 37, 103-4, 153 n. 124
  sola scriptura, 21
  typological interpretation of, 103-4
Second Advent, 87-91, 104-6, 111, 142 date of, 87, 104-5
Sectarianism, 24
Self-dedication in baptism, 31, 40-42, 69-70, 76-77, 83, 91, 101-2, 118-19
Seven seals of the Apocalypse, 87-89
Sin:
  and baptism, 29
  confession of, 29, 122-23
  forgiveness of, 38-39
  knowledge of, 38
Spirit baptism, 22, 26, 30-33, 59-63, 71, 76-78, 85-86, 92-93, 110-11, 115, 119, 125-26, 140-41
Spiritualism, moderate (Zwingli), 26, 30-31, 103
Spiritualists, 25, 113, 120, 122, 125-26, 133, 136-37, 148 n. 19
Suffering:
  a baptism, 42-43, 53-54, 65, 71, 77-79, 83-84, 86, 89-90, 93-94 116-17, 128-29, 133, 141, 172 n. 106
  inner suffering, 60-61, 65, 80-81, 116-17, 137
  in persecution, see Persecution

life of, 72
mystic, 60-61, 65-67, 82-83, 141
See also Martyrdom
Suspension of baptism for two years, 1^7
Sword, Christians and the, 87, 90, 117, 136

Taborites, 161 n. 36
Tribulation, water of all, 80-84
Trinity, 30, 32, 79-86, 88, 103, 121-25, 129, 144, 158 n. 227
Turks, 82, 88-89
Typology of baptism 103-4, 107, 111
  Noah 32, 37, 46, 48, 51, 103
  Exodus, 99, 103-4, 11-12 (See Exodus experience)
  faithful bride of Song of Songs, 99
  Feast of Tabernacles, 106

Universal nature of baptism, 81-82, 84, 95
Universalism, 84-85, 98, 171 n. 89, 174 n. 7
Visions, 97, 174 n. 123
Volkskirche, 24
Voluntarism, 31-32, 34-35, 41-42, 119-20, 183 n. 94
  See also Will, human
Wilderness, 60, 93, 99-102, 105-6
Will, human:
  develops at age seven, 55
  freedom of, 32-35, 97-102, 119-20
  preparation of for grace, 33-34
  restored in Christ, 32-33, 97-102, 118-20
  See also Children, Regeneration, Voluntarism.
Word and Spirit, 33
Works-righteousness, 136, 152 n. 111

PERSONS AND PLACES

Aaron, 105
Abraham, 103, 104
 covenant of, 37, 60, 64, 114
Adam, 84, 98, 103, 129-30, 152 n. 101
 First Adam, Second Adam, 101
Allstedt, 61, 159 n. 2
Allstedt, 61, 159 n. 2
Ambrose, 51-52
Amsdorf, Nicholas, 105
Anna, the prophetess, 104
Anneken Jans of Rotterdam, 172 n. 106
Anshelm, see Valerius Rüd
Anwald, Hermann, 87, 94, 170 n. 71, 171 n. 90
Aquinas, Thomas, 51, 153 n. 22
Athanasius, 50
Augsburg, 52, 58, 64
 confessions of Hut, 78, 92
 trial of Hut, 70, 92
Augustine, 36, 50-51, 139, 157 n. 209
Austerlitz, 122

Babylon, 105
Bader, Augustine, 94
Bader, Johannes, 151 n. 74, 163 n. 51
Baiersdorf, 88
Basel, 22-23, 63, 110, 150 n. 53
Basil the Great, 51
Beningha, Eggerick, 108-9
Bern, 159 n. 233
Bernard of Clairvaux, 66
Betz, Hans, 172 n. 106
Beyer, Matthew, 154 n. 144
Bibra, 58, 87
Biel, Gabriel, 36, 154 nn. 139-140
Blaurock, Jörg, 27
Bonaventure, 51, 155 n. 148
Bucer, Martin, 117
 arguments for infant baptism, 22-23, 30, 49, 129, 153 n. 123, 183 n. 95
 baptisms of Jesus and John, 47, 154 n. 134
Buenderlin, Johannes, 160 n. 15
Bullinger, Heinrich, 26-27, 178 n. 6

Caleb, 102

Calvin, John, 178 n. 6
Charlemagne, 131
Christ, 21, 31, 48, 59-60, 77, 103-4, 114-15, 121, 131-32, 135, 169 n. 50, 173 n. 122, 182 n. 62
 atonement of, 85, 98
 baptism of, 99-100, 133
 baptism of blood, and the, 52-54
 "bitter" Christ and the "sweet" Christ, the, 65
 blessing the children, 22-23, 49, 129-30, 132
 bridegroom, heavenly, 99-100, 106
 buried with in baptism, 56, 77, 118-19, 133
 captain and leader, 40-42, 175 n. 23
 celestial flesh of, 128
 church, and the, 43, 45-46, 122-25
 command to baptize, 27-30, 70-71, 133
 conceived within, 80
 confession of in baptism, 23, 43
 covenant with in baptism, 41, 63, 69, 77, 99, 106, 112, 118-19, 138-39
 glorified and unglorified, 124, 128
 Great Physician, the, 40, 116
 Keys, and the power of the, 43, 45-46, 122-25
 mystical union with, 100, 106, 175 n. 25
 participation in the sufferings of, 65, 77-78, 80-82, 84, 105, 116-17, 127-29, 141
 relation to John the Baptist, 38-40, 45, 47, 63, 132
 See Body of Christ
Chrysostom, John, 21, 173 n. 122
Constantine, 106
Cyprian, 52
Cyril of Alexandria, 51
Cyril of Jerusalem, 50-51

Daniel, 104, 171 n. 83
David, 82
 See Key of David
Denck, Hans, 38, 62-64, 99, 147 n. 1
 atonement, view of, 98
 baptism, view of, 62-64, 69-72, 75, 99-100, 118, 120, 130, 166 n. 105, 173 n. 109

203

baptized by Hubmaier, 64
confession to the Nürnberg **Rat**, 62-63, 83
covenant idea, 62-64, 69-71, 75, 77, 99-100, 114, 118, 138, 180 n. 37
creatures, Gospel of all, 166 n. 94
David, Key of, 160 n. 15
discipleship, 168 n. 14, 169 n. 49
God, view of, 168 n. 10
mystical ideas, 111, 120, 128, 136-37
Basel recantation, 63, 110
relation to Hubmaier, 63-64
relation to Hut, 58, 62, 64, 77, 79-80, 83-84, 91, 94-95, 168 n. 10, 172 n. 97
relation to Müntzer, 62 f., 163 n. 44
Dionysius (Pseudo-), the Aereopagite, 109-10
Dorsch, Jörg, 88

Eberlin Johann, von Günzburg, 41, 61, 139, 155 n. 153
Eckhardt, Meister, 60, 66
Egypt, 99-100
Elijah, 105
Hofmann as, 97
Emden, 108
Emmius, Ubbo, 108
Enoch, 105
Ephesus, 47
Erasmus, 19
baptism as a pledge, 40-42
discipleship, 25
inner and outer baptism, 25
military imagery, 40-42, 100
Esau, 63
Ethiopian eunuch, 32
Eusebius of Caesarea, 157
Eve, 103, 129-30

Frankenhausen, 62, 86, 90
Froschauer, Christoph, 147 n. 12

Grebel, Conrad, 22, 27
baptism, view of, 42
baptismal suffering, 42, 53-54
followers in Zürich, 19, 25-26, 139, 147 n. 12, 186 n. 3
moderate spiritualism, 30
Müntzer, Letter to, 25, 42, 150 n. 53
reform of Zürich, and the, 62, 139, 147 n. 12, 148 n. 18
Scripture, interpretation of, 20-21, 28
Gross, Jacob, 99, 118

Haug, Jörg, 87
Herod, 93
Hoen, Cornelius, 175 n. 25
Hofmann, Melchior, 47, 96-112, 174-78
atonement, universal, 98
baptism, administration of, 107-9
baptismal covenant, 99-102, 106
Elijah, as, 97
eschatology, 102-7
free will, 97-99
Strassburg recantation, 109-10
regeneration, 97-102
relation to Catholic doctrine, 102
relation to other leaders: 135, 137-38, 140-41
Denck, 98-99, 100-1, 110-12
Hubmaier, 97, 99, 100 102, 108-12
Hut, 97, 100-2, 107-8, 110-12
Luther, 98, 100, 102
Müntzer, 100-1, 111
Rothmann, 108
typological hermeneutic, 102-4
Hubmaier, Balthasar, 19-57, 147-59
baptism:
administration of, 54-56, 109
baptized by Reublin, 19
Christian life, and the, 53-54
circumcision, 36-38
church, and the, 43-47
first written rejection of infant baptism, 22-23
free will, 32-35
infant baptism abandoned, 19-24
infants, dedication of, 23
inner and outer, 30-32
instituted by resurrected Christ, 39, 48
influenced by Catholic tradition, 33-34, 39, 45-46, 52-53
influenced by Erasmus, 25, 42
influenced by the Grebel group, 25, 42, 53, 150 n. 63
influenced by Karlstadt, 25
influenced by Luther, 24, 42, 44, 54
influenced by Müntzer, 24-25
interpretation of Scripture, 20-21, 28
John and Christ, of, 38-40
pledge in baptism, 40-44, 70, 76-77
Keys, view of the, 69, 167 n. 2, 181 n. 57
Oecolampadius, correspondence with, 22-24, 49
regeneration, 32-35, 44, 118-20
relation to other Anabaptists, 99, 102, 108-16, 118-20, 125, 127-33, 135,

137-41, 147-59, 166 n. 99
Zurich recantation, 153 n. 131, 159 n. 242
Zwingli, meetings with, 19-20, 22, 147 n. 6
Hübner, Hans, 88, 170 n. 68, 171 n. 90
Hugh of St. Victor, 154 n. 140
Hungary, 88
Huss, John, 98
Hut, Hans, 47, 58-96, 137-41, 147 n. 1, 179 n. 12
  baptism, administration of, 94-95
  baptismal suffering, idea of, 43, 71, 77-83
  baptism, distinction between the "sign" and "essence" of, 83-84
  baptized by Denck, 58, 64
  covenant and baptism, 63, 69, 76-79, 83-84
  covenant and the church, 69, 77
  covenant, inner, 69-70
  creatures, the Gospel of all, 68, 73-74 81-83
  eschatology, 86-92
  Geheimnus, authorship of, 64-75
  infant baptism, rejection of, 58
  "John the Baptizer," 90-91
  Latin, knowledge of, 72-74
  occupations, 72
  regeneration, 79-86
  relation to:
    Denck, 69-72, 75, 77, 80, 83-84
    Hubmaier, 43, 92, 69-72, 75-78
    Luther, 98, 102
    Müntzer, 58-76, 79-86, 90, 93-96, 137
  repudiated revolution, 62, 186 n. 5
  Spirit baptism, 85-86
  universalism, 84-85

Irenaeus, 109
Isaac, 175 n. 14
Isaiah, 60

Jacob, 63
Jerome, 50-51, 157 n. 209
Jerusalem, 33
  New Jerusalem, 105-6
Joel, 105
John the Baptist, 60, 89-90, 141, 154 n. 139
  baptism, 28, 30, 44, 47, 63, 78, 84, 154 n. 144, 173 n. 109
  baptism compared to Jesus' baptism, 38-40, 45, 48, 51, 93-94, 132-33, 185 n. 123

Jonah, 61, 80, 82, 116
  sign of, 61, 65, 82, 116, 168 n. 15
Jörg of Passau, 87
Joshua, 102
Jost, Leonard and Ursula, 97, 105
Judas 83

Karlstadt, Andreas, 25, 150 nn. 53-54, 159 n. 1
Kautz, Jacob, 99, 118
Kern, Melchior, 95
Kessler, Johannes, 54
Königsberg, 170 n. 63
Küssenberg, Heinrich, 147 n. 1

Lambert, Francis, 149 n. 30, 153 n. 123, 157 n. 195
Langenmantel, Eitelhans, 88-89, 170 n. 71
Lefèvre, Jacques, circle of, 67
Lindauer, Fridolin, 26, 30, 149 n. 30, 152 n. 102
Louis IX, 131
Luther, Martin
  baptism as a covenant, 40-42, 61-62, 100, 119
  baptism and church discipline, 44
  baptism, lifelong, 42, 54, 84
  Bible, 24, 63, 67-68, 152 n. 94, 165 n. 88
  criticisms of, 65
  fides infantium, 130-31
  justification, 34, 120, 135-36, 161 n. 30, 169 n. 54
  law and Gospel, 38, 40, 114, 116
  relation to:
    Hofmann, 98, 102
    Hubmaier, 19, 24, 34, 38, 40, 42, 44
    Hut, 54, 65, 84
    Marpeck, 114, 118-20
  translation (I Pet. 3:21), 63, 118, 152 n. 94, 180 n. 38

Mantz, Felix, 62, 139, 150 n. 53, 154 n. 133
Marpeck, Pilgram, 113-34, 178-86
  baptism, administration of, 133
  baptismal suffering, view of, 116-17
  baptism, inner and outer, 120-27
  the church, view of, 122-25
  concept of "co-witness" (**Mitzeugnis**), 121-27, 134, 137, 140
  dedication of infants, for the, 132
  infant baptism, arguments against, 129-32

Law and Gospel, 114-15
man, view of, 125-26
regeneration, 115-19, 135, 141
relation to:
  Denck, 114, 118, 120, 128, 130
  Hofmann, 97, 118, 120, 125, 134
  Hubmaier, 32, 35, 38, 114-15, 118, 120, 128, 130-31
  Hut, 77, 116, 118, 120, 125, 127-28, 133-34, 168 n. 9
  Luther, 114-16, 118, 131-32
  Müntzer, 116
  Protestants, 113, 119, 122, 125-26, 134
  Schwenckfeld, 125-26, 128, 130
  Spiritualists, 113, 120, 122, 125-26, 134
  Strassburg Anabaptists, 118
use of Rothman's Bekenntnisse, 129 f., 178 n. 5, 181 n. 48
Mary, 59, 80, 143
Mayer, Marx, 87
Meinhard, Christoph, 165 n. 80, 173 n. 109
Meiningen, 58, 159 n. 2
Melanchthon, Philip, 36-37, 40, 147 n. 8, 154 n. 144
Moses, 105, 114
Mt. Sinai, 99
Münster, 108, 112
Müntzer, Thomas
  baptism, view of, 59-62, 173 n. 109
  covenant, 61-62, 161 n. 36
  characteristic expressions of, 65
  regeneration, 169 n. 54
  reform of Christendom, and the, 62, 139
  relation to:
    Denck, 62 f., 163 n. 44
    Grebel group, the, 186 n. 3
    Hofmann, 100-1, 111
    Hubmaier, 24-25
    Hut, 58-76, 79-86, 90, 93-96, 137
    Marpeck, 116

Naaman, 30
Nadler, Hans, 170 n. 64, 171 n. 88, 173 n. 120
Nehspitzin, Ursula, 171 n. 83
Nicodemus, 154 n. 139
Nicolsburg, 52, 54, 143
Noah, 32, 37, 46, 48, 103, 114
Nürnberg, 62, 64, 83, 87, 163 n. 44

Occam, William of, 51
Oecolampadius, 26, 49, 50, 148 n. 27, 150 n. 53, 157 n. 195

questions infant baptism, 22-24
Origen, 50-51, 109
Ottin, Gerhard, 170 n. 76

Paris, 67
Paul the Apostle, 22, 47, 53, 68, 84, 101, 103, 109, 114, 127
Peter, 35, 121, 182 n. 68
Pfeiffer, Heinrich, 161 n. 36
Pharaoh, 103, 106
Philips, Dietrich, 186 n. 132
Philips, Obbe, 108-9
Pilate, Pontius, 143
Poldermann, Cornelius, 105
Pope Eugenius IV, 132
Pope Gregory the Great, 36
Pope Leo I, 157 n. 209
Pope Siricius, 157 n. 209

Raymond of Sebonde, 64, 66-68, 72, 81
Rebecca, 175 n. 14
Reublin, Wilhelm, 19, 24, 26, 99, 118
Rhenanus, Beatus, 131
Richard of St. Victor, 100-1
Rinck, Melchior, 62
Rothe, Martin, 94
Rothman, Bernard, 108, 115, 117, 120-23, 129-33, 161 n. 36, 162 n. 42, 178 n. 5 et passim
Rüd, Valerius (Anshelm), 159 n. 233

St. Gall, 54
Salzburg, 171 n. 83
Satan, 42, 99, 175 n. 23
Schiemer, Leonhard, 92-93, 96, 140, 166 n. 94, 167 n. 114, 168 n. 11
Schlaffer, Hans, 93, 95, 166 n. 94
Schrenzin, Katherine, 170 n. 76
Schuster, Nisius, 170 n. 68
Schwenckfeld, Caspar, 105, 124-26, 128, 130, 134, 180 n. 38, 185 n. 123
Scotus, Duns, 51
Servetus, Michael, 95, 173 n. 122
Simeon, 104
Simons, Menno, 186 n. 132
Solomon, 33
Spittelmaier, Ambrosius, 68, 74, 89-90, 95, 169 n. 50
Storch, Nicholas, 25, 59
Strassburg, 23, 27, 30, 97, 99, 107, 109, 118, 120
  the New Jerusalem, 106

Strieglin, Margaret, 170 n. 76
Stumpf, Simon, 148 n. 17

Tauler, Johann, 65
Tertullian, 50, 52, 122, 131
Theophylact of Orchrida, 51, 95
Toulouse, University of, 64
Trijpmaker, Volkertz (Jan), 107

Vadian, Joachim, 22, 27
Valentinian II (Emperor), 52
Vienna, 56
Volck, Jörg, 88

Waldshut 23-26, 28, 54, 58, 99, 147 n. 3,
  baptisms, 19
  Hubmaier's proposed disputation, 21
  reforms introduced into, 21-22
Walpot, Peter, 95
Weigel, Hans, 171 n. 89
Weischenfelder, Hans, 170 nn. 63 and 68
Weischenfelder, Martin, 74, 166 n. 94, 170 n. 64, 171 n. 90, 173 n. 115
Weischenfelder, Veit, 74, 166 n. 94, 170 n. 68, 171 n. 90
Weissenfels, 58, 159 n. 2
Wittenberg, 58, 72
Worms, 168 n. 10
Wüsten, Wolfgang, 88, 91
Wyttenbach, Thomas, 26

Yugoslavia, 51

Zeiss, Hans, 61, 168 n. 14
Zerubbabel, 107
Ziegler, Clement, 30, 70, 97, 129, 148 n. 19
Ziska, John, 161 n. 36
Zurich, 19, 22-25, 27, 30, 38, 52, 56, 139
  Anabaptists 24-27, 29, 38, 62, 147 n. 12, 148 nn. 18-19
  controversy over reforms, 20-21
  disputations (see Disputations)
  Town Council, 21, 27
Zurl, Hans, 170 n. 76
Zwickau Prophets, 20, 24-25, 59, 70
Zwingli, Ulrich, 27, 56, 62, 113-14, 148-55, 163 n. 51
  ban, 44-45
  baptism:
    Anabaptist baptism, arguments against, 28-29, 38, 47
    circumcision, and, 37, 49
    covenant, 36-37, 40-42, 44, 119, 139
    infant, arguments for, 22-23, 35, 36-37, 41, 45, 47, 55, 183 n. 95
    infant, postponement of, 19-20
    infant, reported doubts of, 19-20
    inner and outer, 25, 30-32, 38, 125
  church, 44-45
  church and Obrigkeit, 41
  covenant theology, 36-38, 178 n. 6
  influence on:
    Anabaptism, 26, 186 n. 3
    Hubmaier, 26, 28, 30-32, 35
    Marpeck, 184 n. 103
  justification, 34, 135-37
  original sin, view of, 35, 184 n. 103
  predestination, 35
  Scripture, interpretation of, 20-21, 28, 148 n. 16
  Zurich reformation, and the, 21

INDEX TO MAJOR PRIMARY SOURCES

Ausbund: Das ist, etliche schöne Christliche Lieder, 172 n. 106
Bucer, Martin, Grund und Ursache, 22-23, 30, 47, 149 n. 35
Corpus juris canonici, 50, 131
Decretum Gratiani, 36
Denck, Hans, Confession to the Nürnberg Rat, 62-63, 83
———, Von der wahren Liebe, 63
———, Widerruf, 63
Deutsche Theologie, 83
Grebel, Conrad, Letter to Thomas Müntzer (Sept. 1524), 25
Hofmann, Melchior, Bekentnusz (Strassburg recantation), 109-10
———, Die Ordannantie Godts, 97 passim
———, Verclaringe van den geuangenen ende vrien wil, 98-99
———, Das 12. Capitel des propheten Danielis ausgelegt, 98, 104 f.
Hubmaier, Balthasar, Achtzehn Schlussreden, 21
———, Das andere Büchlein von der Freiwilligkeit des Menschen, 32-35
———, Von dem christlichen Bann, 45
———, Von der christlichen Taufe der Gläubigen, 27-32, 37-40, et passim
———, Eine Form zu Taufen, 54-56, 143-44
———, Von der Freiheit des Willens, 32-35
———, Ein Gespräch Hubmaiers auf Zwinglis Taufbüchlein, 27, 30, 47, 48
———, Grund und Ursache, 46
———, Von der Kindertaufe, 28
———, Letter to Oecolampadius (Jan. 16, 1525), 22-24, 26, 49
———, Letter to Zurich Rat (July 10, 1525), 27
———, Oeffentliche Erbietung an alle christgläubigen Menschen, 24
———, Eine Rechenschaft des Glaubens, 56
———, Schlussreden gegen Eck, 28
———, Der uralten und gar neuen Lehrer Urteil, 50-52, 131
Hut, Hans, Buch mit den sieben Siegeln, 89
———, Ein christlicher underricht, 68, 79-81, 85-86
———, Confession at Augsburg, 78, 92
———, Von dem geheimnus der tauf, 58-59, 64-75, 76-77, 81-85, 89-90, 93-94
———, Sieben Urteile, 171 n. 86
Luther, Martin, Ein Sermon von dem heiligen hochwürdigen Sakrament der Taufe (1519), 40-42, 84
———, Ein Sermon von dem neuen Testament, das ist von dem Heiligen Messe (1520), 24
Mantz, Felix, Protestation, 150 n. 53, 153 n. 133
Marpeck, Pilgram, Glaubensbekenntnis (Strassburg 1531/1532), 114-18 f., 180 n. 41, 128-29, 132
———, Letter to the Anabaptists at Austerlitz (ca. 1545), 122-23
———, Von der Tieffe Christi, 116-17
———, Verantwurtung, 124-25, 129
———, Vermanung, 115, 117-33, 178 n. 5
Müntzer, Thomas, Allstedt Liturgy (1523), 67, 162 n. 37, 166 n. 110
———, Anschlag zu Prag, 59

210 / *Anabaptist Baptism*

———, Letter to Hans Zeiss (July 1524), 61, 168 n. 14
———, **Protestation oder Entbietung,** 25, 59-61, 82
Oecolampadius, **Ein Gespräch etlicher Predicanten zu Basel,** 50
———, Letter to Hubmaier (ca. Jan. 18, 1525), 23, 49
———, Letter to Hubmaier (end of Jan., 1525), 23-24, 49
———, Letter to Zwingli (Aug. 20, 1527), 23
Raymond of Sebonde, **Theologia naturalis sive liber creaturarum,** 66-68, 81
Rothmann, Bernard, **Bekentnisse,** 117, 120, 123, 129-33 178 n. 5., et passim
Schiemer, Leonhard, **Das dreierlei gnad,** 168 n. 11
———, **Von dreyerley Tauf im Neuen Testament** 92-93
Zwingli, Ulrich, **Antwort über Balthasar Hubmaiers Taufbüchlein,** 27
———, **Von Klarheit und Gewissheit des Wortes Gottes,** 20
———, Letter to Francis Lambert and Brethren in Strassburg, (Dec. 16, 1524), 22
———, Letter to Fridolin Landauer (Oct. 20, 1524), 26, 152 n. 102
———, Letter to Thomas Wyttenbach (June 15, 1523), 26
———, **Von der Taufe, von der Wiedertaufe und von der Kindertaufe,** 27-32, 35, 37-38, 41-42, et passim
———, **De vera et falsa religione,** 26
———, **Wer Ursache gebe zu Aufruhr,** 22, 37

INDEX TO SCRIPTURE REFERENCES

Genesis
17:10 — 179 n. 18

Numbers
14:24-30 — 102
19:12 14, 19 — 162 n. 38

I Samuel
2:6 — 80-81, 84

Ezra
7:24 — 177 n. 68

Psalms
2:3 — 166 n. 110
31:22 — 82
69:2 — 161 n. 29, 163 n. 46
93:2, 5 — 67-68, 165 n. 84
93:3, 4 — 161 n. 29

Song of Songs — 99-100

Isaiah
44:3 — 59-60
55:1 — 59
55:10 — 148 n. 16
58:11 — 59
34:25 — 180 n. 38

Jeremiah
31:31-34 — 83, 115, 180 n. 38

Ezekiel
1:10 — 176 n. 46
18:20 — 152 n. 109
34:25 — 180 n. 38

Daniel
12:7 — 105

Hosea
6:7 — 178 n. 6

Haggai
1:1-15 — 177 n. 68

Ecclesiasticus of Ben Sirach
15:3 — 161 n. 28
15:14 — 98, 175 n. 11
18:13 — 103, 175 n. 11

Matthew
3:1, 2 — 158 n. 219
3:6 — 151 n. 76
3:11 — 89-90, 171 n. 88
6:11 — 33
15:13 — 21, 148 n. 19
16:13-20 — 46, 69, 91, 182 n. 68
18:15-20 — 23, 29, 43, 76-77, 104
19:13-15 — 22-23, 49, 51, 129-30, 149 n. 35
20:16 — 158 n. 223
20:22, 23 — 172 n. 103
24:13 — 116
24:27-31 — 104
28:19, 20 — 28-29, 47, 63, 110-11, 133, 154 n. 139

Mark
10:13-16 — 22, 49, 51, 129-30
10:38, 39 — 78, 80, 92, 172 n. 103
16:16 — 20, 25, 67-71, 73, 147 n. 8 154 n. 139, 158 n. 215, 163 n. 49, 165 n. 88

Luke
3:16 — 89-90, 171 n. 88
10:34 — 53
12:50-53 — 53, 80, 158 n. 223, 172 n. 103
18:15-17 — 22, 49, 51, 129-30
22:28 — 102
24:46 — 53

John
1:9 — 98
1:12 — 97, 174 nn. 2 and 4
1:32 — 60
2:7-9 — 60
3:5 — 59, 89-90, 116, 154 n. 139, 171 n. 88
3:16 — 38

211

3:23 — 60
4:14 — 60
5:7 — 60
5:19 — 124, 182 nn. 62 and 69
6:19 — 60
7:38-39 — 59
8:32 — 98, 174 n. 5
14:15-26 — 125
16:17 — 115
20:22, 23 — 46

Acts
1:5 — 151 n. 85
13:42-48 — 174 n. 10
19:1-7 — 47-48, 93-94, 111
FDK 10-7-66 FDK

Romans
1:19, 20 — 68
6:3, 4 — 49, 111, 133
8:15-17 — 53
9:16-18 — 103
10:14-17 — 125
11:32 — 103

I Corinthians
7:14 — 22
10:1, 2 — 84, 111
15:29 — 131

Ephesians
4:5, 6 — 127
5:26 — 124-25, 127

Colossians
1:23 — 67-68, 73, 165 n. 89
2:11-12 — 37, 48-49, 111, 114-15, 129, 132

II Timothy
3:12 — 53

Titus
3:5 — 180 n. 33

Hebrews
4:16 — 171 n. 88
6:4-9 — 175 n. 35
9:13, 14 — 127
10:22 — 49, 127
10:26 — 175 n. 35

James
5:13-15 — 53

I Peter
2:21 — 80
3:20, 21 — 31-32, 37, 48, 63, 99, 111, 115, 118, 121, 132, 152 n. 102

I John
5:6-8 — 52-53, 92, 116 127, 140

Revelation
4:7 — 176 n. 46
5:1—8:1 — 87-89
7:3 — 87-89, 94
7:4 — 105
12:1-6 — 105-6
12:14 — 105

INDEX TO MODERN AUTHORS

Aland, Kurt, 155 n. 148

Baring, Georg, 145, 165 n. 85
Battles, Ford Lewis, 145, 155 n. 145
Beachy, Alvin J., 174 n. 8, 175 nn. 14, 25, 186 n. 1
Bender, Harold S., 148 n. 13, 164 n. 59, 186 n. 3
Bergsten, Torsten, 20-21, 24-25, 30, 49, 146, 147 n. 3, 148 n. 18, 150 n. 49, 171 n. 86, 179 n. 13, 180 n. 33, 183 nn. 86 and 98, 184 n. 104, 186 n. 1
Blanke, Fritz, 148 n. 13, 152 n. 112, 162 n. 41, 186 n. 3
Blakney, Raymond Bernard, 161 n. 27
Boehmer, Heinrich, 160 n. 9, et passim
Brandt, Otto, 150 n. 50, 160 n. 12, et passim
Brinkel, Karl, 184 n. 106
Bromiley, G. W., 145, 147 n. 10, 152 n. 101

Cairns, David, 157 n. 207
Conway, Walter J., 185 n. 116
Cramer, Samuel, 145

Detmer, Heinrich, 162 n. 36, 178 n. 5, 184 n. 113

Egli, Emil, 146
Eissfeldt, Otto, 161 n. 25
Enders, Ludwig, 155 n. 153
Evans, Austin P., 159 n. 2

Farner, Alfred, 156 n. 169
Fellmann, Walter, 145, 163 n. 43
Finke, Heinrich, 147 n. 9
Foster, Claude R., Jr., 168 n. 10
Friedmann, Robert, 87, 163 n. 44, 165 n. 92, 167 n. 113
Goeters, J. F. G., 171 n. 86
Goetz, Walter, 160 n. 11
Goodspeed, Edgar J., 175 n. 11
Grosheide, G., 177 n. 70

Hege, Christian, 162 n. 36, 170 n. 71, 178 n. 5
Heymann, Frederick G., 161 n. 36
Hillerbrand, Hans J., 150 n. 52, 155 n. 153, 162 n. 41, 163 n. 42, 186 nn. 1, 2
Hinrichs, Carl, 155 n. 153, 161 n. 25
Holl, Karl, 137
Hulshof, Abraham, 177 n. 76

Jackson, Samuel Macauley, 149 n. 46
Jeremias, Joachim, 157 n. 207
Jetter, Werner, 153 n. 120

Kawerau, Peter, 107, 109, 175 n. 10
Keeney, William Echard, 186 n. 132
Kirchberger, Clare, 175 n. 29
Kirn, Paul, 160 n. 9
Kiwiet, Jan, 178 n. 4 ff.
Klaassen, Walter, 160 n. 8, 163 n. 57, 169 n. 55
Klassen, Herbert, 159 n. 2, 166 n. 94, 169 nn. 37 and 56, 170 nn. 59 and 61, 172 n. 97, 173-74
Klassen, William, 179 n. 12, 181 n. 53
Knaake, J. C. F., 146
Krebs, Manfred, 145, 148 n. 19
Krodel, Gottfried G., 150 n. 52
Krohn, B. N., 105, 174 n. 6
Krumbholtz, Robert, 162 n. 36, 178 n. 5

Leendertz, W. I., 176 n. 52
Linden, Friedrich Otto zur, 176 n. 46
Littell, Franklin Hamlin, 157 n. 196, 162 n. 36
Lohmann, Annemarie, 160 n. 11
Loofs, Friedrich, 155 n. 148
Loserth, Johann, 25, 149 n. 42, 178 n. 12

Male, Emile, 164 n. 70
Mau, Wilhelm, 21, 24, 147 n. 9
Mecenseffy, Grete, 65, 146, 167 nn. 115 and 118
Meinecke, Friedrich, 147 n. 9

213

Meissner, E., 171 n. 86
Mergal, Angel M., 145
Meusel, Alfred, 161 n. 36
Meyer, Christian, 146
Migne, J. P., 145
Müller, Lydia, 65, 72, 146, 160 n. 4, 163 n. 59, et passim
Muralt, Ludwig von, 146

Neuser, Wilhelm, 159 n. 2, 160 n. 7, 170 n. 59
Nipperdey, Thomas, 160 n. 24, 164 n. 63, 169 n. 54, 186 n. 1

Petry, Ray C., 145, 169 n. 37
Pfister, Rudolf, 153 n. 113
Pijper, Frederik, 145

Ratcliffe, F. W., 67, 165 n. 87
Roth, Friederich, 146, 160 n. 5
Rott, Hans Georg, 145, 148 n. 19
Rupp, Gordon, 58-59, 64-69, 72-74, 150 n. 53
72-74, 150 n. 53

Sachsse, Carl, 25, 49, 157 n. 209, 171 n. 86
Schmid, Walter, 146
Schornbaum, Karl, 145
Sehling, Emil, 162 n. 37

Staehelin, Ernst, 148 n. 27, et passim
Stauffer, Ethelbert, 156 n. 163, 172 n. 106
Stayer, James M., 170 n. 59, 172 n. 91, 186 n. 5
Stupperich, Robert, 153 n. 119

Trinterund, Leonard J., 178 n. 6

Urner, Hans, 182 n. 73, 184 n. 106
Usteri, Johannes Martin, 147 n. 9

Vedder, Henry C., 24, 149 n. 46
Vogelsang, Enrich, 179 n. 12

Walton, Robert, 147 n. 12
Wappler, Paul, 146
Wenger, John C., 178 n. 4
Westin, Gunnar, 146
Williams, George Huntston, 145, 147 n. 2, 161 n. 27, 186 n. 2, et passim
Wray, Frank J., 178 n. 5

Yoder, John Howard, 148 n. 18, 151 n. 68, 153 n. 131

Zuck, Lowell, 162 n. 36

www.ingramcontent.com/pod-product-compliance
Lightning Source LLC
Chambersburg PA
CBHW051737230426
43670CB00012B/2056